CRACK HOUSE

ABOUT THE AUTHORS

Detective Sergeant Harry Keeble has more than fifteen years experience in inner-city pro-active policing. He joined the Met after leaving university in 1989. In 1999 he joined Haringey drugs squad as a uniformed sergeant and spent the following twelve months planning and leading 100 raids on North London's most fortified crack houses. As a result, he stopped all black-on-black killings in the London Borough of Haringey for twelve months in 2000 – an achievement yet to be repeated in a UK inner city. He has since managed international police investigations that have stretched across Europe, Africa and the Caribbean. He has prosecuted major drug dealers, rapists and child abusers at the Old Bailey and currently works for Specialist Operations at New Scotland Yard.

Kris Hollington is a freelance investigative journalist, author and ghostwriter living in London. He has written for the *Sunday Times*, *Guardian*, *Mail on Sunday*, *Evening Standard*, BBC Radio 4's *File on 4* and BBC1's *Panorama*. He is the author of *Diamond Geezers*, the story of the attempted robbery of the £350m De Beers diamonds from the Millennium Dome in 2000 and *How to Kill: The Definitive History of the Assassin*. He is also co-author of *Line of Fire*, written with Brian Paddick.

CRACK HOUSE

THE INCREDIBLE TRUE STORY OF THE MAN
WHO TOOK ON LONDON'S CRACK GANGS AND WON

HARRY KEEBLE with KRIS HOLLINGTON

POCKET
BOOKS

LONDON • SYDNEY • NEW YORK • TORONTO

First published in Great Britain by Simon & Schuster UK Ltd, 2008
This edition first published by Pocket Books, 2009
An imprint of Simon & Schuster UK Ltd
A CBS COMPANY

1 3 5 7 9 10 8 6 4 2

Simon & Schuster UK Ltd
First Floor
222 Gray's Inn Road
London WC1X 8HB

www.simonsays.co.uk

Simon & Schuster Australia
Sydney

A CIP catalogue record for this book is available
from the British Library.

ISBN: 978-1-84739-152-0

Typeset in Bembo by M Rules
Printed by CPI Cox & Wyman, Reading, Berkshire RG1 8EX

For my children

CONTENTS

ACKNOWLEDGEMENTS

First and foremost my thanks must go to the fellow members of Haringey Drugs Squad. Without your total dedication and sense of humour in the face of adversity, any success would have been impossible.

The Method of Entry Teams (Ghosties), 2 Area TSG and 3 Area TSG who showed resolute, fearless determination whenever they were asked to charge into the unknown; you have my undying respect and gratitude.

I would like to thank Chief Superintendent Steven James (Rtd.) for his steadfast faith in us and his inspirational drive and commitment to making Haringey a safer place.

Finally, the authors would like to thank the people from the other side of the crack house door who shared their stories: Jenni, in particular – we know that wasn't easy.

A NOTE TO THE READER

It is important to ensure that the secrets and histories of some of the individuals encountered through my work (witnesses, police officers engaged in sensitive work and informers, all of whom have good reason to fear retribution) are not set out in a manner that would enable people to recognize them. To be true to both requirements, the authors have, with the exception of names that are in the public domain, protected the identities of these people by changing names and altering some background details. The reader should be left in no doubt that every case is real, however. Of course, those cases which are a matter of public record are reported in their original detail.

crack: noun. slang. Pellet-size pieces of highly purified cocaine, prepared with other ingredients for smoking, and known to be especially potent and addictive. syn: base, ball, bazooka, beat, Belushi, biscuits, black rock, blast, bones, boost, bopper, boulders, brick, bump, cakes, Casper, chalk, cookies, crumbs, cubes, fatbags, freebase, gravel, hardball, hell, hotcakes, kibbles'n'bits, kool-aid, Kryptonite, love, mighty-white, moonrocks, nuggets, onion, pebbles, piece, primo, ready rock, roca, rock, rock-star, Roxanne, Scotty, scrabble, scramble, soup, stones, teeth, tornado, 24–7.

The Yanks aren't coming. At least not to Haringey, rated by US Government experts to be as dangerous as a Latin-American hell-hole. According to State Department mandarins you are as much at risk in Tottenham as in Guatemala, where the streets are stalked by death-squads . . . the State Department has 'Red-Flagged' the London Boroughs of Haringey and Southwark . . . Red-Flagging means American tourists should avoid at all costs, and is normally applied to world's worst trouble spots

From the *Evening Standard*, 5 June 1996

ONE

FROM TOTOPAHANA TO TOTTENHAM

6 NOVEMBER 1999

Dawn in Tottenham is not a sight to stir the soul, more like sicken the stomach. As I drive to our target I see the stolen purses discarded in gutters, the last gangs of stragglers staggering home through the cold wet streets, the pools of blood clotting in alleyways, the fluttering cordons of police crime-scene tape. I park on the edge of a decrepit council estate. Across the street two Jamaican men in hooded sweat-shirts stand guard in front of a four-storey Victorian house controlled by a man they call the Prince of Darkness. They're protecting every-thing that's going on inside, a 24-hour operation. If our struggle against drugs is a war, then these streets are the trenches and the crack houses the fortresses – secured with steel and iron, supposedly impregnable.

We're about to attempt the impossible: to storm the crack house using brute force; beat those inside into submission, drag them down to the station and close their operation down. It won't be easy. Those Victorian doors are held in place by thick bars of iron and steel which are fixed to the floor and wall, the windows are nailed shut and wire mesh covers the glass. Lurking inside are crack-addicted hitmen who kill for as little as £200 (known as 'Bics', like the plastic razors of the same name, they are cheap and disposable; if they ever wind up in court their evidence is seen as unreliable). Besides the Bics, the house is full of dozens of addicts, whores and gangsters armed with God knows what.

Before we move, we wait for the crack to arrive. It's on its way, the last leg of its spectacular journey from Totopahana to Tottenham.

In the early autumn of 1999, as she picked leaves in a remote coca farm in the Totopahana region of Colombia, twenty-year-old Olinda Giron stepped on a 'paw-breaker' blast mine. She was lifted six feet into the air; particles of dirt travelling faster than bullets ripped off her clothes, stones and bone fragments searing through her skin – one pebble smashed into her left eye. Deafened, she struggled to climb to her feet in the crater but her left leg now ended in a jagged bloody stump just above the ankle. In shock, she struggled to find her foot, scrabbling though the earth with her hands, looking for it with her one good eye. If she could find it, she thought, doctors might be able to reattach it.

Olinda was still a teenager when she joined her father and uncle to work for eleven hours a day picking leaves in a remote jungle farm three hours from the small town of San Pablo. Her family was one of thousands who had been forced to find work on cocaine farms after they lost their crops to fumigation as part of a $1.6 billion US-sponsored programme called Plan Colombia, a misguided effort to eliminate coca fields from the air. The poisonous chemicals dropped by US-supplied planes did not distinguish between different crops. Yucca, plantain, pineapple and maize crops were all destroyed and the soil and water poisoned. Some farmers cut down more jungle in an effort to replant; others who could not afford to gradually starved and became sick drinking polluted water. The fumigation programme provided guerrillas with more recruits who were desperate to avenge the atrocities that cost them their livelihoods.

Olinda's employer, who lived with his workers in a collection of wood and straw huts, employed thirty *raspachinos* (pickers), working eleven hours a day, six days a week on his six-hectare farm. He paid them £8 per day with full board and lodging. He also paid a tax of £18 per hectare to the left-wing FARC (the Revolutionary Armed Forces of Colombia) guerrillas, and a further £60 on each kilo of coca base produced, which he then sold to FARC's adversaries, the right-wing ELN (National Liberation Army) paramilitaries, for £600 per kilo. The ELN works closely with corrupt members of the Colombian military to get the coke out of the country.

While Olinda searched for her foot, production continued inside the farmer's *coca-cina* (cocaine kitchen). Inside the long shed without walls, under the roof held in place by six wooden pillars, a team of workers chopped coca leaves into smaller pieces with strimmers. On a large spread-out plastic sheet, more workers trod cement powder into the chopped leaves and mixed them with petrol in large black drums. The resulting coca base, a viscous white fluid, was drained off and treated. The six-hectare farm on which Olinda's family worked turned out fifteen kilos of cocaine base per week – the Totopahana region alone is home to some 60,000 hectares of coca.

The coca-farm owner agreed to help Olinda's father to get his daughter to the nearest hospital, two and a half days away – if they agreed to take a delivery of cocaine with them. The farmer had been squirrelling away a couple of kilos every now and again which he would sell for double the price the ELN paid to an independent trader from Honduras. Olinda's injury gave him the perfect excuse to have them transport the coke to his buyer in Bogotá; it would also give them a good chance of sneaking it past various military and guerrilla checkpoints.

Giron and his daughter were accompanied on their journey by the farmer's son, who drove the small truck in which the coke was hidden. He would also pay the necessary bribes and take them through the secret jungle pathways. At first they bumped and bounced their way along the *calle-coca* for three hours, a straight dust road that cut through the green jungle like a line of freshly chopped coke. Then they passed through an army-controlled checkpoint on the outskirts of San Pablo. The soldiers made a show of searching everyone and everything but at some point a bribe exchanged hands and the small sack of coke passed through unmolested. From San Pablo, they drove to Cuatro Bocas only to discover the village had been deserted. Ten of its inhabitants had been butchered a week earlier by ELN paramilitaries who accused them of siding with the FARC guerrillas.

The farmer's son left his truck in the village and then removed the coke from its hiding place; they boarded a motorized canoe and travelled down the Magdalena River to ELN-controlled San Lorenzo before moving onto El Bagre, a FARC-controlled village. Guerrillas, suspecting he was a government spy, dragged Olinda's father and the farmer's son out of the truck and beat them until they were convinced by the maimed Olinda that they were simple *raspachinos*. Further down the river they were searched by a police unit which had just dug out twenty-eight kilos of cocaine from a ferry boat's fuel tank. With just six policemen, their presence was largely symbolic. Determined traffickers could easily stop a little way upstream, carry their merchandise through a few kilometres of jungle, then reload further downriver. When they saw Olinda, who had by now developed fever from an infection, they sympathized. Most of the victims of landmines tend to be policemen. They were even able to provide some rudimentary treatment at their medical post before sending them on their way.

Finally, fifty hours after she lost her foot, Olinda and her father arrived at University Hospital, Bogotá. In front of the building there stands a statue of a soldier with a metal detector in his hands, a strange symbol perhaps, but the hospital is constantly overwhelmed with landmine victims, and about 1200 mine-clearing soldiers and policemen are on the waiting list for an artificial limb. Colombia has more than double the mines in its rich earth than Iraq does in its deserts and is third in the list of countries with the greatest number of mine victims, after Cambodia and Afghanistan (and it's catching up fast). The Colombian military claims that it is no longer sowing mines, but it has an estimated 20,000 in place.

Both the FARC and ELN sow about 26,000 new devices each year, planted to booby-trap the coca fields. They kill three Colombians every single day.

Somehow, despite developing a terrible infection, Olinda pulled through. Unable to return to the coca fields, she found work at the same clinic that fitted her with an artificial leg, moulding and polishing hundreds of prostheses for other land mine victims – children, policemen, even members of FARC and the ELN. Her father returned to the coca fields.

The farm-owner's son sold his coke to ex-gang member Geofredo Cortes Ortiz, who was branching out on his own after leaving the all-powerful MS-13s. While the farmer's son made the dangerous trip home, Ortiz took the cocaine to the town of San Pedro Sula in Honduras, walked into a greasy downtown bar and waited for his buyer. A few minutes later two ornately tattooed members of the MS-13 gang walked up behind Ortiz and cranked up the volume of the TV set. One had a tattoo of a grenade on his right shoulder and five tears drawn under his eye, the sign of an expert bomb-maker who had taken the lives of five people. The other man bore the design of a long machete, its end marked red with blood; a series of equally grim tally marks had been crudely scratched underneath using a prison-made kit.

They had come to kill Ortiz. He had made two mistakes. The first was his failure, while leading the MS-13 inside San Pedro Sula jail, to defend his members against an attack by rivals from the 18th Street gang. It had been the worst prison massacre in Honduran history; while the MS slept on the floor of their cramped dormitory, the 18 had sneaked in with homemade knives and steel pipes and turned the prison into a slaughterhouse, butchering eleven of Ortiz's homeboys. The attackers then gutted their victims and triumphantly strung their intestines along barbed-wire fences like party streamers. They cut off ears and tossed them over the wall for the stray dogs. After it was all over, the 18s laughed and flashed the gang sign at the prison guards who waited for them to return to their cells – they didn't dare intervene.

Ortiz's second and biggest mistake was to start dealing coke on the side once he got out of jail, creating his own chain of supply, hooking up with Colombian farmers directly. He paid the farmers more than the paramilitaries, but by bypassing his own gang he was able to sell the coke on for great personal profit. A few years ago, this wouldn't have been possible: a cocaine mountain had been piling up in Jamaica, the Caribbean funnel for the export of cocaine from South America to Miami, Amsterdam, Madrid and London. The US market was saturated; the price had been falling and border controls had been stepped up. Besides that the MS-13 ran nearly all cross-border smuggling, and anyone treading on their toes was terminated with extremely messy prejudice. But with the growing demand for crack in the US and Europe, most notably from the UK, the temptation to get rich or die trying was all too great.

It was the day of the big Honduras–Jamaica football match and the blasting commentary covered the screams of Ortiz as the two killers dragged him into the bathroom and hacked him to death with their machetes. Once Ortiz stopped moving, they were joined by half a dozen homeboys in the symbolic rite of methodically cutting the dead man's body into little pieces and flushing them down the toilet; all except for his intestines which they saved in a plastic bag, to be strung across a washing line on Ortiz's turf as a warning.

By 1999, crack had all but destroyed civilized life in Honduras, a country that had once claimed to be the least drug-riddled and most politically stable country in Central and South America. A freely elected civilian government had come to power in 1982 and ruled peacefully. Then, in the mid-1980s, came the MS-13 and, with them, crack. The MS-13 gang is named after La Mara Street in El Salvador and 13th Street in Los Angeles, their two main territorial centres. They initially consisted of guerrillas who fought in El Salvador's civil war. As the war neared its end, the gang moved its criminal operations into neighbouring Honduras and rapidly began tearing the country to pieces. Early attempts by the authorities to stamp out the gang were met with brutal responses; in 1988, two MS-13 members armed with an AK-47 and an M-16 stopped a public bus, boarded and emptied their clips into the innocent passengers, killing twenty-eight, including seven children. Eventually the Honduran authorities all but gave up and by 1999 only one police officer, Magdalenys Centeno, covered gang-related crime. She spent her time going to gang funerals and taking photos; just keeping track of who's who in the Honduran gang world was a full-time job. By the turn of the century the country was in a state of permanent war between the government, MS-13, rival gangs such as the 18 and the Junk and the *Sombra Negra* (the Black Shadow), a group of vigilantes made up of angry cops and local traders who spent their free time hunting and shooting MS-13 members on sight. They had plenty of targets: San Pedro Sula, a city of half a million Hondurans, had over 35,000 MS-13 members, many of them addicts (crack sells for an affordable £1.25 a hit).

The MS-13 moved to the west coast of the United States in the mid-80s, bringing crack with them. Today they are one of the most violently dangerous gangs in North and South America – and one of the most organized, with members in seventeen US states. In the Washington, DC area in 1999, local authorities estimated MS-13 membership to number around 6,000. The most notorious death in the US that year was an MS execution: a sixteen-year-old boy turncoat had both of his hands chopped off and bled to a lonely death in a Washington alley not two miles from the White House.

Ortiz's coke was taken to MS-13 leader Cesar Cortez. The MS-13 used their established smuggling network to ship the coke along with a larger consignment to Jamaica, an island paradise torn apart by the trade in coke and the demand for crack. Jamaica (population 2.5 million) has one of the highest homicide rates per capita in the world, with an average of five murders a day. Jamaica's army and police have been given a free hand to enforce law and order in the ghettos (as a result Jamaica has the world's highest per capita police killings per year). Twenty-seven people were killed in one operation, including several children, when troops backed by helicopter gun-ships and tanks raided a poor neighbourhood torn apart by a gang war. Gang members from all sides united against the police and, most wearing bullet-proof vests, held them at bay for eighteen hours using Uzis, Glocks, Mac-10s, AK-47s and M16s.

In the ghettos of Kingston, the capital, criminal militias are loosely allied to one of two political parties: the left-wing People's National Party (PNP) or the right-wing Jamaica Labour Party (JLP). For decades they have controlled voting in the slums in return for political protection. Drugs had always been part of the Jamaican gang scene but with the arrival of cocaine followed by the crack boom (thanks to the MS-13), the island rapidly became a narco-state. The militias created by the major political parties evolved into highly powerful and extremely violent drug-smuggling networks with an inexhaustible supply of guns. Jamaicans were soon distributing crack all over the US. Areas of Kingston became beyond the control of state authority.

Today, the ghettos are run by drug dons, known as 'community leaders'. They provide potential political patrons with valuable votes, and, since the arrival of crack, valuable financial contributions during election years. In return, the dons expect political protection. One prominent community leader was Donald 'Zekes' Philips of West Kingston. Minutes after his arrest by police officers in September 1998, ghettos threw up barricades and launched a wave of vandalism and looting. When demands for his release were ignored his loyal followers set off on a rampage through Kingston's better suburbs. He was eventually released on the personal order of the prime minister. Although dramatic, Zekes' story is not exceptional.

With an average annual income of just £1500, it is all too tempting for poor Jamaicans to become drug mules who are paid between £2000 and £5000 for each trip to transport between half a kilo to ten kilos of cocaine to North America and Europe. About 65 per cent of all the cocaine in the UK is smuggled through by Jamaican mules. Becoming a drug mule is the most readily available form of employment (unemployment runs at around 20 per cent). It is a job which can earn people more money than most Jamaicans see in a lifetime. Most of the smugglers are women, and many are single parents struggling to raise three or four children and put them through school. Others are coerced by threats of violence.

In late October in 1999, in a flat in a run-down block in Tel-Aviv, a ghetto community in Kingston, Julia looked at the forty 25-gram latex lozenges packed full of Cortez's coke, each about the size of a thumb from the knuckle to the tip. She had done this a few times by now, but it was not something she had, or would ever, get used to. For a start, her life was in the hands of the dealer who wrapped them. The smallest hole, the tiniest defect in one of the lozenges and a lethal dose of cocaine would gradually be released into her stomach and she would die. Julia thought the risks were worth it. She didn't want her own kids to grow up in an area where every child has seen the body of a murder victim by the age of ten; where children as young as eleven or twelve called 'fryers' join the drug posses and act as innocent-looking bagmen before graduating to robbery and then murder. The money she would make from muling would pay for a fresh start in the UK.

Julia examined each lozenge carefully; each was made from the fingers of latex gloves, the ends of which were glued, compressed and heat-sealed, before being tightly wrapped in clingfilm. Condoms used to be the favoured wrapping material but they proved unreliable against stomach acid. Finally satisfied, Julia rubbed a little olive oil over one of the lozenges, placed it in her mouth and gulped. It had to be done with conviction every time – any hesitancy and the package could become caught and the swallower could choke to death. When she first started, Julia spent some time practising with large grapes and then smaller lozenges filled with sugar. Occasionally, one had got stuck and although she freed them each time without too much trouble her throat had wound up as sore as hell. After the last was squeezed down her gullet, Julia washed them down with a constipating agent. An attack of the nerves can prove disastrous on the ten-hour flight from Kingston to London.

It's a risky business, but the rewards are high. Julia earned £5000. Dozens of couriers collapse while waiting to board Air Jamaica flights each year; around ten of them die. A few weeks earlier Julia had watched after a bag burst in another swallower's stomach in mid-flight. It was a horrible, agonizing death. The middle-aged woman victim's eyes were full of fear as she writhed in the arms of the stewardess. She had fifty-five bags in her. The stewardesses all knew their plane was full of swallowers (they were the ones who refused food and drink), but there was nothing they could do.

As she travelled by cab to the airport, Julia had to pass by Kingston's dilapidated courthouse. She knew there were dozens of mules awaiting prosecution inside, one of whom was twenty-two-year-old Diane Haddow from Tottenham, North London, who stood in the roasting airless heat of court number five.

Detective Constable Conrad Granston explained to the judge how, after opening her suitcase he found thirty-three plastic bottles of 'medicated powder'. Haddow told him that her daughter suffered from an agonizing skin complaint and that they were for her. But the bottles contained one kilo of high-quality cocaine. She was one of a half-dozen mules in court that morning. Her fellow prisoners included a man who had taken a chance smuggling coke the old-fashioned way – in a false compartment in his suitcase – and a woman who had swallowed ninety-nine cocaine pellets.

Smugglers use a wide variety of techniques apart from swallowing. Some of them employ almost James Bond-like methods – tightly packed into the soles of shoes and suitcase handles; stitched into trouser seams. In one memorable case a woman showed particular ingenuity by weaving half a kilo of cocaine into her hair. British citizen Michael Edwards tried to smuggle out liquid cocaine in a bottle of Sorrell, a local drink made from flower petals. For mules caught in Jamaica sentences are light, especially compared with Britain where a first-time mule can expect to serve a minimum of six years. Lisa Walker was caught attempting to smuggle two kilograms of cocaine out of the country; she was released from a Jamaican prison after serving nine months.

The first thing the mules see when they arrive at Kingston's airport is an infamous poster: 'Drug mules beware: it's a plane ticket to hell'. As Julia prepared to board Air Jamaica (aka Cocaine Air) Flight 223 to Heathrow, she was scrutinized by Sergeant Adele Halliman, Jamaica's number-one mule spotter. But a lack of money and staff meant that Halliman was only able to arrest one mule a day; she reckoned that on certain flights the number of mules was as high as eight out of every ten passengers.

In 1999 the UK's Deputy High Commissioner in Jamaica, Phil Sinkinson, sparked a political row by claiming in a conservative estimate that as many as one in ten passengers were attempting to smuggle drugs. That's (conservatively speaking) twenty kilos a flight. There are four flights a day from Jamaica to the UK flying five times a week, fifty weeks a year. To the drug dealers in England anxiously awaiting consignments from Jamaica, a kilo of coke converted into crack is worth more than £60,000 (up to £90,000 if the coke arrives uncut) – so twenty tonnes of coke worth £1.2 *billion* a year makes it into the UK via Jamaican swallowers alone. If Halliman was right then the true figure may be far higher.

Sadly, not all of Jamaica's police force was as trustworthy as Halliman. In January 1999, 127 Jamaican police officers were transferred after it was discovered that a whole police department had formed an alliance with members of a Colombian cocaine cartel. Eight months later the entire Special Anti-Crime Taskforce was disbanded after its officers were caught smuggling drugs.

On board, Julia buckled her seat belt, closed her eyes and prayed the packets of cocaine in her stomach wouldn't make her vomit during the ten-hour flight. She also prayed she would make it through London customs. While the chances of getting caught at the Jamaican end are quite small, it was a different matter in London, where there are more resources and stiffer sentences, but the odds are still in favour of evading detection. But in a surprise sweep at Heathrow airport everyone was searched and X-rayed for cocaine. Twenty-three swallowers were discovered, including two children (one sixteen-year-old eventually passed fifty-three latex lozenges and a twelve-year-old passed eighty-four). One week later a further nineteen were caught on a BA flight from Jamaica into Gatwick.

The flights were not targeted because of a tip-off, but were chosen at random to give investigators an idea of the problem they were up against, a problem that had been highlighted by Dutch customs at Amsterdam's Schipol airport. They complained that they had been ordered to stop arresting small-time cocaine smugglers arriving from the Dutch Antilles because the courts and prisons could not cope with the high numbers. In 1999 an estimated 20–25,000 drug mules flew into Schiphol, 1200 of whom were caught and convicted, up 60 per cent from the previous year. In a random sweep of one Caribbean aeroplane, Dutch customs officers caught forty swallowers.

Julia was the only one to escape the X-ray, although her bags and clothes were carefully searched whilst a Belgian Shepherd sniffer dog snuffled around her. Julia was heavily pregnant. The law forbade the X-raying of mothers-to-be. As a result she was gold dust to the dealers and commanded top dollar for her services. She left the airport a free woman, carrying a kilo of Colombia's finest in her belly, nestled next to her baby.

Julia was driven to a nondescript council block in Hanwell, West London, just twenty minutes from Heathrow. That night she was given laxatives and the next day, with the help of a home enema kit, the twenty lozenges were retrieved. Julia returned to Jamaica seven days after she landed. She planned another two trips; she figured that once they were done she'd have enough to start a new life as a single mother with her child in the UK. Two weeks later, however, shortly after an early morning landing at Heathrow, a package spilled its lethal contents into her stomach as she was being driven from the airport. She was found, unconscious, propped up against a wall in a suburban street by an early-morning commuter; her jacket, jewellery, anything that could be used to identify her had been removed. The ambulance got Julia to hospital in time to save her but not her baby. As soon as she was well enough she was tried and sent to jail for six years (one third of all women in prison in England and Wales are Jamaican mules) before being sent back to Jamaica, where she found work as a low-paid clerk for a charity that specializes in mule prevention and rehabilitation.

Julia's earlier consignment of coke was repackaged and taken to the flat of twenty-seven-year-old Asad Malajit in Balham, south-west London. Asad, a barrister, had won a prized scholarship to the bar but when he was unable to find chambers he developed his coke habit into a crack-dealing enterprise. Inside his large apartment, Asad mixed the cocaine with a solution of baking soda and carefully cooked the mixture using his microwave. As he cooked the cocaine, the liquid burst free from the crystals and produced a distinct cracking sound. Once all the moisture was removed, a pure cocaine base remained that, when smoked, gave the user the ultimate hit. In only a few minutes, cocaine, the glamour dust of the 80s, had been boiled down to hard mean little pellets of highly addictive crack, giver of euphoria, taker of lives.

A few minutes later Asad opened his door to former postman turned arms dealer Peter Callum, thirty-six. With crack the demand for guns is extremely high. Callum's Mercedes was full of ammo, ready to be sold in a joint deal with the crack to a man known as the Prince of Darkness, a notorious K-man (the boss of several crack houses) based in north London.

Guns and crack go hand in hand. Most serious UK crack dealers are armed and aspire to own the £3000 Mac-10 machine gun which looks similar to the Uzi 9mm but fires 1000 rounds per minute. An extremely effective sound suppressor makes it a very quiet weapon, and gun attacks often go unheard. The rapid fire makes them difficult to hold, and in the hands of the crack dealers they are wildly inaccurate. The Mac-10 is also known as the 'Street Sweeper' and the 'Spray and Pray', an indication of its indiscrimination. On this deal, however, Callum was selling on a stack of bullets for a set of Walther PPKs that the Prince of Darkness had purchased from two South London arms dealers. They bought decommissioned weapons legally from a Bermondsey trader before converting them using parts bought from B&Q.

They were hardly able to keep up with demand from 'Murder Mile', the Upper Clapton Road area near Tottenham. Seventeen men were shot dead there in 1998 and there were sixty-seven attempted murders – the victims were saved from death only by the poor marksmanship of the gunmen or the skill of the medical crews who treated them – and there were at least another eighty shootings (that we knew about) resulting in minor injury or criminal damage. London was displaying the early symptoms of the violent disease that had wracked Honduras and Jamaica. Indeed, at that time a full-on gang war was being fought in North London between the Lock City Crew and the Cartel Crew, which started with an argument over a parking space outside the Bridge Park Leisure Centre near the notorious Stonebridge estate in Tottenham. Bridge Park had been built for the community with government and lottery funding but by 1999 its storerooms were being used as an armoury.

Back in Tottenham, I watch as a car pulls up and two of the Prince of Darkness's lieutenants get out. One has the crack in a plastic bag. The other holds his hand in his coat, and walks backwards towards the house, watching for an ambush. I sit low in the car, holding my breath. After they enter, the door slams with a heavy clang.

And so that's it. That's how a kilo of crack made its way from Totopahana to Tottenham. And it's all been to feed the insatiable cravings of the thousands of addicts on our patch who have spent last night doing whatever's necessary to buy their fix – thieving, mugging, pimping, begging, stealing from each other, selling their bodies, dealing other drugs, hiring out guns, carrying out hits, only to hand their money over to the Prince of Darkness and others like him so they can blow it all on guns, cars, designer clothes and, of course, more crack. These 50,000 addicts are possessed by crack. Crack owns them. Teenagers have told me they decided to become addicts after the first time they used it; they spend the rest of their lives chasing that first God-like high. Nothing else matters. One seventeen-year old said to me: 'Sometimes I stare at myself in the mirror and think, "Who the fuck are you?" I have no idea. No fucking clue. The only thing I live for is another blast. And another and another. That's it.' Right now, she's inside the crack house I'm about to raid, whoring to earn her fix.

The house is full of crack whores, one of whom has just given a blow-job to a dealer in return for a £10 rock. Now she is sitting on a filthy sofa in a room full of twenty addicts and armed Tottenham Man Dem gang members, opposite one of the Prince of Darkness's top lieutenants. He is fondling a handgun he used to blast a rival in a drive-by the previous night. She's heavily pregnant (her son, already a crack addict, will be born with spina bifida). She's so addicted the buzz from the crack will barely register. Nevertheless, she lights her little crack pipe with the legend 'I ♥ London' written on the bowl. I climb out of the car and open the boot. With a grunt, I pick up the enforcer, my trusty thirty-kilo battering ram.

Time I introduced myself.

TWO

FROM HAROLD HILL TO HELL ON EARTH

SEVEN YEARS EARLIER: 12 OCTOBER 1992

As I walked through Clissold Park I noticed the children's sandpit was full of dirty syringes, from a night of jacking up. I made a mental note to sort that out once I'd checked in at the station – but that was soon forgotten when I entered Newington Church Street and came across a dead junkie in a car. Thankfully, some PCs had just arrived at the scene.

I was a constable fresh from probation all set to start life as a real copper at 'Cokey Stokey', aka Stoke Newington police station. By now, as I marched up the steps to the brand-new glass-fronted building in the High Street, I got the feeling that a few syringes in a children's play area were going to be the least of my worries. A group of TV cameramen, sound recordists and various journalists tried not to trip over their equipment and run into each other as they jostled outside. I looked away, ignoring them and ran ahead through the station doors.

I didn't yet know it, but I was about to encounter my second death of the day, only this time, instead of a lonely drug addict, it would be a policeman with a wife and kids.

Journalists from *Panorama* were at Stokey investigating claims that more than forty police officers from the station were facing charges of corruption. They were mainly accused of stealing drugs from dealers they had nicked and then selling them on through their own network of street dealers (hence the station's nickname). The amount of money involved apparently ran into the millions.

Suspicions were raised after officers from Customs and Excise uncovered a massive scam involving the non-payment of VAT on fruit machines in pubs, clubs, arcades, bingo halls and so on. They organized raids in Stoke Newington with the local police but each time they smashed through the doors, the suspects and fruit machines had gone. When they planned raids on their own, the fraudsters were caught bang to rights every time. Customs passed their suspicions onto the Complaints Investigation Branch (CIB) of the Met Police and Operation Jackpot was born, named in honour of the fruit machines. Jackpot began in 1991 and the shit really hit the fan in 1992, just as I arrived at Stokey, when forty-four officers were under investigation.

One of the forty-four was Sergeant Gary Carrol. The night before Carrol had acquired a gun, locked himself in a cell, put the weapon to his head and pulled the trigger. Not the best time to arrive for my first day at work. I was in at the deep-shit end.

My decision to join the police was as much a surprise to me as it was for my parents. I was eighteen, studying for my A-levels, and between lessons one day I spotted a booklet on joining the police in the bin. I was going to walk past it, but something made me stop, reach into the rubbish and pull it out. The idea suddenly seemed appealing. Breaking the speed limit to get to dangerous and exciting incidents, getting into fights and being able to bust the heads of violent criminals with the full power of the law behind you – fighting crime seemed like a worthy purpose and a lot of fun. I gave it a try by becoming a special constable and found myself on the street in police uniform, including baton and handcuffs – an eighteen-year-old who didn't know the first thing about the law. It was brilliant.

My parents were quite surprised but supportive when I told them. I finished my A-levels, went to Middlesex Poly, got my degree and signed up. After graduating from Hendon training college I was farmed out as a probationer to Romford, which seemed to have all of the UK's shittiest social problems crammed into one small area. Determined to make an impact I spent most of my time nicking shoplifters on the High Street, and was soon on first-name terms with the staff and thieves. I later applied for an opening in Harold Hill – which in retrospect was a slight mistake as Harold Hill is in the London Borough of Havering – just north of Romford. It was a new town without an underground service or any transport links to the rest of London. I spent a great deal of time looking for crime by day and twiddling my thumbs by night. I missed my thieves and the Friday night fighting. I was there in a flash when I heard they were suddenly desperate for volunteers at Stokey.

If it was action I was after, I had hit the bloody jackpot.

Even before the corruption had been uncovered, Stokey had already become a dumping ground for 'naughty' and lazy police officers but it also attracted PCs like myself, keen and reckless crimefighters desperate to get their hands dirty wiping the streets clean of drug-dealing scum. It was a dangerous cocktail. Fortunately, all of the eager beavers somehow wound up in the same unit and we policed the streets solidly and legally, leaving the no-hopers to waste their time in the wish for an easy life.

Sadly, while Stokey was the dumping ground for naughty and lazy coppers, the CIB still had more than its fair share of incompetent policemen. One CIB officer had been refused entry into the Flying Squad because of 'serious character flaws' and was later arrested for corruption. Some didn't even have any detective experience and during Operation Jackpot they didn't consider organising a covert operation to collect evidence against those suspected of corruption. They told the officers they were under investigation right from the start, so it was no surprise that only one of the forty-four officers was ever prosecuted. The CIB stated that this was due to a 'lack of evidence'. This was despite an official recognition by senior Met officers that Stoke Newington police officers had been engaged in supplying drugs.

One of those who escaped prosecution was DC Ronald Palumbo. While he was on bail awaiting trial for corruption at the Old Bailey, Palumbo transported four lorry-loads of cannabis worth £10 million from Spain to the UK. Thankfully, although Palumbo managed to fool the CIB, Customs had launched a surveillance operation which eventually netted him and he was sent down for ten years.

The unlucky one who was prosecuted in spite of the best efforts of the CIB was one of Stokey's finest, Detective Constable Roy Lewandowski. Lewandowski was an extremely experienced and effective policeman who had earned the respect of his colleagues for his courage and loyalty. Unfortunately he was also bent. As we are about to see, Lewandowski was a very successful drug dealer – but he wasn't convicted for drug-dealing. He was given an eighteen-month sentence for stealing three grand in valuables from a murder victim whose killing he was supposed to be investigating (this was despite an acceptance in court that Lewandowski had earned up to two grand a week from the drugs trade).

Not all the coppers at Stokey were bent, of course. With hindsight, some officers seemed incredibly naïve but it was almost beyond belief that there was an organized cell of extremely bad apples in our midst.

While the CIB had been investigating, the neighbourhoods had gone to shit. Informers were non-existent – who was going to come forward to a police force full of drug dealers? Plus, there had been a few deaths in police custody, which had done nothing for public confidence. We were chronically short-staffed. Street dealing was off the scale, so much so that normal statistics didn't make sense anymore. About twenty-eight officers were on duty each night; the drug dealers had fifty men on the street around the Esso garage alone (100 metres up the road from the police station).

The new chief superintendent made our mission clear: restore law and order. It was a busy time and, although I thought I knew what it took to be a good copper, my experience at Stokey was a revelation. These were the heady days of relatively paperwork-free policing, although the events at Stokey would usher in a new era of bureaucracy in an attempt to eradicate police corruption. The job was all about action. Every time I came to work something major had happened. A drug dealer died in a scrap with police. A suspect died in police custody. I once chinned a guy only to be told he was a top London Triad (I came across him torturing a young girl in the street), unwittingly risking a vendetta against the police.

I walked into the station one morning when a sergeant barked at me, 'Guard that lorry, Keeble.' Just down the road, in Stoke Newington High Street, was a Luton van that had obviously crashed. Some officers were frantically running round the vehicle with cordon tape, sealing off the road before legging it.

'Why?' I asked.

'Because there's a half-tonne bomb in the back which might go off at any moment. You have to keep people away.' The lorry had been bound for the City of London when a pair of PCs had pulled it over for a spot check. The driver, an IRA commando, had tried to run him down but crashed instead, before shooting one of the unfortunate PCs twice (he survived). I spent the rest of the day arguing with locals who refused to believe their lives were in danger. I eventually gave up, muttering to myself, 'You're going to die, you're all going to die,' as they all pushed past. I made the ten o'clock news – I was a very small, very lonely distant blue dot next to this explosive lorry.

My colleagues and I were always suffering from some injury sustained in the course of our duties and I learned how to fight – hard and dirty. It was excellent preparation for what was to come and I was about to get a small taste of what was on the horizon. Nobody saw it coming, but the inspiration for the fortified crack house came thanks in part to the actions of a corrupt copper at Stokey.

Lewandowski had nicked a petty drug-dealer, Pearl Cameron, and 'persuaded' her that in return for her freedom and his protection, she should escalate her business and provide him with a cut of the profits; he demanded about two grand a week. Cameron began a new type of low-quantity, high-volume drug-dealing, setting up one of the very first home-run crack outlets in the UK. She sold rocks of crack fresh from her microwave through the kitchen window of her house in Sandringham Road, just off Stokey High Street, to more than a hundred people every day.

It couldn't be described as a crack house as such, as punters didn't smoke on the premises and it wasn't fortified against police and rival gang raids (thanks to Lewandowski, there was no need). Addicts simply bought their fix and left – unless Cameron's mother was visiting. Then a red towel hanging from the window would warn customers to stay away until the visit was over.

But other drug dealers had caught on to Cameron's methods. Punters who were turned away from Cameron's place could walk a few hundred yards to 'Jerk Chicken', a grimy Jamaican fast-food restaurant. If you really pushed it you could probably persuade the chef to fry you some chicken – but he much preferred to cook up crack cocaine instead, which would be presented to you sandwiched between two buns in a plastic burger box.

We raided Pearl Cameron's place, arrested her and tried to take her house in Jamaica, claiming it had been bought with her drugs money. We marched up and down Sandringham Road (which had become Stoke Newington's 'frontline', the ultimate clash point) 24-7 and opened a one-stop cop-shop where locals could report crime. We only received about one visit a day (it was there more as a visual statement, a warning that we were back on the case) and it was a great place to study for my sergeant's exams.

We virtually kidnapped street dealers when we arrested them to avoid getting shot and beaten up – timing was everything, so we picked our moment carefully. Our van skidded to a halt; we piled on top of the dealers, arrested them and read them their rights without any pause for breath as they were bundled into the back of the van, which was burning rubber before the doors had closed. If anyone had been stupid enough to attempt to bribe us, we would have added the offence to their charge sheet.

While all this was going on, coppers were being sacked,

demoted and moved away from Stokey. Eventually Cokey Stokey had gone from a hard core of dodgy officers surrounded by a bunch of good coppers to a hard core of some of the most painfully honest policemen you could ever wish to be arrested by surrounded some of the laziest, most useless bods on the force.

The real problem the police faced then, as we do today, was terror. Witnesses of violent crimes were understandably frightened to come forward. They often ran from us so they wouldn't be seen talking to the Filth. They knew the drug dealers would get them – and besides that many believed the corrupt police had given the gangs *carte blanche* to do whatever was necessary to maintain their grip on the drugs market (which they had).

About 60 per cent of all drug-related crimes and nine out of ten armed robberies are solved due to the use of informers and witnesses, so we were struggling to make headway. If you're a witness in a major case then the Met is very good at making you disappear if you decide to enter the Witness Protection Programme, although it is psychologically traumatic. You will lose your identity; the old you will vanish; bank and building society accounts are closed, your National Insurance number is withdrawn, your passport is destroyed and your birth certificate deleted.

But if you were a single mum living in a council block next door to a drug den and whorehouse then you were screwed if you came complaining to the cops of Cokey Stokey. Besides, in London, a witness who wants rehousing goes to their borough, which rehouses them within that borough – which is often only half a mile from where they were in the first place. One woman who was brave enough to come forward was respectable, middle-aged and church-going. She had been one of a number of witnesses to a gun crime, and had gone to court. The guys concerned went down, and since then she had had to move five times – the gang just kept finding her.

We found ourselves dealing more and more with crack dealers. Back then, crack was peculiar to Stokey and new to us because the dealers had become so confident that they were able to market this highly addictive drug with ease. Up until Stokey, I hadn't come across that many gun incidents but, as time went on (I was there for four and a half years), more and more officers came face to face with guns.

A colleague came into the canteen white as a sheet, hands shaking as he sipped on a hot sweet tea. He was a solid copper, not afraid of much or, if he was, he managed to keep it well hidden, but on this occasion he was in bits. He'd waved down a car just off the High Street for a stop and search. The driver had pulled over, good as gold, and wound down the window. When the officer looked inside there were four men wearing body armour, each of them armed to the teeth with Remingtons, Glocks and Magnums. The gunman in the front passenger seat of the car leaned forward and quietly told the PC to 'move away' which he duly did. The gunmen drove on and vanished.

'I don't think I can do this any more,' he said. 'The job's fucked.' We used this catchphrase all the time as we came up against more and more shit from the dealers and addicts, because our job really was 'fucked'.

We also dealt with a rising tide of street robberies carried out by dozens of gangs. A particular problem was that a great many wealthy Hasidic Jews had been violently mugged (almost one a day), so my team began a surveillance operation where we disguised one of our members, Steve, as a Hasidic Jew (we called in the BBC make-up department for assistance) and made an arrangement with a local bank where he would walk in, give a code-word and they would give him £5000. After two weeks we knew he was being watched by a six-strong gang. They were staking him out, carefully making absolutely certain of Steve's routine before taking the bait.

They hit Steve full force without warning, just piled straight in. They weren't expecting such a strong fightback from their prey and Steve got in a couple of meaty smacks before he went down. He was wearing a wire and, as we sprinted towards him, his cries of pain hurt my ears so much I had to rip the ear-piece out. By the time we got to the scene, an elderly Jewish woman was giving one mugger what-for with her handbag. One of the officers, Craig, was belted in the head with a knock-out punch and a tooth went flying across the street. Hands were scrabbling inside his coat for the five grand when we finally steamed in. We didn't hold back and put the muggers down hard and fast using a series of carefully chosen below-the-belt strikes; even so it was a good, frantic sixty seconds before we had five of them down and under control. The sixth escaped and sprinted down the road, but we caught him. We were buzzing like mad, and the atmosphere once we got back to the station was terrific, with everyone saying 'nice job'. That is until Craig, with a swollen eye and jaw lisped, 'Where'th my tooth? Whoth got my tooth?' In the excitement it hadn't even crossed our minds to look for it. Craig was holding out hope that a dentist might save it. He wasn't too happy: 'Thith job ith FUCKED!'

This was a real, violent and prolific gang caught red-handed. The story even made the *New York Times*. I had an even bigger grin on my face later that day when I received my notice that I had been 'made-up', promoted to sergeant.

Five of the six went down. Amazingly, one had the balls to claim that he didn't know the others and that he'd been 'running for a bus' when we 'assaulted him' in a case of mistaken identity. I roared with laughter when I heard this but the judge wiped the smile off my face by acquitting him. Our brave little old lady with the handbag received a commendation from the court; miraculously she had walked away unharmed from the brawl.

The first sergeant's position that became available was in Haringey and I transferred to Muswell Hill, a couple of miles north of Stoke Newington, in April 1997. After Stokey, I thought I would be able to handle anything and I was soon given the chance to lead a drugs raid. I didn't know it, of course, but Haringey was going to make my time at Stokey look like a walk in the park.

THREE

THE FUCK-UP

Dawn, Wood Green, North London. The streets were empty, save for the occasional early riser on his way to work. Our three unmarked family saloons slowly glided to a halt alongside the kerb. We climbed out and shut the doors, handles up; less noise that way. I looked back at the main attack force of eight men and women forming on the pavement, adjusting their ballistic vests which sat hot and uncomfortable underneath their clothes. The dress was varied, from Armani to Primark (with a big mortgage and young child, my brand was Tesco value range). I hated early starts. Black coffee sloshed uneasily in my stomach. Someone had forgotten to buy the milk. The sun broke the horizon behind us; birds and a whirring milk float were the only sounds.

This peace of this delightful warm summer's morning was about to be well and truly shattered.

This was the first time I'd seen the area. A junior officer had put together the raid – a simple job, we'd all done it before, except this was my first time in charge. The intel-packs, passed around our briefing room at Wood Green police station, told us the target was a young kid suspected of dealing drugs. The reason was the stream of constant visitors that had been seen by officers. He was more of a public nuisance than a serious player.

I hadn't visited the scene myself and had relied on the junior officer to get the details. This was lazy, overconfident policing, as I was about to learn to my cost. As it was my first raid in charge I was obviously keen for a good result; I needed to prove myself and was hungry for success even on this small scale. I studied the briefing pack carefully, examining the layout of the street and the position of the suspect's house. Because so many briefing packs have been lost by careless officers, they are now disguised. This is still done in the optimistic but futile hope that a misplaced pack with sensitive info might be mistaken for an old paper and thrown in the bin.

I confirmed by radio that officers were already at the rear, ready to catch any runners or drugs that might suddenly fly out of the windows. After opening the boot I put on the huge mittens that come with the enforcer, a two-handled hydraulic cylinder which packs a quarter-ton punch. The mittens protect you against glass and splintered wood, should you follow the thirty-kilo battering ram through the door. I hoisted the bright-red solid-steel tube onto my shoulder and marched to the front of the attack force. As the only one trained, it was down to me to bash the door. I started a slow jog.

I was brought to a sudden halt by laughter. I stopped and turned around. I was alone. The team had stopped outside another house and were waiting, asking each other, 'Where's he going?' I was already five doors away. What the fuck? I felt like a proper twat and turned back. What an idiot – at least I hadn't crashed through the wrong door. I turned as red as the enforcer as I walked back towards my smirking colleagues – for them this would be the highlight of the raid and would feature heavily in canteen discussions for days to come. Walking back towards them, I felt uneasy. I should have been leading this raid but I clearly wasn't.

On the door was a number five; despite my careful examination of the plans I had managed to stuff it up. I opened the gate and jogged up the pathway. A perfectly maintained blue Victorian door awaited destruction at the end of it. I found it almost painful to destroy a good piece of antique craftsmanship like this. I've lost count of how many of these beautiful doors I've destroyed in my career.

As I swung the enforcer back I was suddenly overcome by a rush of panic. Something was wrong, but what? All the officers were ready to go, right behind me. Two of them had been to see the address before. Was I just feeling stupid? Fuck knows. I had already lost face; but something else was very wrong, I could feel it.

It was too late; the enforcer's momentum carried me unstoppably towards my destiny. The noise clapped down the long, quiet street. The door splintered and buckled. Its glass panes cracked. The small glass windows exploded, the door frame snapping and giving way; the door followed. I caught a glimpse of something that made my heart leap – a child's toy in the hallway. It was all too late, too inevitable; the attack force stormed past into their allocated rooms.

A WPC voiced the words already in my head, words that turned my blood cold: 'Is this the right address?'

It was the wrong fucking house.

The door was not in the place shown on the briefing-pack drawing. Dizziness and nausea kicked in. Oh God, no, I prayed I was wrong. Then I heard them – the cries of children. I took a deep breath and marched inside. The parents were in shock, dad had already managed to cut his feet on the glass and blood was everywhere. The kids were screaming, screaming, screaming. Their mother guessed correctly that I was in charge and stormed up to me. 'You've got the wrong house, you idiot! The postman gets it wrong all the time but I would have thought the police might have been a bit more bloody careful! It's the *other* number five you want!'

The correct house was twenty yards down the road, a slight bend the only dividing line between two streets, meaning there were two number fives only twenty yards apart. I had originally gone to the right house; it was the others who had got the wrong address.

Bright red and sweating, I ordered everyone out except the exhibits officer who took down the details of all the damage. The paperwork had to be perfect as the DPS (Department of Professional Standards) would crawl all over it. An investigation and humiliation on a massive scale – my first raid and an unbelievable fuck-up.

A year later, after a lengthy interview in which I admitted a lack of supervision, the chief superintendent gave me a formal admonishment. He told me the Independent Police Complaints Commission had only recommended this action due to my honesty in admitting my screw-up. He then laid into me about my appearance. I was unshaven and hadn't had a haircut for a couple of months. I told him I was off the next day to assist in an undercover crack operation in Brixton for six weeks. His eyes softened. 'I'm sorry,' he said, 'no one told me. Now get out!'

Despite this I was back in the inspector's office a short time later on a mission. It was early 1999 and I'd applied to become head of the newly created Haringey Drugs Squad. The local squad, Tottenham, had recently been abolished and this new unit was supposed to cover a much larger area of North London, an area home to a million people. A sergeant was needed to manage a team of five officers.

The DI wasn't happy. Here was a guy who had been given a major ticking-off for raiding the wrong house asking to lead North London's only drugs squad. He told me he had submitted a report asking that the sergeant who had previously run the Tottenham squad be allowed to stay on – but it wasn't to be. Officers were expected to change posts every six months; he had done his time and was expected to move on.

The other problem the DI had was that no one else wanted to do it, so, by default, I got the job. I hissed 'Yes!' and balled my fist, throwing out an imaginary punch to the solar plexus. Finally a chance not only for redemption but an opportunity to tackle the massive drugs problem in Haringey.

Some of the wind was taken out of my sails as I strode out of the station. A colleague who had heard the news shouted: 'Oi, Keeble! You'll fuck up and be back in two weeks! See you then.'

Cheeky fucker. I was going to show them.

FOUR

IN CHARGE

I bounded up the steps of Wood Green police station to the detective inspector's office, ready for the job. I kept reminding myself I was head of the drugs squad – well, OK, only by default, but I was ready to take the war to the dealers.

DI Gordon Green was a brusque, well-built Geordie with a goatee and his brief was to the point. 'You'll have a five-man team, work Monday to Friday nine to five and target the supply of class A and B drugs.'

This was perfect for me; lots of room for manoeuvre.

'Where's my office, guv?'

The DI furrowed his forehead. 'Ah . . . yes. Your "office",' he said, placing inverted commas around the word 'office'. 'This is a very busy station, Keeble, two hundred and fifty officers and admin staff in this building all fighting for office space. Your place is on the streets. That's where *your* office is.'

'Sorry, guv, but from where am I supposed to base our ops?'

'Well, maybe there's something.' He thought carefully. 'Drugs squad, drugs squad . . . Ah! I know.'

I raised my eyebrows hopefully.

'Yes, no, definitely no office, nothing's free, I'm afraid. But this might be of some use.' He opened a drawer and rummaged around for a few moments before producing a key. He handed it over.

'There's a room on the first floor of the Portakabin in the yard. There's some equipment too that's been left for you from the old Tottenham Drugs Squad. Good luck, Keeble.'

'Thank you, guv.'

I motored over to Tottenham police station where I met Martin, my predecessor, a good bloke with an excellent reputation. He disappeared into a back room for two seconds before emerging with a 1980s push-button phone covered in mould and a yellowing plastic brick with the legend 'BT Ans__rp__ne'. I'm sure it was pretty groundbreaking in its time, but now . . . These were resting on a blue A3-sized folder that contained the Duty Sheets (used to record police working hours).

'There you go,' he said cheerfully.

'Is that it?'

'Noooo, of course not.'

'What else is there, then?'

He produced a set of keys, leaned forwards over the desk and waggled them under my nose. 'There's a car. It's already in the car park at Wood Green, you can't miss it.'

I thanked him and he wished me luck. Picking up the file, and balancing the phone, answer-machine and an ancient PC unit I'd been told I could have, I staggered back to Wood Green in search of my office. I found it eventually. The 'room', as the DI had described it, was actually a largish stock cupboard full of outdated and forgotten files. I sold it to myself like a Kensington estate agent selling a broom cupboard as a bijou apartment. It was quite roomy (if you didn't stand up straight or stretch out your arms), quiet (isolated and dark), and it had potential for renovation (if you rearranged the boxes you ended up with somewhere to put stuff on). I fashioned together a kind of desk out of the boxes, on which I dumped the PC and plonked down the phone, answer-machine and folder and went in search of the car. At least we had a bloody vehicle, so we wouldn't have to search and stakeout drug dens on foot, I thought.

I emerged into the courtyard where all the cop cars were parked.

There was only one unmarked vehicle in it. I couldn't believe it was all the Met could provide one of its only two drugs squads. I pushed in the key, hoping it wouldn't fit. It did. A manky-purple Ford fucking Fiesta between the five of us. Anyone with any street knowledge would recognize it instantly as the classic CID car: the small aerial on the roof; the dirty interior. It didn't have fluorescent stripes but it might as well have had.

I mooched off back to the 'office' and sat on a pile of boxes that sighed out a cloud of stale dust. I decided to find a wall socket to which I could connect the phone and alert the front desk as to where my team could find me. It was then I noticed that the answer-machine had vanished.

Fuck me. I hadn't been the head of HDS for more than an hour and already someone had nicked my antique answer-machine. I had a storage cupboard for an office, a ten-year-old Ford Fiesta, an ancient computer that worked in kilobytes instead of megabytes, one phone and no furniture. I got the feeling that the chief inspector was not expecting big things from me.

I was both excited and apprehensive as I waited for my staff to arrive. This was a chance for other departments to dump their dead wood. Thankfully, whatever their past experience might have been, they were as keen as me and proved to be the saving grace of the unit. Greg, a twenty-eight-year-old Geordie, grabbed my hand as I welcomed him into the 'office'.

'Hi Harry, er, what're we doing in the storeroom?'

'Pull up some boxes and make yourself comfortable, it's all ours,' I told him. Fortunately he took it in his stride and set about building his own chair.

I knew Greg from my old team; he radiated keen energy. He was level-headed and streetwise and had made a number of good arrests off his own bat. Greg would go on to become my number two once the unit had settled down. He was followed by Adam (twenty-seven), a tall, strapping Nigerian with a deep laugh who hardly ever said a word. A recently married father of two, Adam was an expert at undercover: he'd never be picked out on the street as a police officer. He looked understandably puzzled as I told him to pull up a box.

Next to pull up was Darren (twenty-five), a ginger Mancunian engaged to Holly who worked as a station officer at Wood Green. He looked just like a trendy student; again, he would never stand out as a police officer. Colin (thirty-one) was a muscular London skinhead who turned the air blue every time he opened his mouth – he was renowned across North London for coming out with potentially career-ending politically incorrect statements. He would respond to horrified looks by raising his palms up and saying, 'What? What did I say?' in a mortified tone. He was the hardest police officer I'd ever encountered – if I was ever in a scrap I wanted Colin by my side. He shared my philosophy exactly. Hit dealers hard and aggressively. Put the fear of God into them. Push 'reasonable force' to the limits. Then treat them on the level. A crack dealer should never feel that it's personal, but respect the fact that they have been overpowered and are in our power. Colin had this uncanny knack of being able to communicate with criminals, calming them down in record time before cajoling a confession out of them. A human lie-detector, Colin knew exactly when even the most crafty ones were bullshitting him.

Finally the last man arrived, Charlie. I could tell he didn't really want to be in the drugs squad; he soon told me that he was a petrol-head and more than anything he wanted to be in the traffic police. This was of some concern to me as traffic cops and drug cops are very different breeds.

So there we were: the first union of Haringey Drugs Squad. I explained the situation with the office and that it was tough but we'd have to make do. Next, although I already knew the answer, I asked the guys what they thought the main problem was that we should be tackling.

The answer came back straight away.

'Take a look at our fifteen most-wanted,' Greg said. 'All crack-heads.' Most crime is committed by what we call nominals. On the walls of every single police parade room across the country there are photographs of the key criminals, the most-wanted. These aren't the Mafia dons or Triad leaders but the violent thugs who terrorize ordinary people.

They are all male, in their teens and twenties – and nearly all of them are either dealing crack and depend upon the crack houses for their trade or are simply addicts whose habit drives them on to commit an extraordinary amount of crime. Their ugly, bitter faces are scarred by the drugs. Next to each picture are ever-expanding biographies where notes have been added of aliases, addresses, sightings and recent activities. They all have thick criminal records going back several years.

The same faces are there year after year – occasionally one will disappear for a while, when they've been *really* unlucky and have wound up in prison. But soon a new evil bastard with a virtually indistinguishable face and an almost identical record pops up on the wall.

Take Sam Stockton, twenty-nine, from North Tottenham, a crack addict with thirty-three court appearances for sixty-eight offences including burglary, car theft, dangerous driving, damage to police cars, drug-dealing, actual bodily harm, ad infinitum. He had been banned from driving for five years but had recently been spotted behind the wheel of a 4X4, stolen only weeks after his release from prison for dangerous driving. On this occasion he overtook a marked police car and crashed into a set of traffic lights after driving the wrong way up a one-way street, much of that with half the car on the pavement. Once cornered he reversed into two police cars, doing two grand's worth of damage, before taking off and running another police car off the road. Oh yes, he also stole a £35,000 BMW which he sold to feed his crack habit. He got eighteen months and was out terrorizing the streets in six.

The Met tends to talk a lot about going after the big dealers. These operations often involve lengthy trips to the Caribbean and lots of zipping about in fast boats playing Crocket and Tubbs – more fun than bashing down the doors of local crack houses.

Anyone can see the sense in this of course – stopping the drugs at source, or as close to the source as possible, is obviously the logical thing to do. But we simply can't match the resources of the major drug dealers. It's not because of a lack of commitment or incompetence; as we've seen in the first chapter, the volume of drugs being imported is too high, the methods varied and ingenious and demand remains as insatiable as it's ever been. For example, less than three tonnes of cocaine was seized in 2006–07 compared with over nine tonnes in 2004–05, and one tonne of heroin seized in 2006–07compared with nearly 2.5 tonnes in 2004–05, according to official government statistics.

A lot of time and money is spent on chasing the 'Mr Bigs' but, as we shall see, the networks are set up so that the Mr Bigs are distant from the drugs and cash – linking them to crime is nigh impossible. They're also smart, have the best solicitors and even if a conviction is secured there are a dozen more like them waiting to take their place. I'm a keen and obsessive amateur student of international conflict, particularly World War II. The war against drugs is like fighting legions of secretive soldiers led by invisible generals – in this type of war you can only defeat the general by destroying his army.

Going after the Mr Bigs doesn't address the everyday issues that concern most people. If you have been mugged, or if you spend your life dodging the detritus of drug users in your stairwell or local park, you know exactly who you want targeting and they don't live in the yachts. They're the faces plastered on our wall. They live in your neighbourhood and they burgle and rob anyone they can; they batter old ladies for their pensions, steal benefit books from the mentally handicapped and extort money from kids. In recent years they'd started shooting each other without worrying too much who was caught in the crossfire. They've no respect for anyone and yet they are free to go about their business virtually unchallenged.

This sorry state of affairs was largely due to the crack-house phenomenon. We'd been warned that crack was coming ten years earlier, back in 1989 when the Association of Chief Police Officers had their annual drugs conference. The guest speaker, Bob Stutman, head of the US Drug Enforcement Agency's New York office, told a stunned room that crack had transformed the United States in four years: 'People said it's you crazy people who live in New York. You're all nuts. It can't happen anywhere else and it will certainly never leave the ghetto. The only thing I ask you is learn from our mistakes. We have screwed up enough times. Don't be like the people of Kansas and Texas and California who said "It can't happen here", because it did. I will make a prediction. I will personally guarantee that two years from now, you will have a serious crack problem because we are so saturated with crack in the US that there ain't enough pipes to smoke all the crack that's coming in.'

The week after Stutman gave his speech, a senior official at the US embassy's visa department in London was stabbed to death as she prepared to inform on a colleague illegally supplying visas to Jamaican crack dealers. A few weeks later a Jamaican hitman shot two men dead in separate attacks. This was followed by another six hits carried out in as many months by gunmen working for Jamaican crack dealers. But the strongest warning of what was to come had already been given the year before Stutman's warning, when Britain's first major crack dealer was arrested.

The market had been ripe for exploitation since the Brixton riots sparked civil unrest throughout the UK in 1981. The Toxteth riots that followed Brixton, and the endless recession that blighted Liverpool in the 80s and 90s, helped promote organized crime with a veritable army of disillusioned but bright and ambitious kids who left school with no hope of a job and a normal life. As the inner cities seethed, rejecting law and order, they turned inwards, embracing the criminals who at least seemed to be in control and kept some kind of order while offering a future to those willing to take a chance, especially in Toxteth.

The main players in the drugs trade at this time were the middle-aged blaggers who had made fortunes from robbing Liverpool's docks before containerization forced them to turn to

banks, extortion, smuggling and drugs. Liverpool was well suited
for this purpose; it had traded contraband through its docks for
hundreds of years and had long-established criminal networks that
covered the country. The blaggers formed new alliances with the
young generation of Afro-Caribbeans in the Toxteth ghetto who
helped with importation and distribution. Soon Liverpool, an
international trading hub, became Britain's Amsterdam for
cannabis, heroin and cocaine.

It was here that crack first hit the UK in the mid-eighties, when
Colin 'Badger' Borrows stole a street dealer's coke after watching
him hide it on a patch of waste ground. Borrows, who was fresh
out of jail for burgling a policeman's house, sold some to a Yardie
who taught him to 'wash up': how to mix the coke with baking
soda to take out all the impurities. In an interview with journalist
Graham Johnson for his book *Powder Wars*, Borrows recalled: 'I had
a go and it was perfect first time – we dried it on the cooker. I was
buzzing and not just from the crack. I knew what this was going to
be worth. I sold it in a few days and had £1000 profit. People ate
it up.'

Borrows, the son of a lorry driver and father of two, compared
himself to Alan Sugar and Richard Branson (except he is quick to
make it clear that he made his money a lot faster than they did) –
he was an entrepreneur, and if it were any other business Borrows
would have been fêted by Margaret Thatcher as someone who had
taken the Tories' advice and 'got on his bike'.

Borrows peddled for all he was worth. After selling crack for a
few days on Toxteth's frontline he had a regular demand from the
area's first addicts. He then squatted a house and got a production
line going. Soon he was making three grand a day and had set up
a team of crack-addicted street dealers who ferried people to one
of his three houses, which were open for business 24/7. Within
weeks he was taking in £40,000 a day and in a few months he was
an Armani-wearing millionaire with a BMW, a Jag, Merc and a
Bentley who blew two grand in Liverpool's finest Chinese restaurant every night of the week.

He realized that by getting prostitutes addicted to crack they'd move into his houses and work for free (today 95 per cent of prostitutes are crack users). He also bought shops and had dealers selling rocks out the back. Borrows the Badger then started burrowing away into other cities as yet untouched by his business – Manchester, Birmingham and London.

'People thought crack was a fad that would die out. But I made it big so that it will run and run and be there long after I die. No one can take that away from me. I created an industry, I made something from nothing. I feel a sense of fucking pride in that. It's an achievement.

'It's just like someone selling cigarettes from a pub or alcohol from a pub. It's given a lot of people jobs. There are whole communities who rely on drugs to make a living. It generates billions. I'm proud of that. I've contributed to society. Without me, they'd have fuck-all – no cars, no tellies, no trainers, fuck-all.'

Borrows was arrested and jailed in 1988 for dealing crack cocaine. But the epidemic he started was already sweeping the country. His multi-million-pound business was torn apart as gangs fought for control of various crack houses. The money was so good that it got violent very quickly and old criminal codes were rapidly abandoned in the desperate struggle.

Unlike other mainstream drugs, such as smack (heroin) and cannabis, crack is a pick-me-up, a big rush. So the punters were as wild as the dealers, flooding the criminal world with violence, guns, muggings, rape, prostitution, random shootings, torture and contract killings. Guns poured into the country as gangs were desperate to arm themselves. In August 1988 a guy called Rohan Bailey, known as Yardie Ron, got shot to pieces in a row about crack in Harlesden. Seven different people took shots at him; he was hit by twelve bullets. His was the first official crack killing in London.

The dust never settled as various wars were begun and never resolved, turning the UK's criminal community into one of the most violent of its kind in the world. Back in Stokey in London in

1990, DC Roy Lewandowksi was way ahead of his law-abiding colleagues (perhaps because he thought like a criminal) and was one of the first to spot the potential dangers (and profits) of crack cocaine. By creating his very own crack house he had got in early and was on course to make millions until he was rumbled. With the violence and 'tie-ups' and 'have-offs', raids by other criminals on crack houses in the hope of robbing drugs and cash, crack houses became very efficiently fortified – not because the dealers were afraid of a police raid but from fear of losing their precious business to another gang.

In 1989, after Stutman's speech, the Met set up a Crack Intelligence Co-ordinating Unit (CICU). It was shut down twelve months later when big seizures failed to materialize. The problem was, along with Customs and Excise, they'd relied too much on stopping crack getting into the UK. But the crack houses were right there, destroying our neighbourhoods under our noses;[2] they had been allowed to flourish until they became virtually impregnable.

One of the first fortified crack houses in London had been set up on the North Peckham estate in 1988. It was secured with iron bars on the windows and an iron grill on the door. No one came in. The buyers made their deals through a little cat-flap in the door. Pretty soon, there were crack houses all over London, from Kingston to Notting Hill, from Brixton through Harlsden to Clapham – where one dealer called Redman washed his crack in a little house in a cul-de-sac with his pump-action Remington shotgun, two pistols and collection of 9mm Brownings by his side. When he was shot, he refused to testify in court against the woman who pulled the trigger so he could kill her himself after she was acquitted.

---

2 In one memorable case, it took the police in Sutton's Worcester Park area four months of surveillance to amass sufficient evidence to shut down a notorious local crack house. The property was located directly above Worcester Park police station, but splendid work for all that.

At this time, the police's solution to the drugs problem was to have very small drugs squads (or, better still, don't have any at all). The idea behind it was, of course, that if you make fewer drug arrests, surely you've got a smaller problem? Crime figures are there to attempt to make the police look good. If you have an effective drugs squad tackling crime then the crime figures for drug-related crime increase and overall crime goes up.

In the late 90s drugs squads were out of vogue with the police. This was post-Stephen Lawrence and the focus was on forming large murder and robbery squads. But most robberies, shootings and murders were committed by drug addicts and no one was getting tough on the causes of these crimes, the major one being, as many victims knew, the crack house. By 1999, ten years after Stutman's warning, there were only two drugs squads for the whole of London – us with five policemen and one for the whole of East London.

Raiding fortified crack houses is not the glamorous end of British policing but it does create massive results as you are targeting the crux of crime. But the big problem with the statistics is that it is impossible to estimate how much crime is prevented; for example, if a crack house is raided, leading to the recovery of weapons and drugs, and several arrests are made, we can't then say we saved so-and-so's life tonight and so may robberies and burglaries were also prevented. Many of those arrested will get off for one reason or another and those troublesome negative figures for gun crime and drug-dealing go up.

If the addicts who are committing crimes are pleading their addiction to crack as mitigation and it is working and if we can't stop the importation of drugs into the UK then that leaves one (rather obvious) option. The answer: terminate the source with extreme prejudice – close the crack houses by any means necessary. The crack house is the shop floor of the international drugs business. If there are no outlets from which to sell crack, guns and sex then less drugs will be sold, leading to fewer addicts and a decline in the need for addicts to commit crime to feed their addiction. It will also remove the base from which so many nominals seem to operate.

Without worrying about conviction rates (obviously we wanted to send as many crack dealers and criminals to jail as possible but we couldn't expect the CPS (Crown Prosecution Service) to be bothered with a small-time drugs offender, especially as only 0.3 per cent of all crimes result in a prison sentence) and with gang wars raging on the streets around us (this was before Operation Trident was set up, so there were no specialist units dealing with black-on-black crime), I decided that our job would be to take out the gangs' fortresses, eliminate their bases, scare them shitless and drive them out – and hopefully we would also pick up some weapons caches (and not get shot in the process).

That was another thing: the crack gangs were fearless, not just because they were high on crack but because they had so little to fear from the police. The gangs see us as another gang – but whereas we used to be the strongest gang with the most resources we're now all too often seen as the weakest, restricted by the law rather than empowered by it.

How can a drug dealer possibly take seriously the police force that writes to everyone in the neighbourhood telling them, 'There is a crack house in your area and we will be raiding it soon. Sorry for the inconvenience, etc., etc.' Unbelievably, this technique was used by the police in one South London borough.

While I understand the rebranding of the police 'force' as a 'service' – we are here to serve the community (as we have always been) – we are not here to serve the criminals. I was determined that Haringey Drugs Squad would be a force to be reckoned with.

Of course this was big talk for five men armed with one A3 folder and a clapped-out Ford Fiesta; not the best equipment to tackle the 50,000-odd problem drug users in one of the poorest areas in the UK, containing one million people. When we typed 'crack house' into CRIMINT, our crime intelligence database, our PC (eventually) came back with precisely 100 addresses.

'Well,' I said, snatching up the car keys and the print-out, 'we might as well have a look, mightn't we?'

FIVE

CRACK IN THE COMMUNITY

We drove through the cold wet streets at 7 a.m. with our print-out and an A–Z. As we approached each crack house we saw the evidence of crime all around. Stolen purses and handbags lay in the gutter, the occasional addict hurried past us with his freshly purchased rock hidden under his tongue, his hood up, paranoid and rightly so. Balls of foil sat in congealing pools of blood in alleyways; every now and again we passed a yellow police board appealing for witnesses to a shooting or murder.

Even at 7 a.m., outside a decrepit council block, two Yardies in hooded sweatshirts were standing guard in the stairwell. Anything could have been hidden beneath their thick, heavy coats. Never mind Operation Trident, set up to deal with black-on-black crime – there should be a unit for crack-on-crack. Seventeen men had been shot dead in London over the past six months while there were sixty-seven attempted murders by gun on our patch alone (victims were typically saved by the shooter's inaccuracy) and another eighty shootings resulting in minor injury (these were just the ones we knew about) – all crack-related.

Just two days previously a hitman from the Tottenham Man Dem had opened fire on a man and his girlfriend in Southgate, hitting her in the arm. The gun had been found later the same day by cops in the City of London who stopped a car full of black youths.

Although the gun was linked to the shooting, it couldn't be linked to anyone in the car and no one was prosecuted.

Already by 1999, in what had so far been the worst year ever for crack murders, the media had tired of black-on-black killings and almost none of these made it onto the news. People had already forgotten what it was like a decade earlier in 1989 when we had six crack-related shootings in the entire Metropolitan area for the whole year. Shooting had become an everyday crime, like mugging and burglary.

One thing about the crack houses that particularly worried me was that they appeared to be impregnable; my stomach knotted at the thought of trying to get past that door and facing whatever was inside. Because fortified crack houses had rarely been raided, our intelligence was severely limited. The raids you tend to see on the telly are for good publicity, council flats with a Yale lock where one tap of the enforcer pops the door open. I remember watching a publicity raid on TV and the third man, dressed head to foot in riot gear, charged in carrying a clipboard. What was he planning to do – force the armed crack gang inside into submission with a multiple-choice questionnaire? Besides, it'd be a bit embarrassing if the press were there and after half an hour the cops were still struggling to get past a steel door while the criminals smoked all their gear.

What we did know was that as well as armed guards, the front door of a crack house was often reinforced with something called a New York latch. This was a metal bar which slotted into a plate behind the centre of the door. The bar would then be fixed to the wall at a forty-five degree angle. Any force directed at the front door would be displaced along the bar and into the wall – trying to smash the door down with a battering ram would be like trying to knock over an elephant with a toothbrush.

The room where the crack would be dealt from was usually upstairs, behind *another* reinforced door, often with bouncers manning it. To actually arrest someone for dealing crack we would have to catch them with it on their person. If a dealer drops their stash on the floor in a roomful of people, even if it is their own house, we can't charge them with anything as we can't prove to whom the crack belongs (unless a witness is prepared to talk or they can be linked to the evidence in some other way, such as DNA). As incredible as this sounds, all we can do is pick up the rocks and destroy them.

Despite this, some dealers kept a coal fire burning so they could throw the crack in it, or would flush it down the toilet or simply chuck it out the window (if they weren't reinforced by steel wire – but reinforced windows tended to only be on the ground floor, something we later used to our advantage). Some dealers employed 'catchers' who would hang round the back of the house explicitly for this purpose and would catch drugs, guns and sometimes even people trying to escape a police raid. The windows were always blacked out so there was little chance we could find out what was on the inside. So to actually bust someone we would have to be through two reinforced doors and up a flight of stairs, all the while fighting to get past whoever was in our way before the dealer could drop or destroy his stash.

As we looked at what seemed to be a fairly ordinary terraced house in Culvert Road, I wondered just who were all those addicts, whores and dealers – what was going on behind all those blacked-out windows?

A teenager, who couldn't have been more than fifteen years old, wearing loose-fitting clothing, walked up the path. 'This can't be a crack house,' I told Greg, thinking this girl was far too young. 'Look at her.' The girl knocked on the door. The letter-box flipped up, she stood back and the door was pulled open. She slipped through the narrow gap and was inside, the door instantly slamming behind her. A few minutes later there was a young man, then another girl, then a couple. We watched the lost souls coming and going and counted thirty in less than an hour.

Greg said, 'I think this is the right address, Harry. Look at them.

They've lost all sense of what's going on. They're like zombies. They're out there standing in the pouring rain. If it were cold and snowing a blizzard they'd still be walking up and down out there. They're at the point where they'll rob people, set up family, friends . . . anybody; they've reached the point where they don't care any more.'

As we toured the streets we rapidly discovered that once-pleasant neighbourhoods had gone to hell. We were dressed in civvies, so I tried to talk to the people who lived near the crack houses. Most were too scared. But some opened up. A woman told me that her neighbour had been shot while on her way to a takeaway when an argument between two crack dealers turned into a gunfight. She survived, just.

A young mum was terrified of losing her kids to crack: 'If I don't get my children out, or drugs don't get out, then they'll eventually get my children. I'm sure. I've seen it all around me.'

A middle-aged man said: 'I've had an old friend, an old lady, phone me in tears because she wanted a pint of milk and they were on the stairwell and she couldn't get out. You can't go out any more and if you're out you can't get home. In a block on the estate one woman spent four nights with a friend. She was too frightened to go back home. Why should people have to live like that? God help us.'

A father told me, 'I tell my sons to go to school and study hard so they can make something of themselves, but they just laugh in my face. They say, "Why should we study? So we can end up like you? No thanks."' His kids were peddling drugs, making more money than their father. How was he supposed to convince them he knew best? You can't explain it to them, it's impossible.

As doubt swam around my mind about the impossibility of the task, I remembered: 'You'll fuck up and be back in a week.' I balled my fists. Fuck it. It was going to be one hell of a learning curve. For now, at least, I thought I had found a couple of small, relatively unsecured outlets we could warm up on. But I needed to know what the hell went on inside those crack houses. Who was in there? How many people? What were they all doing? How was the dealing system set up?

There was only one way to find out.

SIX

INSIDE A FORTIFIED CRACK HOUSE

The first thing fourteen-year-old Jenni Doyle did when she woke up was reach over for her crack pipe with one hand and fumble for her lighter with the other. She sucked on the 'glass dick' without checking to see what was in it. She knew only too well that she had smoked the last of her supply sometime around dawn. Jenni checked her watch. It was 4 p.m.

She lived with her mum in a small council estate on Woodstock Road, in a slightly better part of Haringey called Stroud Green. Her mother worked as a cleaner for a large firm in the City of London, where she was now. Her father had vanished four years ago.

After a bit of 'ghostbusting' – scanning the carpet for pebbles or pieces of lint that might be crumbs of crack carelessly dropped the previous night (there never were any; crack addicts are rarely that careless) – she clambered into her loose-fitting clothes and was out of the house and on her way to Culvert Road in just a few minutes.

Jenni looked much older than her fourteen years and easily passed for eighteen. She couldn't remember the first time she'd had sex but she sure could remember the first time she had taken crack. She hadn't been a bad kid, although she had always hated school. When her parents split up, Jenni gave in to peer pressure from the wrong crowd and started truanting, spending her days drinking and smoking.

The first time Jenni saw crack she didn't know what it was but when she sucked the pipe she felt she could keep breathing in the fumes for an eternity. Every single cell in her body felt like it had been pumped up with air. The guy she was with had to pull the pipe away from her – all she could think about then was having more. Every stress had gone – her life, her parents, none of it mattered; this feeling made it all so . . . unimportant. She was alive, every molecule rippling with pleasure. She had to have more.

The only place to get some was a crack house. Her friends knew of one in South Tottenham, an area where the streets were plagued by the Craven Park Man Dem and the Edgecot Boyz, two of the thirty-odd street gangs in Haringey at the time.

But they didn't have any money. That's when Sara, Jenni's friend, told her that she was a prostitute. They went to a house in Tottenham and Jenni waited outside while a pimp came outside and collected Sara. The pimp, who controlled twenty girls, stared at Jenni long and hard over his shoulder as he led Sara inside to have unprotected sex with four men for £150.

By now Jenni was coming down. It was the worst feeling in the world; all she could think about was getting more. She had blisters on her lip from chewing but she couldn't stop. It was agony.

When Sara came out she had spent the £150 on crack. They smoked it together straight away. Jenni kept trying to hit the pipe again and again until it got so hot it popped and she was left with a tiny piece of glass stuck in her skin next to her left eye. She didn't feel it.

Some people can afford a crack habit for a while at least – they have jobs, possessions, homes and bank accounts that can be pillaged. For a fourteen-year-old the most 'valuable' possession is their body, which can be sold quickly and easily. Sara took her to her pimp. He made a 'coolie', a cigarette laced with crack, and told her to put on a slutty outfit he gave her. As she smoked he approached her from behind; he was touching her. Jenni didn't care – he had crack.

That day, while her classmates studied for their GSCEs, Jenni was on her way to the crack house in Culvert Road to earn her fix by having unprotected sex with as many men as her pimp sent her.

The house in Culvert Road[3] was desolate, uninviting, dank and smoky. And that was just from the outside. It stank of piss; human shit was in the garden and the alley; foil, tissue, beer cans, newspapers and rotting clothes surrounded the property.

The door was opened by a young man dressed in jeans and an enormous coat that could have housed several guns of varying sizes.

In the dimly lit hallway there were wet bloodstains along the edges of the dirty lino. On the second-floor landing a sharp odour swept out through the door – the rancid chemical smell of crack.

The carpet in the first room was shit-brown, heavily stained and pockmarked by so many burns that it looked like abstract art. In the dim light, dozens of people were standing, sitting and lying down; they seemed almost motionless.

But jaws were moving, voices barking hoarsely into mobiles, talking deals; their speech was jagged, nasal and riddled with slang. In a corner near a window, a shadowy figure moaned as if ill. Bizarrely, one woman sat with her skirt pulled up over her head, her legs apart. A man was blowing smoke into her, between her legs; a variation on the hit-kiss ritual. After inhaling deeply users put their lips together and one blows the smoke into the other's mouth. That way not even the merest puff of the precious smoke is wasted. This alternative version of the kiss extends to another orifice.

New methods and new exotic rituals crop up all the time to increase the length of a smoke. Some users are called 'balloon-heads' because after sucking on their pipe they exhale into a

---

3 We later raided this address; the characters and the stories that follow have been reconstructed from the people we found inside.

balloon and then hold the balloon closed with a finger until they are ready to inhale its contents.

Doors hung off their hinges, giving the house a lop-sided feel; it was still possible to see the faded door numbers from the days when each room was a separate bedsit. In an adjacent alcove, a couple were copulating. In the hall, a man and a woman argued feverishly, competing with the loud rap music blasting out from one of the bedrooms.

The smell was a nauseating combination of stale sex, sweat, urine, crack, cigarettes and filth. Two men argued over who had the last hit from their pipe; two others were on their hands and knees looking for crack particles they claimed they'd lost in the carpet.

In the kitchen, flanked by his protectors, sat the man behind the scales – the 'K-man'.

He was unrepentant. 'I've got hundreds of people addicted but why the fuck should I care? So they've fucked up their lives or maybe died, I couldn't care less. Why should it matter to me? Kids come to me, I tell the boys to bring girls next time and I get them addicted, so soon enough they're whoring for me so fast you wouldn't believe, sometimes the next day. Then they tell their mates and the plague continues. There was one girl, a teen, so beautiful she could have been a model. One week it took me. She's on the street now. Why should I feel anything? I need to get paid.'[4]

This K-man had been caught on the street with some rocks on him and the judge ordered him to be tagged. But he simply threw a bag of sand (a grand) to a friend who went to the centre to get tagged for him. Amazingly, *unbelievably*, the companies didn't think

---

4 Smoking crack reduces inhibitions and leads young teenage girls to have unprotected sex with men for more drugs. Also, men who control the drug control the sexual play around crack. So even though a girl might insist on using a condom, the man with the crack can simply refuse and the addict soon gives in. HIV is on the increase again thanks to crack, with one in twenty-five crack users carrying the virus according to the UK's Health Protection Authority.

of asking for a photograph of the offender they're supposed to be tagging!

It wouldn't be long before Jenni moved into the crack house with the other girls – life would be easier that way. Someone who had already crossed that line was Maria Arundel, an eighteen-year-old prostitute. As Jenni arrived at Culvert Road, Maria was crawling around in her underwear on the floor of the crack house's master bedroom, ghostbusting along with several other women. This surreal, pitiful ritual started every morning and continued sporadically throughout the day.

Maria choked as she inhaled the smoke from a bit of crumbled plaster and twitched uncontrollably. Everyone was desperate for a client, desperate to take them into the whoring room onto one of the five filthy mattresses so they would share their smoke. These were not attractive women. One had lost half her face and most of one arm in a fire; she had passed out chasing the dragon (smoking heroin) and had not felt the fire started by a dropped cigarette until it was almost too late. Another woman never washed and stank (the others had got used to it). One other lady was in her forties, overweight with an over-bite. Somehow, despite the scars and smells they all managed to sleep with enough men to each get through at least £500 of crack every week.

Amongst those in the house that evening was James Matthews, a twenty-eight-year-old law draughtsman at Wood Green Crown Court. James had enjoyed experimenting with drugs ever since attending university and had been partial to a few lines of coke every now and again. That is until the day he and a friend decided to cook themselves some crack.

Sitting in his basement flat at 2 a.m. one Saturday morning, illuminated only by candles, James opened the wrap that held the gram of powdered cocaine. Excitement buzzed around them like a static charge. His friend watched intently as James began cooking up the hits. James flattened the open bag and let about four rocks and some powder fall onto the table. He crushed the rocks with a bottle cap and then worked them into six separate piles. He had already gathered his tool kit, which consisted of a spoon, a tiny bit of baking soda and a glass of water. He put a drop of water on the spoon and heated it briefly, after which he added one of the small piles of coke.

The two men hadn't spoken for a good five minutes, the suspense rendering them silent. They watched as the cocaine fell into the water, clouding it as it sunk to the bottom. He then proceeded to heat it until about half of the water dissolved, and quickly added a tiny sprinkle of baking soda. The concoction bubbled up. James heated it slowly, careful not to burn any of it off. The sweet caramel smell told him that the coke had been cut with a type of sugar. The two men smiled as the mixture made a loud pop, separating itself from the spoon, and crystallised into a brittle, clear yellow puddle. James immediately scraped it out with a scalpel, and waited for it to harden.

Picking the rock off the scalpel blade, James carefully dropped it into his crack pipe and handed it to his friend. The rock sizzled as it evaporated and disappeared into his friend's lungs until all that remained in the pipe bowl was a tiny bit of black residue from the sugar. He sat back on the couch with a slow nod. His face went from smiling to wonder as he exhaled and the hit fully entered his bloodstream. His eyes closed and his arms went limp. He let out one monosyllabic groan and was gone.

James felt strangely calm and listened to his friend describing how much better this was than any other method of using coke – 'How stupid are we for snorting it?'

When James finished making his hit he threw it in the pipe and smoked. Blood rushed to his ears, his veins streamed and pulsed with cocaine; his lips, teeth, mouth, throat and lungs were all numb, and the rocket he was tied to took off – he was soaring up, up, and up. Eventually, after fifteen minutes, he felt the rocket slow down and stop, at which point he could feel himself lazily descending back down to earth. They had intended to save half a gram for the following day but they couldn't stop and by the time dawn broke they were ghostbusting the carpet. More. That's all they could think about. More.

James had held it together at work for almost a year but it was getting difficult. He had raised extra money by transferring his credit-card debts to another account. Then, instead of cancelling the old card, he withdrew cash until it was full before transferring the balance again. His bank, no doubt pleased to see he was paying off his debts, had raised his limit. By November 1999, it had got to the stage where he had seven cards with about £20,000 of debt and no way of making the payments. The fear his debts caused within him was so strong there was only one thing that brought him relief – crack cocaine. Each day he struggled through, pretending to work, thinking of nothing but how quickly he could get to the crack house in Culvert Road.

Other addicts who had made their pilgrimage to Culvert Road that evening included several normal 'respectable' people – teachers, taxi drivers and civil servants. Mark James Roberts, twenty-two, worked as a shop assistant in the fishmonger's on Wood Green High Street. He hadn't yet been caught with his hands in the till but it was only a matter of time; John Daniels, twenty-seven, worked on the set of *The Bill*, operating the clapper and loading films into cameras.

Mike and Janet started smoking crack together at weekends, then during the week. Mike said it turned him into Superman at work. He was a builder and worked long shifts flying high to raise more drugs money. They started fighting over the crack – Mike wanted the lion's share; it was his money that was paying for the gear and when words failed to win the argument he beat her with his fists. That's when Mike tried to quit the crack but Janet refused; she blamed Mike's attempts to quit as the main cause of their relationship troubles.

Despite enormous debts and the problems crack brought to his workplace, Mike continued to get high until he got fired and the money ran out. Janet suggested Mike offer her up to the dealer for sex in return for crack, which he duly did.

Also in the house was Mikey, an addict who worked for the K-Man dealing on the estates. This was the most dangerous job. On the streets you were vulnerable – addicts would try to rip street dealers off or, worse, 'shank' (stab) them and take their stash. Then there were the cops; no one wanted to get collared with a load of class As on them. Worst of all though were the gangs who robbed the street dealers and sometimes stormed the crack houses.

Mikey kept about twenty rocks in his mouth, little balls tightly wrapped in foil then clingfilm melted shut with a lit cigarette. He'd cough one out when he saw a punter coming and money and crack would be exchanged in a gang handshake, a tap on the knuckles, then the palms open and the fingers scrape along each other's palms. Deal done. If the punter was a woman, then they would kiss and the pellet would be flicked in with his tongue.

Mikey knew of another guy who kept rocks in his anus and whenever he saw a female client he quickly extracted a rock and expertly placed it in her mouth. He proudly called this technique a 'street kiss', until someone caught him and he was beaten mercilessly.

If the police approach or try to arrest these street dealers, the rocks are swallowed. Then, if the cops don't hold onto them and if the wraps don't leak and kill them first, they puke them up a little later; otherwise they sift through their faeces the next day. Other dealers hide their stashes in bushes, sometimes booby-trapping them with dirty needles.

Mikey sometimes had a runner; most often it was Charlie, who was thirteen. Charlie would hang around the estate and take orders, acting as a go-between for dealer and client. Charlie made £50 a day from doing this. Those dealers who recruit teens are following a tradition – adults are more likely to face a prison term if caught with several rocks. Teen runners not only avoid the law but are also relatively easy to frighten and control.

Mikey didn't see the Edgecot Boyz coming until the Stanley knife ripped through his jacket and tore the skin as it sliced down his back. He dropped to the gutter where he was kicked and the gang took his stash and cash. Not wanting to hang around for the police, Mikey staggered towards Culvert Road, blood streaking down his back into his jeans. As he limped up to the door, blood splattered behind him on the pathway.

The K-man later told the whores to scrub the path clean. Blood on the doorstep was bad for business. Crack, the ultimate cure-all, obliterated Mikey's physical pain.

Nigel Brown also worked on the street. He was a full-time crack-related criminal, in that his entire life was based around criminal activities to raise money for crack. This included benefit fraud, pick-pocketing and, when he was in a hurry, a good old-fashioned mugging. Thirty-two-year-old Mary Michaels wasn't a crack addict. She worked at the benefit office in Wood Green as an administrative assistant and was returning home when she was singled out by Nigel. He struck from behind, punching her viciously in the back of the head. For Mary, it was over in a flash – everything went red and her ears rang with the sound of rushing blood. When she came to, a member of the public was comforting her. Her purse was gone, her self-confidence shattered; her cash in the K-man's pocket, the proceeds evaporated inside Nigel's lungs.

Mary was left so traumatized that for months afterwards she burst into tears without knowing why; she shuddered with fear every time a man passed her in the street. Nigel had transformed her personality; from being an outgoing confident individual, Mary became a recluse, unable to do her job, unable to go out after dark, unable to sleep past 3 a.m.; she'd drive up and down her street until a parking space became free close to her door.

One step up the criminal ladder from Nigel was Wayne. The only thing that came close to crack for Wayne was the rush of robbing. As soon as he had got up that morning he was in a trance-like state. 'I don't think about anything else, notice anyone or anything; my mind is so fixed on what's happening. I want to instil terror in the cashier by the look in my eyes, my clenched teeth – absolute eye contact with them.'

Together with his partner they hit Barclays in Wood Green, just by the tube station. Wayne's partner had the shotgun down his left sleeve; it was just a case of lifting and pointing his left arm and grabbing the handle with his right and they were set to go. Hearts thumping, the two men burst into the bank and stormed up to the counter. Wayne's knuckles connected with the back of a customer's head; he passed the cashier his bag and told her to fill it.

The cashier, who had already faced robbers more than once, started filling the bag slowly with low-value notes. 'I told her to gimme the fucking twenties and fifties and demanded more money off another cashier. She told us there weren't none, so I told her there was. "Don't fuck with me," I said, "I know it's there!" She took two parcels of sealed money out of the reserve drawer.

'When you've got a gun in your hands, people are listening to you; they're doing as they're told. You're in full control. It's just brilliant. You're just there. You're the man. You're God. But to *feel* like you *are* God, well for that you need crack cocaine. We got out of there fast, blasted down Lordship on the bike and into Broadwater. Fucking bitch had put in two stacks of blank paper. We thought we were fucking minted. We still came away with three grand. Not bad.'

There are three types of bank robbers: those trying to raise a stake to invest in a business or drug-dealing, those trying to pay off debts, and for many young aspiring robbers, such raids are carried out with an attitude of 'earn and burn'. For Wayne it was the last option.

'Three grand, that's £1500 each, would be gone in no time; then we'd be skint and looking to do over another bank. I used to spend it on silly shit, jewellery, clothes, designer trainers, haircuts, women . . . when it's from a bank and you've got it in your pocket, it's burning a hole. Then we got into crack. Crack will eat £1500 up like it was nuthin'.'

These two young men spent the next twenty-four hours in the crack house. The K-man smiled and watched as he smoked with the robbers and the pile of money steadily crept from their side of the table to his. The robbers then handed over their watches, designer trainers and jeans. They left wearing stinking tracksuits and a pair of slippers so they could walk home – the K-man kept a few pairs especially for this.

These were just a few of the hundred or so people who visited this small crack house on one day in 1999. There were at least ninety-nine more houses out there.

There was no time to waste.

SEVEN

METHOD OF ENTRY

Jenni Doyle woke up in her mother's flat in Woodstock Road and reached for her glass dick. It was empty, as usual. She looked at her clock. It was 9 p.m. Fuck. How could she have slept so long? Her stomach started aching with the desire for crack, her nerves crying out in pain as the ache spread to every extremity. She felt groggier than usual, though. Jenni sat up and swung her legs out of bed. Except that they didn't move. She pulled off her duvet. Chains were wrapped around her ankles; they were fixed to a metal plate screwed into the wall. On the floor was a plastic washing-up bowl, a large jug of water, some toilet paper and a bowl of cereal.

Jenni screamed.

I drove along Woodstock Road with a smug grin on my face. I'd discovered that I'd been the victim of crime yet again at the station. The Ford Fiesta I was driving wasn't ours; it belonged to the CID. They had 'exchanged' it with the drug squad's car and hoped we wouldn't find out. It wasn't exactly Starsky and Hutch but the Nissan Primera was big enough for the five of us and, even better, it was mocked up as a taxi, making stakeouts and recces easier.

The previous afternoon Greg and I had sailed down the same road on the back of a rubbish truck disguised as bin men. We had wanted to get some solid evidence of coke-dealing from a basement flat (we had to convince the courts for a 'ticket', a warrant to forcibly enter) so I decided to 'borrow' the occupants' rubbish bin. Stealing rubbish is actually a crime; there's nothing wrong with borrowing it, however, so as long as we returned it to the owner after we'd raided his flat, we were within the law. After collecting the street's refuse we threw the stinking bin-bag in the back of the Primera, dashed back to Wood Green police station, donned two sets of rubber gloves and sifted through the rubbish in the yard. Inside we found a load of wraps, drug bags and flyers – our man was dealing for the club scene and not for crack-heads. This wasn't the kind of hit I really wanted to be doing – recreational drug users tend to have much less of a negative impact on neighbourhoods – but I decided that it was a good warm-up for Haringey Drugs Squad before we stormed our first serious fortified crack house. We re-bagged the rubbish so it could be returned later and stored it in the evidence room with a note warning anyone intending to throw it away that it was vital evidence.

Although the front door looked quite flimsy, I asked Greg to book a Method of Entry team just in case the dealer had invested in a New York Latch. These priceless units are made up of civilians who specialize in finding speedy ways into buildings they themselves will never enter. They're commonly known as the 'Ghostbusters' or 'Ghosties' because they sometimes burn their way through doors with oxy-acetylene torches strapped to their back, so they look similar to the stars of the film of the same name, except the Ghosties dress in black, not green.

Their main weapon is the enforcer. Usually it takes just one or two strikes to obliterate even the sturdiest door. In extreme situations, a firearms team will load pump-action shotguns with 'Hatton' rounds. These fire a burst of compacted lead powder which disintegrates anything it hits – including door hinges. A favourite of the Ghostbusters' is the door-jammer. This great piece of kit is a hydraulic ram that rips a door from the frame. It makes a wonderful hum, especially during a dawn raid. After a few seconds the door can be smashed in.

We pulled up across the road at 7 p.m.; this was when the dealer would be at his busiest so he should have a good stash ready to sell. A couple of guys from the CID had tagged along just in case we needed them and they stood by watching. I needed this to go well; if it didn't, then they'd soon let everybody know and our reputation would be shoddy right from the outset.

The Ghosties pulled up in their red van, debussed and crept down the steps in the darkness with their red enforcer.

The door popped open after one swing, and as the Ghosties pulled back I charged in with my torch screaming 'POLICE!' more in the hope of not being mistaken for a rival and getting shot than anything else. The dealer was standing up in the lounge, a big pile of coke, Es, scales and cutting equipment on the coffee table. He looked petrified. 'It's all right mate,' I said; people do stupid things when they're terrified. Greg appeared behind me. 'Nice one. Shall I tell the Ghosties they can clear off?'

As the Ghosties packed up, we searched the flat and photographed the evidence; we had about two grand's worth of coke. The CID guys were impressed so I was overjoyed, as they'd spread good news round the station. We had done so little damage to the door that I was able to close it behind them as they left. The dealer, meanwhile, was sat in the lounge in shock, quiet as a mouse. I was just thinking this was a nice uncomplicated result for us when the doorbell went. Putting my fingers to my lips I called out, 'Come in, bruv, it's open.'

A moment later a guy in an army jacket appeared in the room; he saw me and two other officers. 'Aw shit!' He turned as if to run but Greg was behind him. A quick search revealed a small piece of coke. We cuffed him to his mate. The doorbell went again. 'Come in, bruv, it's open.' And we had another one.

'We've timed this one well, eh Harry?' Colin said as the doorbell buzzed once more. Several 'Come in, bruvs' later we were outnumbered seven to six and were out of handcuffs. The guys all knew each other and we were having a jolly old chinwag as we marched them out of the house in front of their stunned neighbours and into a van we had called to take them all to the Factory (police station). This lot was going to take us all fucking night to process, particularly as the dealer came up with a beaut of an excuse to try to beat the dealing rap. He told us he was an addict and claimed the gear was for his personal use. He was bagging it up so he knew how much he was using. Nice try but it wouldn't wash. Overall, not a bad start for Haringey Drugs Squad but the next raid was going to require something special – talk about going from one extreme to the other.

Jenni wouldn't stop screaming. Eventually the neighbours, fearing a murder was imminent, called the police. Jenni's mother, who couldn't afford to lose her job, had doped her daughter and chained her to the wall in an effort to keep her at home and get her off crack.

The police constables were utterly stunned when they saw the chain and steel plate. Jenni, at her wits' end from crack deprivation, begged the police to save her from her 'cruel' mother. The officers nicked Jenni's mother for false imprisonment. Jenni was handed over to the Haringey's Child Protection Service – as it turned out, she would have been better off chained to the wall.

EIGHT

TENSION TOWN

Twenty-nine-year-old Patrick 'Nookie' Smith had hired a gun partly for self-defence (he owed his own gang, the Lock City Crew, money for drugs) but mainly because he was planning to pay off his debts by robbing another dealer. The problem was that his cunning plan of stashing the weapon in his girlfriend's rubbish bin for safe-keeping had backfired. After a night on the tiles, Nookie turned up at his girlfriend's place and was horrified to find the bin men had been and his gun was gone.

Nookie's girlfriend, twenty-eight-year-old Laverne Forbes, should have known better than to have been with a man like Nookie. She had a job and a seven-year-old daughter and a decent home in a low-rise block of flats in Kessock Close, Tottenham, overlooking the River Lea and the Warwick reservoir.

Two days after Nookie lost the gun, on 25 May 1999, Laverne walked out her front door with her daughter ready for the school run. Two men in their twenties, both wearing dark clothing with their baseball caps pulled low over their faces, were waiting. One was carrying a pistol. As they ran towards her, Laverne turned, pushed her daughter back into the hallway and into the lounge before returning to the hall. One of the men kicked the front door open and burst in firing the pistol – three bullets tore into Laverne's back and she dropped at the bottom of the stairs.

Climbing over her, the two hitmen bounded up the stairs just in time to catch Nookie clambering out of the bedroom window. They dragged him back inside where they beat him to his knees. The assassin placed his pistol's muzzle between Nookie's eyes and pulled the trigger. Meanwhile, their daughter had run into the street and was screaming, 'My mummy and daddy have been shot!' As neighbours ran out of their homes to help, the gunmen sprinted down Yarmouth Crescent before crossing a footbridge into an industrial park where they disappeared. An air ambulance rushed the couple to the Royal London Hospital. Nookie died later the same day; Laverne followed twenty-four hours later.

The hit rocked London with its brutality; why would anyone shoot a mother in front of her seven-year-old daughter and then execute a man in his bedroom? Most witnesses refused to talk to the police out of fear; one frustrated detective said, 'With these guys it is like the gunfight at the OK Corral. They go round doped up to the eyeballs and open up with handguns or Uzi machine guns. We just come along and pick up the pieces. We know there are people out there who heard and saw what happened but they're too afraid to talk.'

The murders of Laverne and Patrick were just the latest in a sequence of killings that had been sparked off after a row over bad car-parking.

The Lock City Crew (LCC) were from Brent, just to the west of Haringey, and they used the Bridge Park Leisure Centre (funded by Brent Council and opened by Prince Charles) as their base and armoury – a safe meeting place where they stored weapons and drugs. The centre was managed by forty-nine year-old David Lewis, who had convictions for robbery and who had hired a security guard who was a member of the LCC.

On 1 May 1999 the wife of a prominent member of rival South London gang, the Cartel Crew, arrived at the centre to meet a friend; she left her BMW parked at an odd angle, blocking part of the centre's entrance. The security guard couldn't resist and wound her up about her bad parking, insisting that she 'try again'. The woman responded by throwing a bottle at him. Someone called the police and she was forced to leave.

Twenty minutes later she returned with her husband, Dion Holmes, twenty-nine, who brought along a few of the Cartel Crew with him.

When Lewis saw the Cartel Crew rolling up he ran inside the centre and told Lock City member Winston 'Escobar' Harris. Harris, 38, a Jamaican who had done time in New York for GBH, scrambled his gang, telling them to grab guns from the armoury and wait for him inside the centre. Harris got hold of a 12-gauge shotgun. With him were fellow Jamaicans Stephen 'Beamer' Murray, 26, from Kensal Green, Jermaine 'Mylord' Hamilton, 22, from Kilburn and Leonard Cole, 27, from Finsbury Park (who were all in the UK illegally).

Harris then slipped out the back door and watched as Holmes and his crew swaggered into the centre. Harris had a set of keys; he ran round to the front, entered and locked the door behind him, trapping the gang inside – along with about a dozen women and children attending a playgroup. The plan was for Harris to pick off Holmes but as he made his way deeper into the centre he heard a gunshot. One of his crew had fired their gun by accident; women and children were running screaming towards him, to get to the exit. Harris shouted at them to calm down but no one listened, the women begging him to let them through. Instead he shouted, 'Shut the fuck up!' and blasted a hole in the ceiling with his shotgun. Suddenly men were running around the centre brandishing handguns and firing at each other in a Wild-West-style shoot-out as women and children ducked for cover. The Cartel Crew escaped by throwing furniture through windows and running towards the high street. When it was over Dion was flat on his back in a corridor, a bullet in his heart. People slipped on the blood that covered the floor; two other LCC members were bleeding badly from bullet wounds.

One of the guns belonging to the Lock City Crew matched the shells recovered from the murder scene in Tottenham.

Two days after the double murder, on the evening of 27 May, twenty-three-year-old Adrian Roberts aka Buds, Blessed or Popeye2, was the victim of a drugs robbery which took place at the hostel where he was staying. He was forced to lie on his bed and was shot in the back. Hours later one of the gunmen, Clayton King aka Loose, was ambushed by Roberts' gang, the Kick Off Head Crew. King left a nightclub with Marlon Abrams aka Chuggie at about 2.45a.m. As he came to a stop at traffic lights in Acton Lane, gunmen pulled up alongside and blasted the car with two 'pray-and-spray' Uzi 9mms, hitting King five times. Abrams was also hit but managed to drive away to hospital. King died on the way.

Once again the police were left to pick up the bloody pieces and, as ever, faced a wall of silence. A public meeting was called by Brent council and the local police. No one knew how many people would turn up – everyone seemed to be terrified by the gangs. But it was packed and the police were given tremendous abuse by an angry crowd. A woman said her innocent son had been caught in the crossfire of a gun battle but the police had treated him like a criminal. She told them: 'You're tarring everyone with the same brush, even when they're victims!' The community was seething.

I didn't know it yet but my decision to take out every one of our borough's 100 crack houses would become an all-consuming obsession, taking us into situations I could never have imagined. But for now I was concerned about the effect such aggressive tactics would have; after all, it was the aggressive and prejudicial stop-and-search tactics that had led to the 1985 Broadwater Farm riots which had spawned today's gang system. Recent events echoed those in the lead-up to the 1985 riots – the area was a tightly wound steel spring – and I was about to give the key a few good turns.

People welcomed Haringey's Broadwater Farm Estate when it was built in 1976. The new tenants had previously lived in houses without a bathroom and hot water but it soon became apparent that the estate was a perfect place to operate if you were a criminal. The concrete walkways were a rabbit warren with plenty of corners for muggers to wait for victims before losing any pursuers with greatest of ease. The estate deteriorated into a hard-to-let ghetto and in 1985 the unrest that had been spreading through London since 1981 hit with an intensity unlike anywhere else.

'The Uprising', as it popularly became known, started in Brixton in 1981. A council housing waiting list of 18,000; a third of the housing sub-standard; high unemployment with two out of every three of the unemployed being black; the highest robbery figures in London (twice the second highest); no social amenities. Add to this the police's aggressive tactics in Operation Swamp, where 1000 black men were stopped and searched (including three members of Lambeth Community Relations Council) in the three most deprived streets in the area. The fuse was lit. It was just a matter of time before the bomb detonated. When officers tried to help the black victim of a stabbing, their van was surrounded and the victim rescued by angry youths convinced that the police were letting him bleed to death. The next evening, an officer arrested a man outside a mini-cab office on the notorious Atlantic Road, and Brixton exploded. The fighting lasted for two days and there were almost 300 police injuries, 65 serious civilian injuries, 56 police vehicles destroyed and 30 buildings that had to be demolished. More riots would follow throughout Britain's cities that summer, most memorably in Liverpool's Toxteth in July; the area had collapsed under the weight of 80 per cent unemployment as the docks closed and relocated.

Lord Scarman's 1982 report on the Brixton riots was the first official recognition of institutionalised racism in the police: '. . . many believe that the police routinely abuse their powers . . . The damage done by even the occasional display of racial prejudice is incalculable.'

Four years later, Brixton's communities had been turned into no-go ghettos when another incident threatened to plunge the area into pandemonium. Inspector Douglas Lovelock was firmly in the mould of the Sweeney; kicking in doors brandishing guns, while not common, was considered normal practice when hunting a dangerous armed robber. In this case he was after Michael Groce, a blagger who'd recently waved a gun at one of his officers. As Lovelock ran though the flat a shape shifted in a bed and then leaped up as the Inspector ran into the room. He fired. To his horror, he had shot Groce's mother, Cherry, in the chest. She was rushed to hospital – she pulled through but was left paralysed from the waist down.

One week later, on 5 October 1985, a young black man, Floyd Jarrett, was arrested in Tottenham by Haringey police, having been stopped in a car which they thought might have been stolen. The tax disc didn't match the vehicle. Four officers went to his home on the Broadwater Estate to search for further evidence. Floyd's mother Cynthia opened the door and while she might not have been best pleased to have four police officers in her home, she nevertheless allowed them to conduct their search.

The situation deteriorated as soon as Floyd and his brother Keith arrived along with their sister Patricia. They shouted at the police to get out and some pushing and shoving started. Cynthia, who was twenty stone, collided with a detective, fell to the ground and stopped breathing. She was pronounced dead on arrival at hospital.

No stolen property was found in the house, and the vehicle Jarrett was in when he was arrested wasn't stolen. Cynthia's death, seemingly at the hands of the police, sparked outrage. The next day Haringey's black mayor, Bernie Grant, said, 'For the second time in a week, a black woman has been killed by officers of the state. Police behaviour is totally unacceptable. The force is out of control.' Like Brixton, the area suffered from high unemployment (up 82 per cent within ethnic minorities in one year), high crime and poor housing.

Violence began after a coach-load of black and white youths arrived on the estate to be greeted by locals. At 6 p.m., at a packed meeting held on the estate, Grant appealed for calm. Someone shouted, 'It is too late for words!' and the meeting erupted.

Police were attacked with bottles, stones and petrol bombs; cars were overturned and set on fire. As one officer fell trying to escape a hail of bricks a concrete slab was dropped from the second floor of a tower block; it landed on his back and ruptured his spleen.

A few minutes later shotgun blasts sent the police scrambling for cover; two journalists were hit with pellets. Every time the police tried to advance they were sent packing by a hail of petrol bombs and bricks thrown by more than four hundred rioters. At 9.40 p.m. Scotland Yard's firearms squad were issued plastic bullets and CS gas (the first time the police had been authorized to use CS gas on the UK mainland).

Nine minutes later a policeman was shot and seriously injured. By 10.10 p.m. the first floor of a block of flats was on fire but the fire brigade couldn't get close enough to tackle the blaze because they were pelted with missiles. A team of policemen led by thirty-four-year-old PC Keith Blakelock, a father of two, were despatched to attempt to clear a path but were overwhelmed by dozens of men who appeared on the smoke-filled landing. Blakelock suddenly found himself cut off from his colleagues and surrounded by several masked men (and some boys) armed with machetes and baseball bats. His head was practically severed in the attack. The dying PC's helmet was taken as a trophy.

The rioting continued; as PC Blakelock lay dying a gas explosion ripped through a nearby house and another officer was shot. It was not until 4.35 a.m. that the police finally began to take control.

Winston Silcott, known as 'Sticks', who had been sent to borstal twice and who was on bail for another murder, was charged and convicted in 1987 for the murder of PC Blakelock. But his conviction was overturned four years later after a new technique (electrostatic document analysis, ESDA) proved that pages of Silcott's confession had been replaced at a later stage. Silcott had not appeared on any of the 1000 police photographs of the riot and his fingerprints were not found on the weapons recovered from the scene. Teenage witnesses who said Silcott was there had been put under tremendous pressure. Stories appeared in the press that they were held in cells naked for days, without access to their parents or solicitors.

In 1991 Silcott was awarded £50,000 compensation for being wrongly convicted (the police officer's widow, Elizabeth, received £15,000). Detective Chief Superintendent Graham Melvin and Detective Inspector Maxwell Dingle were charged with fabricating evidence but were acquitted in July 1994. Detectives are still trying to gather fresh evidence on the murder. In October 2004 the blood-stained, slashed uniform PC Blakelock was wearing was removed from Scotland Yard's Black Museum for DNA testing.

The riots of Broadwater Farm did irreparable damage to the community. As in Toxteth, the young turned their backs on civilized society and embraced crime, forming organized gangs. Crack, introduced by Burrows the Badger, came along at exactly the right time as the younger and more ambitious gang members realized that here was a chance to get rich quick.

Perhaps the most extreme symptom of the changes wreaked by the Broadwater Farm riots and the rise of crack cocaine was Mark Lambie. Lambie was fourteen years old when he was arrested and held naked in Wood Green's police cells until he confessed in desperation that he was a witness and party to the murder of PC Blakelock. One can only imagine what an effect such an accusation and treatment could have on an innocent fourteen-year-old boy's attitude to the police — and society in general.

Fifteen years later, in 1999, twenty-nine-year-old Lambie had become one of the most feared gang leaders in the UK; known as the Prince of Darkness, he was the head of the Tottenham Man Dem, an organization responsible for countless shootings, several murders and horrific tortures, which controlled dozens of crack houses that brought misery to thousands of people.

I didn't know it then, but I would eventually become a major thorn in Lambie's side. I would also encounter one member of the Jarrett family in my quest to close the crack houses. I hoped that the majority of people would see that we were targeting the serious criminals and that our war would be with them alone, but there was always a chance something might go wrong. A hundred per cent success rate was unlikely; if an innocent person was hurt or killed as a consequence of our aggressive tactics then the community might explode as Broadwater Farm had in 1985. The police were already hardly the flavour of the month as it was.

The public's confidence in us was at an all-time low. And not only because we just seemed to be mopping up after the gangs. On the night of Monday 11 January 1999, two policemen were called to a house in Tottenham where they found thirty-year-old Roger Sylvester, a local government employee, shouting and beating his fists on the door of his house. When the officers tried to approach Sylvester he threw himself on the pavement and stared pounding it with his fists and legs. He was eventually restrained by eight officers, detained under the Mental Health Act and taken to hospital where he suddenly stopped breathing. One week later Sylvester's mother switched off his life-support. While an inquiry cleared the police of any wrongdoing, Sylvester's family were rarely out of the local newspaper and TV news, demanding a public investigation.

Then in September 1999, Harry Stanley was shot dead by the Yard's elite SO19 officers when a table leg he was carrying in a bag was mistaken for a sawn-off shotgun by a member of the public. Although it wasn't on our patch, it was just down the road in Hackney and only served to increase the 'us and them' divide.

Besides this, Haringey had a unique problem. The borough consistently scored highly in the crime figures and was always in the top five worst criminal areas in London; in fact it was usually in fifth position after Lambeth, Westminster, Southwark and Hackney. But there was one crucial difference between Haringey and these other boroughs. They were all inner-city areas – strictly speaking Haringey didn't fit this category as it included the distinctly leafy outer-London boroughs of Archway, Crouch End, Stroud Green, Alexandra Palace, Highgate and Muswell Hill. Unsurprisingly, no crack houses were to be found in these areas.

On the other hand, when we plotted our 100 crack houses' position on an A–Z we found that 90 per cent of them were confined to the area to the east of the railway line to King's Cross that bisected the borough; specifically the wards of Noel Park, White Hart Lane, Coleraine, High Cross, Bruce Grove, South Tottenham, Seven Sisters and Tottenham Central. So Haringey shared the characteristics of both an inner-city borough and an outer-city borough. When we recalculated the crime figures for the inner-city part of Haringey without the outer-city areas then it leaped straight to the top of London's crime chart – by a long, long way.

Take burglary, for example. In Haringey in 1999, there were 31.2 burglaries for every 1000 houses, behind the inner-city boroughs of Hackney (38.5), Islington (35) and Lambeth (38.2). But remove the three 'crime-free' outer-borough areas of Haringey and you are left with 45.5 burglaries per 1000 houses. The results were the same for mugging, GBH, ABH and shootings per 1000 people and, of course, drug-dealing and possession. The troubled boroughs of Lambeth, Southwark, Westminster and Hackney have their hot spots but generally crime is much more evenly spread throughout these boroughs than in Haringey (Westminster is an anomaly because criminals are drawn there from boroughs all over London to prey on tourists, so street crime is always sky-high).

While I am distrustful of crime statistics generally, they do help give an overview of the area you're policing and can make you aware of particular hot spots, criminal frontlines and peculiarities. These following facts are unadjusted for the crime-free areas of Haringey.

Fifteen years after the riots, the borough remained one of the most deprived local authority districts in the country. Around 17 per cent of the population was black, with 43.2 per cent being from ethnic minorities. Unemployment (particularly long-term unemployment) was racially disproportionate, with black people and people from other ethnic minorities twice as likely to be unemployed as white people. The divisions were even greater among young men.

Educational achievement was among the lowest in the country. Pupils from rival schools gathered in Wood Green shopping centre, in particular the bus terminus opposite Wood Green tube.

Disturbing confidential police reports from 1999 expressed concern about the growth of a teenage gang culture (there were at least thirty gangs with fifteen members or more in the Haringey area, with dozens more 'clicks', smaller gangs made up of school-kids affiliated to the adult gangs in a criminal version of a mentoring programme).

Between 1998 and 1999 sexual offences had increased by 23.9 per cent (one-third of these were rapes), drug crime by 32 per cent and robbery by 54 per cent. Mugging had risen by 58 per cent; overall, street crime had gone up by 51 per cent. Violent crime had increased by 80 per cent and Grievous Bodily Harm was up 65 per cent.

Haringey had a greater proportion of robberies than anywhere in London. The vast majority of these occurred close to train stations along the Tottenham High Road, in particular to the south around Seven Sisters where the illegal drugs market was largest. Commuters leaving the station were often followed to quieter streets where they were mugged.

Processing all this information, along with our list of crack houses, I calculated that the most dangerous part of London was the 'Tottenham Triangle', the half-mile between South Tottenham and Seven Sisters train stations, specifically the area where Tottenham High Road, Seven Sisters Road and Amhurst Road met – this was one of the main junctions of North London, the Piccadilly Circus of the drugs world.

At its apex was a house on Ashmount Road, a Victorian terraced crack house from hell. Greg and I knew we were getting close when we came across a junkie chasing the dragon (smoking heroin) behind the wheel of her car round the corner in Harold Road. We walked past and after a quick discussion we decided to nick her; we were hopefully just far enough away from the crack house to get away with it. I tapped the driver's window and flashed my warrant card. She leaped in her seat and turned her head towards me. She would have been a pretty girl once. Her eye was black, her nose was red and freshly broken and her skin was pale and veiny, almost translucent – heroin chic. A quick search uncovered her stash. We were stunned to discover that she was the daughter of a senior North London cop.

'You won't tell him, will you?'

Fuck me.

'Please, he knows nothing about this; please keep it this way.'

We had no right to interfere, but if it was my daughter I'd want to be told. Greg suggested an informal meet in a pub should be arranged with her father, but eventually I decided against it; if we did it for her, then we should do the same thing for every addict we come across. They're adults, it's up to them. I have no idea what happened to her.

On our next recce we got close to the crack house. The front garden was full of rubbish, broken glass and the odd needle. The stained and peeling door was manned by two hooded bouncers who stood guard leaning on the doorposts with their hands in their pockets. I guessed that in a house of this size, the dealing room was upstairs, probably behind another reinforced and heavily guarded door. I felt murderous aggression radiating out into the street; the neighbourhood was paralysed by fear. No one had dared to report this house to the police; it was incredible that something like this was able to exist alongside a 'normal' community but it was a measure of how impotent people believed the police to be.

What really amazed me was that the punters who were flooding in and out at a rate of forty an hour were coming from all over the south of England. It was the perfect location; its reputation had spread way beyond London's borders, deep into the Home Counties where it was known as the 'One-Way Crack House' because it was situated right in the middle of Tottenham's one-way system. It was two minutes' walk from Seven Sisters Tube and Seven Sisters mainline (which runs from Liverpool Street to Cheshunt in Hertfordshire) and two minutes from South Tottenham station (which runs from Gospel Oak to Barking in Essex).

Outside the house an argument was raging between two men with strong Jamaican accents. I stole a glance: one was short and stocky, while the other, dressed in loose-fitting and low-hung jeans, dark puffer jacket and baseball cap, turned, caught my eye and frowned, looking me up and down. I shoe-gazed, kept walking and hoped that my attempt to look like a junkie was convincing – I was sporting a nose-ring, earrings, a filthy army coat, boots and unwashed hair (which I was growing). My appearance had caused some consternation amongst some of our neighbours in the little village which I had recently moved to with my family. I was certain I was at the top of the Neighbourhood Watch's most-spied-upon list.

As we walked Greg said, 'There's fucking guns in there, Harry, you know it.'

'Yeah, but if we go in armed then the job's fucked. No drugs and no arrests.' Raiding a crack house with guns would be a waste; if we're armed we have to do a 'dig out' – shout a warning through a megaphone that they are surrounded by armed police and should walk out when they're ready. That would mean all the drugs would be destroyed, any weapons wiped clean and hidden (that way they had a good chance of denying all knowledge of their existence) and we would probably end up letting everyone back in to carry on. I badly wanted the element of surprise and I wanted to be quick enough to get some drugs, which would give us a chance of shutting the house down.

I said, 'There's no evidence that we can see that guns are inside, so going on that we're doing this unarmed.' I could see Greg didn't like this but it was the only way. From my brief recce of a crack house I knew there was no way we could risk sending in one of our team as an undercover officer to buy crack in an effort to find out about its inner workings. I knew that large-scale and mass market crack dealers used a variety of methods to root out UCs in their midst, and, although most officers were able to deal with them, I thought in this case it would be too dangerous.

Anyway, even if we wanted to work undercover, we couldn't afford it. UC work takes time and money and requires expensive equipment which is not always available. And before we could even approach a suspected dealer we needed evidence of dealing, otherwise they claim they never thought about selling drugs before this nasty policeman came along and put them up to it. And then you have to buy off them two or three times. Closing 100 crack houses this way would have taken us years.

When we got back to the station I started putting together a plan as to how we would get in – this would require some out-of-the-box thinking.

We headed for the smoky canteen (one area with luxurious comfy chairs had been put aside for smokers – this used to be the senior officers' canteen but those are all extinct now). But before we could grab a tea, someone told me that gunshots had been fired at Ashmount Road.

My mind flashed back to the two men arguing outside and the guy who had eyeballed me. An Armed Response Vehicle (ARV) went to the scene, ambulance following. Although the crack house carried on regardless, the gunman was long gone. The armed officers followed the trail of blood and caught up with the short stocky fellow who was limping down the road in the direction of Seven Sisters Station. He refused medical attention, claiming he 'fell over' and would sort it out at home. Sometimes gunshot victims check their wounded limb with a nightclub's metal detector. If the bullet has passed through the machine won't beep; so if the bleeding can be stopped then the chances are they won't need to go to casualty. Without any witnesses and the injured party extremely uninterested in any investigation there was nothing to be done.

I decided that we would still treat the house as gun-free as the shooting was on the street and there was no reason to say that the shooting was anything to do with the people in the house. I also had a bright idea as to how we were going to make this raid a success.

NINE

MASSIVE ATTACK

So here I was. From stuffing up what should have been a routine raid of a small-time dealer to leading 100 unarmed officers on a dangerous mission to raid and close down a house full of crack-heads armed with God knows what.

Yes, that's right – 100 officers. I had taken advantage of my wide-open guideline-free brief (i.e. my boss hadn't mentioned our budget) and put in a request to the Territorial Support Group for as many officers as they could spare. The TSG (also unfairly known as the Thick and Stupid Group) are the Met's muscle. They roam the capital, six to a van, ready to provide a rapid response to any emerging situation where brute force might be needed to restore the peace. I tried to impress their commander with the fact that I was the Head of Haringey Drugs Squad (without mentioning there was only five of us, a Nissan Primera and a stock cupboard) and that this was a big operation (which it was), neglecting to mention that it was also our first. Fortunately, I didn't have to try too hard. 'This is right up our street,' their commander told me. 'They're gonna love this.'

Although still 100 per cent up for it, their tone bacame deadly serious at an early briefing when I told them they were about to take part in an impossible raid on a supposedly impregnable crack house which contained up to fifty crack-heads and dealers. 'Oh yes,' I added, 'we've received information that there's a bucket of acid kept in the hallway to throw over raiders.'

Then there was the possibility that the building was secured by a New York latch. The only way in would be to totally obliterate the door. I booked a team of Ghostbusters for this; they would charge the house carrying an enforcer *and* oxy-acetylene torches. I also requested a few sniffer dogs, an ambulance, a fire engine and, for good measure, a police helicopter with a powerful search beam.

From what we could tell from the outside, the house was going to be packed. The pressure was unbelievable. Everything was down to me, including risk assessment. If these men went in there and got shot to death by a gang of crazed addicts, then it was my responsibility.

At 7 p.m. on 11 November 1999, the briefing room at Wood Green police station was packed to the rafters. People had spilled out into the hall, I spotted my DI and DCI at the back of the room. Fuck, I better get this right, I thought. As I pushed my way to the front people called out 'Jimmy' and 'Smokin'!' in reference to Hollywood actor Jim Carrey's catchphrase in *The Mask* (I really do bear a striking resemblance). I spoke to the team supervisors, explaining strategies, outlining the route, showing floor plans and possible contingencies. I also briefed them on the shooting and the bucket of acid that might have been left in the hallway. I'd called the fire brigade as I had wanted them to attend but they said to just give them a call if they were needed as the station was just around the corner. They then went and discussed tactics with their respective units. I was buzzing with excitement – I'd hardly slept the night before and had got up at dawn but didn't feel the slightest bit tired as we lined up our vehicles. Everything had to be perfect, even the order in which we pulled up at the address – we had to give them as little warning as possible and it was vital that the Ghosties and the TSG arrived in the correct sequence. I called one of the observation team for their report on the latest activity at Ashmount. 'Fucking busy,' he replied succinctly. The hit was on.

We drew stares as our multi-vehicle convoy snaked through Wood Green to Tottenham. It was clear that something big was going down and I was worried text messages would be fired off to all the dealers of Tottenham warning them that we were coming.

As soon as our vehicles pulled up outside the Ashmount Road house, all eyes were on me to launch the operation. Once the crews all stated they were ready, I turned and took stock. Nearly 100 officers in full riot gear. I called the helicopter and told the pilot to start his descent towards the target.

My heart was pounding, my mouth totally dry, as I began to jog slowly towards the house. As I turned the corner, a couple standing outside the address backed away and then sprinted off sharpish. Finally, we were about to show the dealers there was no fucking with the police now. A blue curtain flicked back from a first-floor window and a face peered out at us. We'd been spotted; I sped up.

It was a rush like nothing else – me in civvies, looking like an addict, charging with the Ghostbusters, one wielding a bright-red enforcer, the others with full cutting equipment; behind me twenty TSG officers in full riot gear, ready to beat the crap out of anyone who dared to put up a fight; the helicopter coming down from above as the searchlight lit up the windows, hopefully blinding, deafening and terrifying those inside. The street behind me was packed with police. The Ghosties swung the enforcer. As they did, one thought flashed into my mind.

Please God, no gunshots.

TEN

THROUGH THE LOOKING GLASS

Time didn't exist inside the Ashmount Road crack house. It was irrelevant. All the windows were blacked out and for those who hadn't left for days it could have been six in the morning or six in the evening, they neither knew nor cared. Acrid smoke dominated every room, a suffocating thick haze that sunk into every corner. Burns marked all the surfaces and users had at least one burn hole in one or more items of clothing, the signature of a falling spark or ash from crack. The furniture was broken and improvized. A large blue wooden door had been rested across two milk crates to form a table. Cupboards were full of rubbish, pizza boxes, takeaway tins, empty cans of Nutriment (a milky vitamins and minerals drink), broken ashtrays, plates, cups and glasses.

Jayne sat on a sofa on the ground floor, facing the wooden cutting board on the door-table, her pregnant belly overshooting her jeans. She was five months gone. With a frown of concentration she began. All the ingredients were spread out on the table: a small glass bottle, razor blade, bag of baking soda, alcohol, clipper lighter, a chipped cup full of water and, of course, the cocaine.

Using a tiny spoon she carefully dropped a little coke into the bottle, adding a pinch of baking soda and a little water. She cooked the mixture with the lighter while gently shaking the glass in a circular motion. After a minute she stopped heating the concoction and shook the glass more vigorously; the powder had become a tiny globule of oil which gradually coagulated into a solid rock.

She reduced her clipper lighter to medium flame and cooked the rock until it started to melt back into oil. Switching off the lighter, she shook the bottle until the rock had reappeared. She then added a few more drops of water, so that it covered the rock which sat at the bottom of the bottle. It pinged off the sides as she shook it and her client leaned forwards, took the bottle from her and studied it against the naked bulb that hung from the ceiling. Thirsty for a smoke, she watched the man tip the rock into his palm and study it with wide eyes. 'Damn, you're good at this!'

Jayne's second skill after preparing a potent rock of crack was as a 'buff' – an expert at oral sex. Her client had promised her crack if she could perform the 'double master blast': make him reach orgasm just as his high from the crack reached its peak. Jane collected her gear (it would be stolen immediately if she left it – in the crack houses, it's every man and woman for himself and addicts often steal crack from one another) and made her way with her client into an adjoining room full of filthy mattresses.

Upstairs in the first-floor dealing room, sitting on a stinking brown sofa, a Jamaican man caressed a Glock 17-L, a 9mm seventeen-shot semi-automatic pistol renowned for its accuracy and stopping power (SO19's weapon of choice). The gun is almost entirely made of high-tensile plastic rather than steel. The urban myth that makes it so popular is that it is the only gun in the world that will pass through an airport metal detector unnoticed.

His companion had an untreated but healing gunshot wound in his arm. They discussed plans of revenge. There was a lot of action going on around them in the corridor outside and in the dealing room. People were cleaning and building their pipes, and jockeyed for position near anyone who was cooking. Others had packed their pipes and were smoking. Some, yet to find a fix, were agitated – their eyes were wide, hands trembling, their bodies arguing with their heads as to what to do. Sit or stand. Move into another room. Ask someone to 'beam them up'. They weren't interested in conversation or sex – at least for now – just a puff on the pipe.

In the fortified dealing room manned by a bouncer, bags of crack and fistfuls of notes were snatched and grabbed as the scales chinked up and down. The talk was frantic, filled with master plans and false promises. Every guy talked about girls, coke, music and guns. The scales on the table were dusted with white powder alongside a roll of foil, a small pile of rocks and a bag full of crumpled cash.

A young woman strode into the room, obviously in the middle of a 'crack attack' (a desperate need for crack) and proclaimed her availability. She unfastened her jeans and pulled them down low enough to reveal a shock of pubic hair, a popular and effective way to generate a sale. Some women wear nothing underneath their short skirts and part their legs, flashing potential clients; sometimes touching themselves. Although too much crack leaves many men temporarily impotent, in the early stages it creates a powerful desire for physical contact – a factor which works in the dealers' and prostitutes' favour.

The sound of an approaching and descending helicopter gradually cut through the noise, the arguments, boasts and screaming-loud sex. A young dealer walked over to the first-floor window, flicked back the thick blue curtain and saw hell coming straight for him.

ELEVEN

TO THE DEATH

To my surprise the door imploded on the first hit. The house was so busy they'd stopped bothering with the latch. The Ghosties went in and the first wave of the TSG burst through behind them. This was the most dangerous moment – we had no idea what would be waiting for us as we dived into the smoky darkness – but guns, knives and the bucket of acid were at the forefront of our minds. We were all screaming 'Police!' in an effort not to be mistaken for a rival gang and get ourselves shot. If you were the first through the door you had to be quick – if the gangs inside could hold the entrance the narrowness of the corridor would immediately create a bottleneck, leaving the two men at the front to fight their way in against the entire crack house while the rest of the TSG stood impotently behind them.

I almost choked on the smell, the acrid smoke though which I saw the screaming prostitutes, the pregnant woman on the sofa, men with their trousers down, dealers cursing, the drugs, the filth.

The TSG were on the stairs in a flash, rotten and without banisters; size tens banged heavily on the boards. A massive bouncer who was closing the reinforced door at the top of the stairs saw them coming and hesitated, frozen with shock. Big mistake. That was the dealing room; that was where the main fortifications were. The TSG leaped forwards, kicked the door open before he could close it, and they were into the unknown. A group of men and women stared wide-eyed as the TSG grabbed the nearest guy, pushed him into the wall and yelled 'Police! Nobody fucking move!' For a second, nobody reacted. Then came the madness. It was like a fight from a Wild West film, only those were real chairs being broken across backs and fists were really breaking noses; the addicts high on crack didn't feel punches and contorted themselves until their bones cracked in an effort to get away.

As the leader of the operation, I ran from room to room, walkie-talkie in hand, ready to call for extra help or medical assistance. The noise was phenomenal, the helicopter and its blinding searchlight, the screaming – the prostitutes just didn't stop. Fighting is an exhausting experience. Besides that the TSGs were wearing heavy armour which made it all the harder to hang on to a writhing addict. While most officers soon overpowered their targets, some were still struggling and one unfortunate officer was rolling around on the floor, wrestling with another man who was naked from the waist down. But after cracking a few ribs, we prevailed and had thirty men and women in handcuffs.

I wanted to put the fear of God into those bastards that terrified the community and it worked – some of them pissed themselves. But I was friendly afterwards: there's no point acting tough as they clam up or just give much worse abuse back. On the ground floor, most of the people were crack addicts, not players, and were quite friendly – the TSG kept pointing at me and saying 'Who does he look like?' Soon the criminals were yelling 'Jimmy' and 'Smokin'!' and cracking jokes.

Although most people calmed down pretty quickly, the heavily pregnant woman continued to scream and shout. This was the last thing we needed so, to be safe, I called in the paramedics. As they approached she screamed, 'Fuck off, don't you fucking touch me!' The paramedics were (quite rightly) not impressed; there was obviously nothing wrong with her but if by some chance she lost her baby then all the good publicity generated from this raid would vanish. She spat in the general direction of the paramedics, a lump of phlegm that arced through the air and landed near my feet. It was black.

As I tried to talk to her, a male voice from the next room called out, 'Don't bust her, man, she cooks my coke just the way I like it!' This got a roar of laughter from cops and crack-heads alike. Even the woman smiled and started to calm down. 'Who's the dealer here, then? Where did you get your gear?' I asked. Unsurprisingly, she told me to fuck off. But she had flicked her head to her right, raising her eyebrows as she did so. I followed this reflex and saw a thirty-year-old guy, well built, surrounded by prostitutes. He hadn't moved since we crashed in and the women seemed to be drawn close to him, as if he were their protector.

Looking round the house, I saw hundreds of little crack rocks covering the floor. The addicts eyed them hungrily. One of the TSG yelled that they'd found a good amount of crack and some scales on a table along with a handgun and a load of ammo under the sofa on the first floor. He coughed as he did so – the smoke was that thick in there. I went upstairs where the atmosphere was a lot harsher, colder. I ordered a firearms unit to come in and make the gun safe and got the Ghosties in to take the metal grills off with their blowtorches. As they started to work, the man surrounded by prostitutes said, 'Hey, you can't fucking do that! This is my fucking house!'

'Exactly. And we need them as evidence to prove that this place is – sorry *was* – a crack house.' We didn't really, but I knew these grills cost £800 apiece and this would piss him off because if he was bailed and wanted to set up again somewhere else he would have to get hold of new ones.

Because the gun was under the sofa and in no one's possession we couldn't link it to anyone in the room – there were no finger-prints and DNA science, although very much a part of police work, wasn't nearly advanced enough then to link a gun to any one person. Even if it had been the chances were that the gun had been handled by dozens of people and therefore carried so much DNA that it could not be linked to any one of them.

A TSG officer came into the room. 'Harry, come and take a look at this.' In the hallway there was indeed a bucket but instead of containing acid it was full of water. It had been placed there to catch a leak from the upstairs bathroom. So much for our intelligence! I looked around and saw the sniffer dogs having a field day; they ensured every last crumb of crack was collected.

I ordered everyone in the house arrested and strip-searched. We cleared a room especially for this and it proved to be a useful exercise in getting to know our targets. Each person was searched in private, giving us a valuable chance to talk to them informally on a one-to-one basis without their mates watching. This way we could build relationships and pick up snippets of information.

Most people didn't want to talk and those that did gave us false names and addresses but some of the prostitutes opened up. I had no idea whether they were trying to get us to go soft on them or if they just liked having a sympathetic ear. One told me that she'd been pregnant while a crack addict. 'I haven't seen my daughter for fourteen months. I was doing a lot of crack cocaine at the time before she was born. The night I was to give birth I was getting high in a crack house. Just as I took a hit from the pipe, I felt like a rubber band snapped down there; and all of a sudden this water came out.

'I said "Oh shit! What am I gonna do now?" So I got up and the water was trailing behind me, and my girlfriend says, "That baby is coming. You better go to the hospital." Do you know what I did? I said, "No, I want another hit." It was about midnight then and I didn't get to hospital until 2 a.m. My baby was born with asthma and a weird cough. I remember I used to smoke the pipe – I used rum at first, then rubbing alcohol, dipped with a cotton ball, to make the flame last longer. I think that's why her lungs are damaged and she has that cough.'

I was tempted to say, 'So, nothing to do with the tonnes of crack cocaine you've been smoking then? All down to the rum, was it?' But I thought better of it and kept my mouth shut.

We were interrupted by a sudden commotion coming from the

bathroom. Darren and Colin were trying to strip-search an already agitated man and it had suddenly kicked off. I joined in as it became apparent there was something in his mouth; rocks, no doubt. I grabbed his neck: 'Don't you dare fucking swallow it!' Darren tried to prise open his jaws while the suspect grunted and dribbled saliva. Finally he coughed up and a bunch of white rocks fell to the floor. 'Look at the size of those rocks!' I said.

Colin bent down and picked them up. 'They ain't rocks, Harry.'

'What are they then?' I asked.

Our prisoner straightened up and shouted indignantly, 'They're me fucking falth teeth and you'th buthted them!'

My initial smugness vanished as soon as I realized he was right. That's all I fucking needed; we were bound to get a complaint out of this. Darren and Colin searched him. My despair turned to relief when we found a good collection of rocks in his pockets. That should balance any complaint about damage to false teeth nicely. Two weeks later he was sentenced to seven days for possession.

Next, Adam stuck his head round the corner. 'Harry, I've got the owner of the house over here.'

Fifty-three-year-old Lesley Ballantine was the only other person who gave us verbal grief. Oddly, although he was Afro-Caribbean, he racially abused Adam relentlessly. A stocky five foot eight inches, Ballantine didn't look like he was capable of running a crack house, and it soon became clear that he wasn't. He'd inherited the property from his mother and had developed a crack habit which dealers had taken advantage of by offering him free crack in return for the use of his perfectly located, large house. They'd 'cuckooed' him – taken over his nest like the bird of the same name. We nicked Ballantine for possession of crack and some forged cash we found in his bedroom. Nevertheless, Ballantine would make bail and return home where he might be cuckooed again.

The custody sergeant couldn't believe his eyes when we showed up at the nick with a load of crack addicts with the jitters. His mouth hung open as they flooded the custody office, all of them demanding this, that and the other.

Processing a prisoner is an unflinchingly bureaucratic task; the prisoners had to be interviewed and their details taken and entered into as many as six forms. The interviews took for ever, as it was at times impossible to get any sense out of our subjects, who mumbled false names and addresses and asked for solicitors. We had been on duty for sixteen hours and it took another thirteen hours before our prisoners were all processed. 'Just think of the overtime, lads,' I told the squad, prodding Adam awake as he collapsed over his umpteenth form of the night.

Finally, I drove home. It was 3 p.m., over twenty-nine hours since I had clocked on. I pulled up at some temporary traffic lights down the road from my house and, as I waited for them to change, fell deep asleep.

TWELVE

KILLERS COME TO HARINGEY

It occurred to me that perhaps the neighbours would like to know more about what had happened at Ashmount Road. Now that the dealers, pimps, prostitutes and addicts had been carted off and the house boarded up, I called round to some of the people I had spoken to earlier. They were genuinely overjoyed. It was as if we had plunged a stake into the heart of Dracula; the once-fearful villagers could move about freely, even in darkness.

That didn't mean the entire area was now trouble-free, of course. Although the crack house in Ashmount Road had gone we still had ninety-eight properties left to deal with. Apart from this, a massive street fight had recently broken out between two rival gangs just down the road near South Tottenham train station, which had resulted in some quite serious injuries – incredibly, the vicious battle had been fought between two rival schools.

Pitched battles involving bats and knives were regularly occurring between schools (particularly bad were the conflicts fought between White Hart Lane and Park View Academy, St David's and St Katherine's – a team of UN peacekeepers would have been hard pushed to sort that lot out). Large gang fights had also been breaking out during lunch breaks and immediately when school finished, with gangs meeting up to fight one another in certain areas: the arena of choice was Downhills Park.

Besides schools, there was also marked rivalry between different estates, particularly in South Tottenham in the Campsbourne, Tiverton, Moselle, Stonebridge, Chettle Court, Noel Park and Culvert Road estates, where serious criminal damage, intimidation of residents and violent behaviour had become part of everyday life. Some teenagers were living impossibly violent lives, fighting wars with other estates, school-kids and street gangs.

It was around this time that one of the most feared men in America, a crack dealer and enforcer called Maxwell Bogel, arrived in London. Bogel, an utter monster, was on the FBI's Most-Wanted list – the likes of him had never been seen before in our capital (which already had its fair share of monsters).

Bogel, a short, stocky and tiny 5ft 4in thirty-eight-year-old Jamaican originally based in New York, was nothing much to look at. He made his name as an enforcer with the Shower Posse, once the most feared drug gang in New York's Bronx, so-called because they 'showered' victims with bullets from Uzi sub-machine guns.

In 1998 Bogel came up with a novel and utterly appalling way of persuading a young couple to cough up the dough he claimed they owed the Shower Posse; he broke into their house at night with an accomplice and tied them up before repeatedly raping and sodomising the man's wife while pistol-whipping him until he found the money.

Bogel was arrested for this attack but was incredibly granted $100,000 bail (Bogel illegally made ten times that amount each year). He committed two more horrifying attacks, raping and sodomizing two girls, twelve and fourteen years old, both in front of their families.

New York's finest, along with the US Marshals, tracked Bogel to a block party in New Jersey but the cops were spotted as they approached the apartment. Bogel immediately opened fire with an Uzi – not at the police but at his fellow partygoers. Pandemonium erupted as other gang members went for their guns just as the police crashed through the door. Bogel escaped in the bedlam, leaving one man dead and a two-year-old child seriously injured.

He escaped from New York using false documents and travelled via Jamaica to the UK, from where he planned to re-enter the USA using a false passport. In the summer of 1999 he was tried and convicted in absentia of attempted murder, kidnapping, rape, sodomy, robbery and possession of firearms. He received a sentence of sixty-eight years. But by then he was a free man in our capital city (the Shower Posse had clicks in several of the world's major cities and London was no exception), with countless teenage girls in the crack houses with which to amuse himself while he waited for a chance to head back home using easily acquired false IDs provided by the UK's most prolific passport fraudsters, William Horncy and Kenneth Regan.

London-based Regan and Horncy fuelled the drugs-smuggling trade by selling on five hundred completely genuine passports to the crème de la crème of smugglers (one man caught with one of their passports had 500 kilos of cocaine on board his ship). Their scheme was simple: Regan took down the details of the individual who needed the passport and then a suitable 'donor' look-alike was found by trawling local pubs and paid off. Application forms were completed with the help of a solicitor, which were then taken directly to Newport's passport office by Regan and the passports sold to the client for three and a half grand.

Regan, who was also convicted of importing large amounts of heroin, was freed early after he turned supergrass. Two years later he was sentenced to life for the cold-blooded mass murder of a family of five in 2003 after he forcibly took over the ownership of an international haulage firm which he planned to use to import drugs from the continent.

Besides Bogel, other senior members of New York's Yardies that made a run for the UK as the heat came down in the US included Charles Brackett, Mervin Benjamin and Fabian O'Neal Littlejohn. They were all firmly in the mould of Winston Harris of the Lock City Crew – they were Jamaicans who had operated in New York before coming to London. They were key members of the Poison Clan, responsible for thirty murders and the sale of millions of pounds worth of crack, heroin and guns.

The gang's name comes from a cult martial arts movie and refers to its members' willingness to kill their own as well as others. The Poison Clan was founded by Devon 'Chubby' Beckford after he killed two crack-dealing colleagues who had refused to let him branch out on his own.

Following an extensive police and FBI operation, the gang was broken up in 1997 with twenty defendants – including Beckford, who narrowly avoided the death sentence – being brought before the courts and convicted on drugs and violence charges. Bogel, Brackett, Benjamin and Littlejohn, however, were still on the run and out there somewhere in our city, and word on the street was they were hiding out in a crack house in North London.

As well as passports, there was no shortage of guns in the capital for Bogel and co to choose from. That's why eliminating the guns is so important – you remove them from a monster like Bogel and he is nothing, just a puny little pervert that most men could take in a fight.

No one knows just how many illegal guns there are in circulation in Britain. The best estimates vary between 500,000 and 2 million. Whatever the real number, one thing is certain: whereas guns used to be reserved for the criminal elite, today everyone who wants one can get hold of one. An old or reconditioned revolver can be had for £150–£300. These guns are often poorly put together and act like mini-bombs when the criminal pulls the trigger, sending out shrapnel in all directions and more often than not blowing the gunman's thumb right off (the nickname 'Fingers' is almost always given to a criminal that has had this happen to them). A new-ish semi-automatic runs to £700 or so while fully automatic machine guns or assault rifles start at around £1500. Three grand will buy you a top-of-the-range Mac 10, the player's ultimate weapon of choice.

For up-and-coming criminals, guns can be hired from gangland armouries. The terms vary but generally involve a fee plus a returnable deposit. If the gun is fired, the deposit is retained and the renter is obliged to dispose of the weapon themselves. The reason is that no one wants to pick up someone else's history. Modern techniques make it quite easy to link a gun to a crime so great importance is attached to whether the gun is clean or dirty. Despite this, many guns have been used in several shootings by several different people.

For example, a gun that was used in the robbery of a Caribbean restaurant in Tottenham had a long and complicated history; at one time it had passed through the hands of Hyrone Hart, then twenty-eight. Hart's street name was 'Irone', referring to a favourite weapon of punishment for a Jamaican enforcer – branding victims with a hot iron. He was a psychopath in a constant state of crack psychosis; he made English gangsters who liked to wire their victims' bollocks to car batteries look tame by comparison and in 1998 he embarked on a crimewave that revolutionized the way criminals handled guns.

Hart, who had three convictions, one for a particularly violent robbery, tortured debtors and those he robbed with hot irons and electric drills. His nineteen-year-old partner was Kurt Roberts, known as 'Pepe' (he was 5ft 4in). They were both part of a nine-strong Jamaican gang led by a man known only by his nickname 'Marlon Brando', a gang which robbed dealers and innocent people alike for cash and drugs. The gang lived a moment-to-moment existence and robbed drug dealers, relying on tip-offs to get their addresses. The problem was that their information was far from reliable.

On 15 June 1998, a twenty-four-year-old man and an eighteen-year-old woman (they do not wish to be named) were spending a quiet evening together in their flat in Clapham when there was a knock at the door. The woman went to answer it; she could see through the mottled glass in the door that the caller was black and didn't recognize him but she opened the door anyway. Three men barged in, one of them carrying a handgun. They tied up her boyfriend, stabbing him in the chest and neck when he started to struggle. Pepe raped the woman while the third man forced her to perform oral sex. The men, frustrated at finding so little money, kicked and beat the man savagely before leaving. The couple survived their ordeal but the next family would not be so lucky.

At 10 p.m. on 25 June the doorbell rang at Kirk and Avril Johnson's house in Tulse Hill, South London. Kirk left his wife watching television with their two sleepy kids, eighteen-month-old Zhane and six-year-old Ashanti, and went to answer the door. Three men burst into the house, one of whom was waving a gun and shouting, 'What money you got? I'll kill you!' Johnson was forced into a bedroom.

Hart told Pepe, 'Turn up the TV and you,' he said, pushing the gun into Johnson's face, 'don't fucking move.' But Kirk recognized the danger his family was in and grabbed the gun in Hart's hand. As they struggled the third man took out a knife and plunged it into Kirk's neck; he was forced to let go, to try to staunch the blood that was now pumping out of him. Hart yelled at Kirk, 'If you don't give us the money we'll kill you all.' They tore the rings from their fingers; Pepe took a distinctive gold ring with the shape of Africa from a terrified Avril and placed it on his own finger. It fitted. Avril said to Kirk, 'Just give them whatever they want.'

'There's £200 in cash upstairs, in the cupboard,' Kirk told them. One of the men went to look while the others tied them up with electrical cord and forced them to lie on the bed above their children. Kirk saw Hart hand his gun to the man with the knife. The knifeman walked over to Kirk, who was now powerless. Convinced he was going to die, he pushed his head into the bed. The gun was fired twice. Next the gunman walked over to Avril and held the Glock to her forehead. Once again, he fired twice.

Amazingly, both bullets missed Kirk and hit the mattress a centimetre from his head. As he struggled to free himself, he saw that Avril, a successful DJ and the daughter of the famous Jamaican reggae star Tippa Irie, was mortally wounded. She died the following morning.

Four days later, in Stratford, East London, thirty-year-old Michelle Carby was dressed for bed when she answered her door only to be punched in the mouth and repeatedly kicked after she fell. She was tied up with electrical cords and bound to a chair in the living room while her three young children (aged twelve, ten and four) slept upstairs. The gang knew her and wanted her to become an alibi witness for them if they ever wound up in court. She refused.

The following morning the neighbours were awoken by Michelle's children, who told them, 'Our mummy is dead, our mummy is dead.' When the neighbours entered the house they found Michelle still tied to the chair. She had been shot twice in the back of her head. Rings were missing from her fingers and other jewellery had been stolen.

Eighteen days later in Kingsbury, northwest London, drug dealer Patrick 'Fergie' Ferguson answered his door at about 8.30 p.m. to be confronted by three men demanding he give them his drugs. Ferguson told them, 'I don't have anything here!' and tried to push the men back out down the hall. Upstairs Primrose, his wife, and their two-year-old daughter were in the bathroom. Primrose came out of the bathroom to see Fergie holding one of the robbers by the throat while another pulled out his gun. Primrose cried out, 'Oh my God, please, no!' but the gunman shot Fergie in the face, killing him.

The bullets recovered from the bodies linked the guns and the gang to the robbery of the Caribbean restaurant in Tottenham, during which shots had been fired but miraculously no one was injured, and witnesses had given police descriptions of the men involved.

Hart then made the mistake of using the mobile phones he had stolen from his victims, which led detectives to a flat in Balham where they recovered some of the stolen jewellery and spotted a photograph of Pepe wearing Avril Johnson's ring. Police caught up with Hart in Birmingham; his trainers had two tiny specks of blood which matched Ferguson's. Not surprisingly, Irone and Pepe got life. These murders marked a turning point where gunmen started to develop a new level of callousness, where it no longer mattered whether women or children got in the way and were shot dead as a result. If these guys were prepared to shoot women and children, it would only be a matter of time before they started shooting policemen.

THIRTEEN

PUNCH-UP

Our plan was to hit the most massive crack houses every other day. They usually stand out and our next target, which was in Tottenham High Road, was a complete eyesore. We decided to hit it on a Friday night. The curtains were filthy, some of the windows were smashed, and in one corner the window frame and surrounding bricks had been stained black by flames from a recent blaze.

People come to a crack house thanks to word of mouth and sometimes just by searching the street for somewhere that looks suitably druggy. The more decrepit the better; it was the equivalent of a neon sign advertising 'Crack Sold Here'.

This particular crack den was in a block of flats above a parade of shops and was directly over a dentist's surgery. It was just as busy as Ashmount Road. From our recces we estimated it had 250 visitors in twenty-four hours – one every six minutes (although most arrived at night in intervals of less than a minute).

The first obstacle should have been the modern door-entry system but the dealers had taken care of that for us by smashing and melting it into a plastic pulp – no doubt they had become fed up of buzzing customers in every minute. The hallway was wrecked too; the painted walls were pockmarked with burns and stained with graffiti. Broken cigarettes lay trampled on the floor, along with newspapers, a couple of empty lighters, countless matches and matchboxes and a few empty beer cans.

A middle-aged man coming down the stairs saw me studying the mess, a look of disgust on my face. 'I've been a landlord for years and I've never seen anything as evil as this drug, crack,' he said. 'It's like a disease. Kids get addicted and get sick and get their friends addicted – it's like they are killing themselves.'

He was right, of course. But landlords share some of the blame, particularly local councils. Crack houses have proliferated because landlords abandon properties. This feeds the homeless problem by giving runaway kids places to stay – anything is better than the street, even if it is a crack house. Many kids end up working as prostitutes or are hired by the dealers as runners, catchers and look-outs. There are lots of people in crack houses who don't have any other place to go; people who are homeless but are not defined as such (and don't appear in any statistics). They don't sleep in door-ways but they don't have their own place either.

Business really took off at night. People of all ages were in and out, up and down the stairs in a steady stream. I watched as six teenage boys wearing hoodies and crooked caps bounced in. A group of girls with a pair of older women strolled in after them. A black kid led a white buyer to the door; he waited in front of the door until he was checked out – he knew the crack-house routine all right. The area was full of touts and lookouts, kids who ask potential punters if they need to score while keeping an eye out for us. No doubt even the most drug-addled lookout would spot a vanload of coppers in body armour. Fuck it, I think, we were never going to be subtle anyway – just steam in hard and fast on this one. But this door had a New York latch and was going to be a real challenge.

I found a side street where we could probably at least debus without being spotted. On the night we simply parked in the middle of the road after arriving in our usual formation, me up front in the Primera with the rest of the squad, then the Ghosties, the TSG behind them and, lastly, the the drugs dog.

Curtains twitched up and down the street. The police state had well and truly arrived. The Ghosties, all dressed in black with an enforcer and their cutting equipment, formed an orderly line in the street behind me. I started to jog; we turned the corner and hit the building as the helicopter descended.

We passed a teenager asleep, out cold in fact, on the stairwell, his face dirty, his hands limp at his sides, his skinny legs poking out at odd angles; a filthy brown jacket was draped over him. Was he supposed to be the lookout? The putrid smell of crack and urine filled our noses as we ran up the stairs towards the door.

It was then that I saw the bouncer standing behind the door. He had just let someone in and it was open. Perfect. Normally I would have stood aside at this point to let the Ghosties do their job but this was irresistible. The bouncer's eyes widened as he saw me sprinting towards him, the Ghosties right behind me. He tried to slam the door in my face, but I was already flying and I hit the door with every ounce of my weight behind me. It crashed open, smashing into the bouncer, lifting him off his feet; he sailed back down the hallway and landed on a large group of people sitting in the next room. Their job done for them, the Ghosties stood aside to let the TSG storm the flat; I screamed 'GoGoGoGoGo!' at the top of my voice and dived out of the way, leaving them to it. It was a beautiful sight, all this power pouring in, and I stood back, gloating. The TSG were about to take the crack-dealing bastards down; any resistance would be met without mercy.

Inside, the rooms were literally smoking. Even by the front door I was coughing and feeling nauseous from the stinking crack smoke. Then I heard the shouts: 'Support, Support!' What the fuck? How many people were in there? The TSG were being pushed back towards me in a whirling giant ball of fists, boots, sticks and batons. I dived back outside and yelled at Greg and the lads who were waiting downstairs. 'Get up here now! We're outnumbered!' Even though they didn't have batons and were only wearing ballistic vests, the guys didn't hesitate and plunged into the chaotic smoking vortex, screaming their heads off while I screamed for dog handlers and for back-up from any uniformed officers in the area before diving back into the flat.

It was utterly unnerving to see so many people putting up a fight. Supposing we lost this one? We'd never live it down. One guy was trying to clamber out of a window to jump into the street below, but was being yanked back in by two officers; they were holding on to his shirt which was steadily ripping. The floor was covered in drug paraphernalia, including the odd needle – everyone was fighting to stay on their feet, as nobody wanted to fall and play Russian roulette rolling around on that lot.

In the confusion one of the TSG had mistaken Adam, who was in his drug-dealing look-alike civvies, for a dealer and was trying to arrest him. Adam was frantically trying to reach into his pocket for his warrant but that only freaked the TSG officer out. By the time they'd sorted it, Adam was furious and the TSG was mortified but there was no time for recriminations. Bodies were being bounced off walls, a crack-head was trying to bite chunks out of one of the TSG; people were screaming, shouting, groaning, crying in pain. We're going to lose this one, I thought to myself. They're going to fucking kill us. They were fighting like animals from fear – but because of that they were fighting badly; we, on the other hand, made every block and blow count – every second felt like a minute.

The optimal state of 'arousal' – the range in which stress improves performance – is when the heart rate is between 115 and 145 beats per minute. It doesn't take much to push a crack addict beyond this level; in fact it's normal for the heart rate of a crack addict who's high to average 175 bpm. This leads to extremely aggressive behaviour. In many cases, once 175 bpm has been reached, people lose control over their bowels – the body believes that the danger has reached such a point that their regulation is no longer necessary. It doesn't take much to push an addict above 175 bpm, which leads to an absolute mental breakdown, and the midbrain, the most primitive part of the brain that we share with cats and dogs, takes over. Crack also kills off the prefrontal cortex, the part of the brain that inhibits anti-social behaviour,[5] so it's a total waste of breath trying to communicate – it's as effective as trying to reason with a rabid wild animal that wants to bite you in the nuts.

Somehow we held our ground and started to push back in. Officers were shouting for extra handcuffs and eventually we had control of the den. While I struggled to catch my breath I assessed the situation. It was a scene from hell. Some crack-heads had pissed themselves; rocks, crack pipes, glass, broken furniture and blood covered the floor; half-dressed prostitutes were either sobbing or cursing. Fortunately there were only minor injuries; the relief was enormous. Everybody struggled to get their breath back.

We gradually worked our way through each of the rooms with the sniffer dogs, collecting all the drugs and paraphernalia, and followed that by strip-searching everyone. The TSG had to hang around while we did this and they became quite pissed off; there were over thirty people and the job took us over two hours.

Amongst those we arrested was a twenty-year-old female addict who was impossibly skinny, her bones threatening to poke through her almost translucent skin. She was a 'chaser', an addict who sacrificed food and sleep in the endless quest for crack. Her skin was covered in red blotches, the result of too much sodium (from the bicarbonate of soda mixed into the cocaine to make crack). She cried when the female officers took her pipe and extracted her stash from her loose-fitting bra. No doubt this would mean another night without food; she would have to find a way of replacing her stash once she'd been bailed.

Crack creates a kind of psychosis which makes people perform obsessive tics. These people, known as 'twitchers', can't take the stimuli crack gives them sitting still. One bloke had torn his ear apart from rubbing it too much. He screamed when officers cuffed him, effectively cutting off access to his tic.

---

5 An American study found that 40 per cent of crack addicts committed senseless violent crimes when high. In the UK in 2001, when a gang of crack addicts robbed a pizza restaurant they shot the owner even after he co-operated.

'He pisses *us* off as well,' said one addict who called himself Brian. 'He never fucking stops. He's gonna lose that ear one day. See him, over there,' Brian said, nodding towards a twenty-something white male with scraggly dreadlocks. 'Every time he gets high he says there are things in his body and keeps trying to push them away. The other day he said there was a man coming out of the wall. Fucking nuts.' Brian didn't stop scratching his scalp the whole time I was speaking to him and even when cuffed he rubbed his head up against the wall.

Other twitchers feel the urge to rub a particular object, such as a snooker ball, sometimes for hours. Some just have to look out of a window. Some are searchers who rummage through their handbags or pockets in never-ending searches for I-don't-know-what. Others spend their entire high ghostbusting.

I always tried to ensure my relations were good with the people I arrested; besides making everyone's job easier, I also got to learn lots of interesting stuff about the people I was after. Brian and I had a chat about the ghostbusting phenomenon. 'People always say the crack high is over in a flash,' he said passionately; 'Well, if it's so bloody short why in hell are those fucking idiots crawling round on their hands and knees for hours ghostbusting? They are high as fucking kites when they are doing that stupid shit.

'They never find anything because somebody else has ghostbusted before them. And I mean some folk look like they're at work, searching all around. Hell, if they weren't high they wouldn't be doing that.'

One of the people we arrested was a sixteen-year-old boy who had some cannabis in his pocket. I was certain he was a runaway and was quite probably working in the crack house. Unfortunately he had the presence of mind to give us a false name and address, so we were unable to locate his parents or get someone to come and pick him up. Once he'd been processed he'd be bailed and back on the street – another lost soul.

Eventually, we were able to send the TSG home and took our bounty down to the factory for processing. With a smile that wasn't entirely friendly, the custody sergeant said, 'Oh, for fuck's sake, not you again, Keeble!'

I smiled testily and thought: We're nicking loads of criminals – isn't that what we're supposed to do? Out loud I said, 'Get used to it. The next lot will be here in forty-eight hours.'

Unfortunately, I turned out to be wrong about that. A suspect house on Brunel Walk was a short distance from Seven Sisters railway and had, according to what little information we had, been a crack house for quite some time. Once again, it was obvious – the front garden was a mess of beer cans and other debris. The curtains had mould growing on them and I was convinced I could smell the stink of crack from the street. Two days after our pitched battle at the High Street I texted Adam with enough info to get the warrant. Although we were able to call on other departments for help, we weren't able to get ourselves any equipment, such as police walkie-talkies, and so relied on our own mobile phones and text messages for communication. Crack dealers operated the same way, using coded texts.

Later that night, Colin and Darren were in an observation position and texted me updates as I approached in the convoy with the TSG. 'All quiet,' they said. We Ghostbusted the door and ran in screaming, 'Police!' only to discover, rather embarrassingly, that the place was empty. Very strange. We had watched this place and seen that it was a fairly busy crack house. Our timing must just have been off. The TSG left us to it and as we ran the dog around and searched the house the occupiers turned up; one of them was a badly scarred prostitute.

She was with a friend and they'd just stopped off to collect a Chinese takeaway on their way home. She was extremely pissed off to find we'd trashed her door. With nothing to show for our efforts (and no overtime because we didn't arrest anyone), we headed home for the weekend pretty satisfied with our week's work, even if it did end with a damp squib. We'd need our rest because we were raiding our next house on Tuesday – it was going to be a real education into the horrors of crack.

FOURTEEN

THE CRACK KIDS

I stood dumbfounded in the middle of a small crack house in Dunloe Avenue, deep in the heart of Tottenham. I was in a small bedroom on the first floor; we had just turned the place over searching for the occupants but had so far drawn a blank – until I threw back the bed's duvet covers to reveal two small children huddled together shaking with terror. They clearly thought we were the bogeymen.

My first thought was that we had stormed the wrong address. It was unusual in that it had none of the normal external physical signs of an active crack house but Adam, who had done the recce, was completely adamant.

We had decided to hit the house at daybreak with just us five and the dog squad. Dawn raids were a rarity (I hated early starts) but the big advantage was that we wouldn't have to spend all night booking criminals in; we would be able to do it within our normal shift. The guys and I were fed up and exhausted with night-long sessions spent booking in prisoners with grumpy custody sergeants who worked eight-hour shifts while we had searched and arrested more than 100 people and spent hours filing forms in our dusty, daylight-free stock cupboard of an office. And, as reluctant as I was to start early, I did want to spend some time with my newly pregnant wife and my six-year-old son.

After a black-coffee-fuelled early-morning breakfast briefing with the dog handler, we bundled into the Nissan and wove through the misty December morning to the address. The Ghosties heaved the enforcer out of their van boot with a groan and jogged towards the property. The door flew open at their first swing and as usual we piled in screaming. It was pitch black inside and I'd forgotten to bring a torch; luckily Greg had had the presence of mind to bring his and we picked our way through to our allocated rooms, hitting light switches as we went.

I had taken the bedroom and now stood nonplussed, wondering what on earth to do with these two terrified children.

'Hi kids, have you got a mummy or daddy?' I asked. They nodded.

'Do you know where they are?' They shook their heads.

'Do you want to go to school?' They nodded.

The children were seven and nine years old. They were lovely kids and, like so many we would encounter, seemed totally unaware of just how extraordinary their circumstances were.

Adam gave me a shout. 'We got something!' It was possible to enter the house's integral garage from the hallway. I smelt the crack as I approached. Inside were two large stinking grey-green sofas covered in burns and worn shiny from age and sweat. Homemade crack pipes were everywhere along with a bunch of stolen credit cards and other personal documents. Matches, beer cans and newspapers covered the concrete floor. 'They've hotwired the leccy too, Harry,' Adam told me, pointing at the lethal DIY bodge job of exposed wires that could easily have killed the kids if they'd wandered in and brushed against them.

Bill the dog handler, a six-five, seventeen-stone skinhead, was one of the most terrifying-looking policemen you're ever likely to meet but he soon managed to get the kids smiling with the Jim Carrey routine and, after a few 'Smokin's!' from me, they were giggling as they washed, dressed, ate and played fetch with Bear the police dog while I rang their school and arranged for a teacher to come and pick them up.

After the kids had been taken to school, we hunted for their mother. Greg came up with a set of mobile-phone numbers dialled from their landline and we left messages on all of them. Over breakfast we got a call that their thirty-one-year-old mother had turned herself in to Hornsey police station. We interviewed her alongside social services before she was bailed. She was allowed to keep her kids while social services weighed the evidence against her, but it was likely they'd end up being taken into care.

It sickened me (and still does) that so many children are in these circumstances. Crack cocaine is thought to be responsible for sending 20,000 children into care (in 2006 there were 60,000 children in care in the UK, costing the taxpayer £1.6 billion). Researchers at Brunel University found that 34 per cent of child-care cases were drug-related. In another study, out of 186 children taken from a 100 cases, 67 had one or both parents addicted to crack.

The pregnant prostitute we had picked up from Ashmount Road later gave birth to a boy with spina bifida (one of the many risks of smoking crack while pregnant), who was taken into care straight from the hospital. It wasn't the first child she had lost this way – and it probably wouldn't be her last. Incredibly, I discovered that this was an all-too-common occurrence.

In one of the worst cases of its kind fourteen children born to the same mother were put into care because of her crack addiction. This was thanks to the unreported phenomenon of mothers who have more children after their first has been taken into care. They fill the emotional vacuum of having their children taken away by embarking on a stream of replacement pregnancies. Sometimes these women had started out as young crack-house prostitutes who had had unprotected sex and ended up keeping their baby. Apart from the human cost of the damage to the children's upbringing, the bill to taxpayers to look after fourteen children was more than £2 million. It also cost an average of £25,000 to hear each case of care proceedings.

Other extreme cases included an addict who had her first three children taken away and then went on to have seven more by three different fathers. One by one they were taken away until she had lost all ten. Another woman had fifteen children in the care of family and foster homes. Nine children were removed from one mother; many were taken directly from the maternity unit because of drug and alcohol problems of the mother who had her first child at fifteen.[6]

Apart from the huge financial cost, there is an enormous emotional cost in the long-term emotional damage to children; when children are taken into care beyond the age of eight or nine years, they are likely to suffer from psychological disorders which lead to anti-social behaviour (and further economic cost), not to mention physical and mental problems which crack dealers are only too happy take advantage of. Babies who are breast-fed by mothers with crack addictions also soon become addicts and can die from an overdose.

And the care system itself was, in 2000, deeply flawed, as I was later appalled to find out. At that time, though, whenever we found kids in a crack house we were happy to hand them over to the care of social services, naïvely thinking that at least then they would be safe; that the care of the state would be the very best. Boy, were we wrong.

Shortly after this raid, North London's murder squad were called to a churchyard near an industrial estate in Tottenham. The body of a black man in his thirties was lying face-down in a pool of his own blood. He had been there for about twenty-four hours by the time forensics got to him. They carefully rolled the body over. The victim had an old machete scar on one arm, deep scars on his face and a gold tooth with a diamond stud. But what immediately

---

6 It's essential to rescue kids from crack addicts for a number of reasons but most addicts don't realize how much damage smoking crack does to the baby: at the least they will end up with asthma; at the worst they will die from acute cocaine intoxication. I'd heard of a case where a five-month old baby born to a pair of crack dealers had died in their bed. They claimed they had accidentally smothered her but toxicology tests showed the baby died of acute cocaine intoxication – from the crack smoke.

grabbed the detectives' attention was the fact that the man had been gutted like a fish.

His stomach had been sliced open and apart in what looked like a savage attack by a psychopathic killer. It wasn't until three days later that the autopsy report revealed that he had fatal levels of coke in his stomach.

The man, whose identity was never established, was probably being driven straight from the airport by gangsters so he could 'unload' his stash of coke when he became ill on the way. Once he had died from an overdose, the 'mule' was butchered and the valuable cargo retrieved and sold on. It sickened me to think that thousands of people had by now snorted and smoked the contents of this dead man's stomach.

That same day we were on our way to raid thirteen – we'd had ninety minutes to prepare and I briefed the TSG in the back of the carrier as we weaved through the chaotic traffic of the Tottenham Triangle to our target.

'This is going to be a very public raid,' I told them. 'I don't need to tell you that Seven Sisters Road is one of the busiest streets in north London. The property we're looking at is a very popular black hairdresser's which, like many others, acts as a sort of social club so they're always busy, lots of people coming and going, especially in the late afternoon and early evening. We have intelligence it's being used as a base to deal crack. We're taking a chance hitting it in the early evening but apparently that's when it's operational.'

I hated rushing jobs but the team had each been assigned their tasks and knew well enough what to do. Greg did the surveillance, Adam got the warrants, all of us worked on the plan of attack and then I prepared the briefings. The only thing I was worried about was that we were relying on an anonymous tip-off. At least it wasn't an informant. Although I understand their usefulness – many brave people have informed at no small risk to their own lives, leading to some high-profile arrests – I have *some* reservations about collaborating with the enemy in the war against crime. The problem is that by definition, grasses are inherently untrustworthy. Sometimes information comes from those who have dishonest motivations for giving information to the police, from setting up a rival dealer to getting revenge on the bloke who insulted their girl-friend in the pub the night before.

For those who do inform, it's high-risk work with small reward. Even reliable, top-notch informants make an average of only £1000 a year. Eventually their criminal colleagues and associates will catch up with them and, as a result, they have to be given a new identity – a costly process that often backfires. West Yorkshire Police spent £100,000 on plastic surgery, a new identity and a home for an armed robber who had grassed up the rest of his gang. Five months later he was robbing banks again. No official figures exist for re-offending informers, but I suspect they are no better than those for ordinary criminals.

In the worst-case scenario, the criminal informer can take us for a ride. Probably the most extreme example of this is the 1995 case of an armed robber codenamed 'Selector'. The thirty-one-year-old West Indian man, already in jail for armed robbery, convinced detectives from London's Flying Squad to release him from prison for two days so that he could take part in another armed robbery. The idea was that Selector would lead the detectives to a danger-ous pair of robbers they had been after for some time. They would catch them red-handed, making a lengthy conviction a certainty. In return, Selector would get a reduction in his time left to serve.

But Selector sent the officers to the wrong location while he took part in a £1.5 million security-van robbery and stashed his £200,000 cut. He even asked the Flying Squad officers to pick him up from his brother's house afterwards, persuading them that the time and location had been changed at the last minute. Shortly after the Flying Squad officers returned him to prison, Selector contacted the anti-corruption branch, CIB3, telling them that the officers were corrupt and had stolen the money. The officers, already professionally embar-rassed, were put under intense scrutiny as a result.

If this tip-off job went pear-shaped and we got complaints then it would be my arse under intense scrutiny. But I wanted to keep our momentum going: we had so far closed twelve crack houses and it felt as if the fog of misery brought about by crack cocaine was already thinning. Word had got around that HDS was after blood; we had nicked some dealers more than once and even though most of those we had arrested had been bailed, we were making it very hard for them to operate.

We pulled up around the corner. The TSG stormed in and met no resistance. Although when I stepped into the room the first thing I saw was quite possibly the biggest man in London. And he wasn't happy. 'All yours, Harry,' said Greg and patted me on the shoulder.

'What the fuck? What the fuck is this, you muthafuckin' shit-heads?' The chair groaned as he quickly spun round. 'Who the fuck is you?' he said, nodding in my direction. I wasn't going to be intimidated, although I didn't want to be the first person on the receiving end of his enormous fists; his mighty biceps flexed like a pair of black cabs jostling for a parking space.

'Sergeant Harry Keeble, Haringey Drugs Squad. We have a warrant to search the premises for drugs. Just sit tight . . .'

'Sit tight! Sit fucking tight? You gonna close this place down with me like this?'

It was then that I realized why he was so pissed off. I had some sympathy; he was in mid-haircut. Tough shit really, but to keep the peace I promised that the barber could finish the job as soon as we finished ours. We turned the place over. Everyone was very co-operative and we found zero drugs but when we checked for any outstanding warrants, the big guy's name came up with a sheet of traffic offences. Luckily, thanks to the persuasiveness of the other people in the hairdresser's, he calmed down and came quietly. Unfortunately, while we were inside, some idiot slashed all the tyres on the TSG's carrier. Not one of our best jobs. Working on the basis of other people's information is always tough. You have to take all the shit when you don't find anything.

FIFTEEN

RAIDING AN ESTATE

Greg and I pulled up in the Nissan Primera a few streets away from our target. Deep in the Stonebridge estate, a property in Helston Court was an established crack address and we were there for a recce. Greg went to take a look while I waited in the 'cab'.

This area was bitterly contested by various gangs. The estate had been sown up by the Edgecot Boyz although rival gangs, including the IDA Boyz, the Tiverton Man Dem, Ferry Lane Man Dem and Stonebridge Manz regularly left the area in a mess. Cars were blown up with fireworks, tyres were slashed in front of the neighbours, windows were broken and locals were threatened and robbed – I didn't need a police incident report to tell me that there was a huge amount of gun and violent crime in this area.

The place was some kind of hell. Junkies attached used syringes with their needles exposed to the underside of the banisters. Children threw shopping trolleys from the roof. The teenage perps had stopped running away from police. A twelve-year-old held the record, having recently been arrested for the fifty-fifth time. His mother, local schools and social services had given him up for lost. One resident claimed he'd opened his front door one morning to find a teenage girl giving a man a blow-job in full view of the street.

This estate was a city within a city, hidden from visitors' eyes; a city where decent, proud and law-abiding residents were kept prisoners in their own homes through fear of the gangs that ruled the streets. In these estates, where deprivation and violence were commonplace, kids' lives were typically bleak and hopeless.

These teenagers were the third generation of drug addicts who had no idea of what it meant to live without violence and squalor. They were practically feral. They had no belief that their lives could be different from the poverty-stricken, aimless, drug-addled existence of their parents. Home Office statistics say that most criminals on these estates strike within 1.8 miles of their front door.

This time I got out and did the recce. I needed to see it for myself to plan a route and assess the door quality and fortifications, as well as check for dangers such as dogs, guns, booby-traps and so on.

This estate was a typical 1960s low-rise block, drab and covered in menacing but incomprehensible graffiti. The temperature seemed to drop the deeper I got. A wave of paranoia hit me – was I being watched? I strode along concrete walkways, my shoulders hunched and my eyes down, hands in pockets. Looking confident here would only increase the chances of a confrontation.

The alleyways that connected the blocks and led to the surrounding roads were a real rabbit warren, perfect for muggers to lurk, strike and disappear with ease. The local newsagent had recently been robbed by a teenager high on drugs, wielding a plank of wood spiked with nails. Teenagers had pulled up paving stones from the playground for use as missiles, dropping them on cars, throwing them through windows. The few people I saw were mainly elderly, pulling wheeled baskets. Their heads were down; they didn't dare make eye contact.

Apart from the pensioners, young men were hanging around at various corners and they all scrutinized me as I ambled past. A series of weird catcalls followed me around the estate; whistles and words just beyond my hearing. My pulse went up a notch – was I compromised? Or were they announcing a stranger or a customer?

I felt pretty certain about my appearance. I wasn't wearing the usual undercover crime-squad uniform of clean Timberland boots, nicely pressed jeans, designer top, short, neat haircut and expensive aftershave. This is usually topped off by the biggest giveaway of all – the wedding ring. Even if you are in the most convincing undercover gear, that little flash of gold will tell any dealer you're a stupid cop. Addicts are married to the pipe, not other people, and besides, rings make good crack money. Another dead giveaway is a beer belly. Addicts don't have the time, money or desire to overdose on beer and McNuggets. Luckily, I was thin and pasty and wearing loose clothes; pipe burns dotted my discoloured shirt, which accentuated the effect nicely. To complete my crack-head ensemble, I hadn't shaved or washed my hair for a few days.

The noise was really unnerving; I caught the word 'stranger' being repeated. Making my way straight to the crack-house door now would attract far too much attention. Instead, I memorized the route and planned to come back very early in the morning when no one would be around.

'So Harry, what d'you reckon?'

'Fucking well dodgy. Even I got the wind up just walking through there in broad daylight. Can't imagine what it must be like to live there.'

A few days later I arrived at the estate just after dawn. All was quiet and I was able to walk right past the door of the crack house and get the details of the locks and the quality of the door. Didn't look like it would give the Ghosties much trouble. The walkways on the estate were broad enough for them to run down two abreast in all their protective gear.

Greg nipped down to the court for a warrant while I put together the intelligence packs for the briefing. I was confident we wouldn't need the TSG this time. Our intel said this was a one-man band operation and so we decided to tackle this on our own with a little help from a sniffer dog. I booked us in for the following evening. This suited everyone except Charlie, who wanted to go and play in a football match with his mates.

'What time's the match?' I asked him.

'Eleven a.m. Harry.'

'Can you get back by four for the briefing?'

'No worries, I'll see you then.'

At four p.m., we met the dog handler and Ghostbusters at the factory. There was no sign of Charlie. This really pissed me off because on a small raid like this one person can make all the difference. Charlie's absence left me with no one to cover the back windows. The flat was on the first floor, and there was always the chance someone might jump from a window to escape (a crack addict had once tried this from a third-floor flat – he didn't survive), but it was far more likely that a load of drugs would come flying out. Luckily, I managed to grab a couple of enthusiastic uniformed constables who were prepared to tag along after they'd changed into their civvies.

We pulled up on the edge of the estate. This time it was the gangs' turn to feel the fear; as we pounded our way to the target the lookouts and street-dealers fled. The Ghosties hit the door running and it flew open on the first strike; they stood aside and in we poured, screaming as the chopper came down.

I spotted movement at the other end of the hallway, and we piled into the lounge to find five guys in here, the same number as the squad. Fortunately they were so surprised that we had them cuffed before they really understood what was going on. Also in the house was a pregnant woman. 'I'm due to give birth tomorrow,' she told me. I prayed that our surprise visit hadn't shocked her enough to start giving birth right now. I leant out of the window and yelled out, 'Anything?' to our catchers below. They shook their heads. 'Come up and give us a hand, then.'

I was a bit concerned to see that all the guys in the flat were clean and wearing good clothes. I couldn't smell any crack. They were pissed off all right and were all asking, 'What the fuck's going on?' There wasn't any smoke, or any smell of crack. Had we just arrested five friends having a chat?

Darren tapped me on the shoulder. 'Harry,' he said quietly, 'come and have a look upstairs.' When we got to the upstairs landing,

Darren put a finger to his lips and tiptoed into the room. He pointed at the bed and mouthed, 'Someone's underneath.' I nodded and indicated that he should take one end while I took the other. In a swift movement I dived down to see the face of a shocked man staring out at me. 'Out you come, it's the cops,' I said.

A muffled voice came from under the bed. 'I thought you was a gang who's looking for me.'

'That's brave, mate,' I sneered. 'Left your pregnant girlfriend to fight them off for you, did you?' He looked to the side and sucked air through his teeth. We turned out his pockets; his name was Otis 'Oral' Bryan, a twenty-five-year-old Jamaican. It was a good sign that someone was after him; it was most likely that drugs were involved.

Meanwhile Colin had found a knife in the back pocket of one of the guys in the room. This wasn't technically an offence at the time – you could carry a knife in your own home – but with a confident 'What the fuck's this, then?' from Colin, the guy started to squirm in his seat and Colin pocketed the knife without any further ado. If he had kicked up a fuss we would have handed the knife back and let him leave the property – then he would have been breaking the law and we would have nicked him.

As we were unable to find any sign of drugs I called in the dog handler, who after a few moments turned up a package the size of a squash ball in Bryan's coat which was hanging in the hall. It was crack. Now all we had to do was prove it was his. The fact that it was in his jacket in the hall was not enough. But I had an idea.

I walked into the lounge and said, 'We've found the crack. If no one owns up you're all going to be arrested, and –' I added, pointing at the pregnant woman '– that includes you. Your name is on the lease so these drugs have been found in your house, in your possession. If, however–' and at this point I deliberately looked Otis in the eye '–someone owns up, then the rest of you will be free to go.'

Otis's girlfriend was rightly peeved to hear this bit of news. 'What?' she screamed at Otis. 'You're dealing?'

Sometimes we found that the man of the house was a crack dealer while his girlfriend didn't know – sometimes even if they were living together. She might not let his friends smoke fags in their house, but behind her back a constant stream of his mates came to visit and buy crack behind her back. It soon became clear that despite his cowardly behaviour, Otis cared for her deeply. 'Listen to me, I'm gonna sort this out.' He looked at me and said, 'Can we talk privately, please?'

'What, you and her?'

'Yeah.'

'OK. We're going to wait in the same room but we'll give you enough distance to whisper.' This might seem like a strange situation – it was – but it was worth a gamble. We could arrest everyone for the crack but if they all denied possession we wouldn't be able to charge anyone. Either Otis knew this and he was explaining it to his girlfriend or he was telling her that he was going to take the rap. If he did, he would go down and wouldn't see his kid until it was walking.

Otis confessed, much to everyone's relief. Two hours later we were back at the station and booked him in. He got two years.

Just after we were done, Charlie showed his face. I was rightly pissed off and so I took him into an empty charge room and threatened to sack him from the team, a threat I carried out after his behaviour failed to improve. He was replaced by Taylor, a softly spoken twenty-eight-year-old Jamaican who would become a real asset to the team.

The Met's motto, in the wake of the ballsed-up investigation into the Stephen Lawrence murder, was 'Integrity is non-negotiable'. I meant to make sure that Haringey Drugs Squad stuck to that motto, no matter what.

This was something I would later come to regret.

SIXTEEN

THE CRACK PYRAMID

Whenever we raided a house, we were only able to study the outside and so sometimes we found little surprises waiting for us when we crashed through the front door. At one address we reckoned there were only two dealers, so it was just me and my famous five. On a wet morning, I charged the door using the enforcer; it popped open with so little resistance that I pounded through the corridor way too fast, followed by the rest of the squad. Struggling to control my momentum and put the brakes on I stepped onto an old lino, which, although covering the floor, wasn't stuck down. I glided down the hall like an amateur ice skater scrabbling for traction.

It was only then that a hysterical bloke suddenly appeared and bounded downstairs with a cricket bat and began knocking me for six. Fortunately, he dropped the bat as soon as he realized we were cops. Cedric (who also had what was probably the largest stash of coprophilia porn in existence), like all wannabe K-men, had been expecting an attack from a rival.

Organizationally speaking, crack houses are set up just like a fast-food franchise. A major player, normally known as 'K', runs several crack houses. He pays one of the 'Board of Directors', a senior member of the drugs gang that has overall control of the area, for the right to sell drugs on this patch.[7]

---

7 Interestingly, while the operational side of crack-dealing is a tightly run enterprise, the

The K-man employs an enforcer, who assures their safety, a treasurer responsible for taking care of the finances, and runners for the transportation of crack, cash and anything else. Beneath these are those who run the crack houses. While typically men, one was a mother of two known as 'Angel'.

'I worked my way up. I had a rep for being reliable. I used to work for the guys upstairs, running errands and opening the door for clients. I made £100 a day and all the crack I could smoke, which was pretty cool for a twelve-hour day. I didn't take anything while on the job; if you got too high you were sent home without pay. They had three other people working in that room – the kid working the scales, the doorman and the guard who carried a gun.

'The scale boys kept accounts, amounts sold in grams alongside the price paid by the customer. At the end of their shift, the scale boys added everything up, including how much had been given to house staff for personal use. John would give the cash to the treasurer, who paid John his share. The treasurer would compare the final figure against the amount of crack bought and the amount sold. If everything checked out, everybody got paid.'

As the crack trade became more lucrative street gangs started to prey on crack dealers so often that most dealers got armed guards. Women were almost never behind the scales, although a wife or girlfriend sometimes took over if their man wound up in prison or dead. Dealers aren't convinced that women have what it takes to prevent robberies. Angel was the exception to the rule. She was given the opportunity by a K-man after he'd been ripped off by two brothers. They had been giving crack away to girls, partying, showing off with friends and generally doing things that were not good business. Angel seemed like a solid alternative. She leaped at

customer side is more like an aboriginal society, its members busying themselves with day-to-day survival, like hunter gatherers: finding the right dealers, talking about how to get money for drugs, discussing where the next opportunity to get the best drug will come from, searching out the best tools, devising their own inexpensive techniques for preparing and using the drug. And then there are all the rituals – the preparation of the drug, the smoking methods, the bargaining of sex for drugs and so on.

the chance: no more sleeping with strangers to get what she needed. Angel turned the business around – she literally cleaned up the crack house, somehow managing to keep order, and the profits rolled in.

Angel's job came to an end once a rival dealer began a violent campaign to take over her boss's crack house. She lost her kids and became a crack whore until she somehow made a new life working for a charity that helped women involved in prostitution break free of the drug/whore cycle.

Below the K-men are the foot soldiers, whose aim is to become the manager of a crack house. Then there are mercenary fighters who can be called on in an emergency, such as during a gang war or a raid on a rival's house. Below them are the 'bics', the addicts who can be hired to do anything, even kill, for a few rocks of crack.

Then there are runners who earn a small percentage running errands, dropping off and picking up deals. Transporters move large amounts of coke through the country while babysitters may keep watch over drugs in safe-houses. Add to these the lookouts, bouncers and catchers and you have a multi-billion-pound industry that employs thousands of people. And like any big business, the junior employees were constantly vying for a place inside the house, behind the scales.

Some who join the crack trade are real entrepreneurs and create a well-paid niche for themselves. 'Spider' worked in quality control, a job he claimed to have created. 'I met these big dealers and suggested they make a position where a person would test the drugs before they distribute them. They thought it was a great idea and thought I should be the one to do it. Now I only do this one thing instead of doing too many things at one time. This is my job,' he said proudly.

Jez, an intelligent young man who became a successful young dealer simply because he could see the rewards were better than regular employment, scoffed when he heard this. 'Spider ain't goin' anywhere. He's like the man who invented chicken nuggets, just some fucker in the basement thinking up stuff to make money for the real players. Does he think his boss is gonna go down there in that basement and say, "Hey, Mr Nugget, you the man, we're selling this chicken faster than we can kill them, so I'm gonna sign my name on this fat-ass cheque for you?" Fuck no. The man that invented them things is still working in the basement spending years on his regular wage trying to make those sandy fries taste better.'

Jez is right. Except for those that run the crack houses and the K-man, all of the employees in this chain are poorly paid. For every big earner, there are hundreds more just scraping along. A foot soldier is the equivalent to the burger-flipper or a supermarket shelf-stacker. Sometimes they even have one of these jobs to complement their meagre earnings from crack. Along with bad pay, the foot soldiers have the worst job conditions – they are closest to the addicts, and hence the most likely to get arrested or murdered. Statistically, they are as likely as a UK soldier in Iraq to suffer Grievous Bodily Harm. And many of them aren't even old enough to join the army.

'Derek' was a well-known face on the streets of his estate. He was always in trouble, and had recently been acquitted on two counts of robbery when he was tailed and then arrested by four plainclothes officers in November 1999. When searched, he was found with crack cocaine, heroin and £400 cash in one pocket and a packet of Chewits in the other. He was charged with possessing Class A drugs with intent to supply. Derek was twelve years old.

Many of these kids are reluctant gang members. A recent study of fifty-nine teenage gang members in Harlesden, northwest London, carried out by Professor John Pitts, makes bleak reading. Although this kind of study has problems in that you can't always trust that what these kids are saying is the truth, it was sobering to read that 40 per cent of these fifty-nine claimed to be reluctant gangsters. Pitts found that they had no previous record and were good pupils, and that many of them didn't like what they were forced to do. But the gang culture is strong; they are frightened to be seen as a 'pussy' or to become a target of violence. Pitts cites the story of a brother and a sister; he was fifteen and she was fourteen. They'd never been in trouble until a local gang told them to do a robbery. They said no. So they beat him up and raped her. Other children are intimidated in other ways: 'So he tells 'em "fuck off". Anyway, the next thing he knows, someone's shot up his mother's flat. There's lots of families round here can't use their front rooms because of this sort of thing.'

Those dealers who recruit teens are following a tradition – adults are more likely to face a prison term if caught with several rocks. So child runners not only avoid the law: they are generally trust-worthy and relatively easy to frighten and control. It's still worth busting them, of course – even if they get off they get cut out of the business. There was one fifteen-year-old known appropriately enough as 'The Kid', who was an aggressive dealer selling from both the street and crack houses in the hope of rapid progression up the dealing hierarchy. One evening he was stopped by the police – he looked older than he was but he was driving and his pockets were full of rocks. Although he threw the drugs on the floor to try to beat possession, he was still arrested and lost his coke, and although he got the charges dropped, his solicitor cost him £2000. Once his scustomers heard about the arrest most of them went elsewhere and were afraid to come to his flat. They thought his phone might be tapped or that he was being watched. Being arrested put him in a position where he was hurt financially, where he was no longer trusted by his community. Where once he might have shifted an ounce in a few hours, it now took him a week.

Crack led to the mass employment of out-of-work teenagers and truanting school-kids. Today the underground economy, and the drug trade in particular, is probably the single biggest employer of teenagers. For the teen dealer, staying on top requires handling often unstable personal relationships, dealing with a constant stream of people of different ages, personalities, genders, ethnicities and mental states. He could be with a wealthy well-educated banker at one moment and an escaped mental patient the next. There is no privacy: as long as he's selling crack, he must contend with the phone ringing day or night. A constant stream of visitors makes the operation very visible and at some point he will be called upon – by us, if he's lucky, and if not then a rival with a gun.

Teen dealers start in lowly positions and move up through hard work, skill, intelligence and a little luck. A kid who can routinely handle money, control personal use of crack, deal with buyers and handle a weapon may make it out of the street and into the world of a player. It's this hope that keeps them going and the streets full of teenage dealers.

John worked near Tottenham Hale. In the summer of 2000 he spent six nights a week between 6 p.m. and 1 a.m. glancing over his shoulders as potential punters approached. It was a great summer; he began by selling 200 £6 deals of crack and ended up selling £500 a night, every night except Sunday, until the cops caught up with him.

'The minute the coke's gone the money stops,' John recalled. 'The moment this happens the girls stop coming round. I've seen this happen many times. My brother was one. Every time somebody starts to make crazy money they discover the girls, they discover the big ride, and they want to take control. I have a problem keeping myself together, but not many people listen to you when you tell them what you've seen. They got to go through it by themselves.'

Wise words for a seventeen-year-old.

'I don't know what's wrong with everybody. Yesterday, everything was fine; today there are motherfuckers everywhere. In your job, you go in, do what you have to do, and then it's over, right? Not me. I'm glad you're seeing this, because most people think it's just sniffing and spending money all the time. This is hard work. It's hard because you've got to deal with so many different and dangerous people.'

Besides the dealers, it was becoming common for us to pick up young crack addicts and kids caught in the middle of the druggy lives of their parents. To fund their addiction (it was not uncommon for them to have a £160-a-week habit) these kids resorted to shoplifting, theft, prostitution and dealing. Some got a miniature protection racket together in which eight-year-olds were forced to hand over money as the price of avoiding being beaten up. Crack was creeping into the borough's rougher schools: one child beat up four teachers after turning up high; another sprayed cleaning fluid in a teacher's face and a fourteen-year-old tried to sell a realistic replica gun at school to buy crack.

A six-year-old brought some rocks of crack to Show and Tell at a local primary school. I'm not kidding – the child was so used to it at home, he didn't even realize it was illegal. This was common amongst youngsters in this area – they didn't even realize that you could go to prison for taking or owning crack. This is why drugs education in schools is imperative – but some schools have already gone far past that stage.

At one North London primary school not far from the Tottenham Triangle, the crack trade had infiltrated the playground, with kids holding dealers' stashes. Incredibly, when the head teacher tried to remonstrate with the older dealers as they came to pick up their stash, they held a gun to her head.

Installing a higher perimeter fence and a buzzer entry system failed to deter them. The head teacher pleaded for help for months from the Local Education Authority, writing almost fifty letters. She received six replies. It was far too late by the time I got to hear of it (and her school was just outside Haringey Drugs Squad's turf, so it was unlikely that we would have heard about it earlier in any case). It pissed me off. People needed to know that they could come to the police. We could have put a stop to that immediately. What parent wants to send their kids to a school that has Yardies walking around it carrying guns?

For a few years in the 90s crack was a new drug and there wasn't much competition among dealers, but by 2000 it had reached saturation levels in inner cities. Prices became so low that while the players at the top of the pyramid still made fantastic money, the profits dwindled away for junior gang members. So why are kids still trying to get a piece of the action today? It's because they want to become a player as much as a teenage girl wants to win *Pop Idol*. Dealers give kids the impression that you have the choice of working long hours flipping burgers with no respect or taking a chance selling crack for a couple of hours a day, wearing designer clothes and driving a BMW. The reality was quite different – foot soldiers are the crack equivalent of burger-flippers – but it's not just about money, it's also about respect. No one wants to do well at school because you don't get any credibility for that. You don't get MCs in a club saying, 'Let's all big it up for John who got top marks on his chemistry homework this week.' This is a strong motivating factor – the desire to show friends and families that they can achieve something by generating loads of cash. Mothers readily accept money from sons they know haven't worked a day in their life because they aren't in a position to refuse dirty money.

There isn't much that can be done about this; the opportunities are too good. I heard the same stories time and again. Jez the dealer said he got into drugs because the rewards were simply too irresistible. 'What the fuck could I say to this twenty-year-old making *nine grand a week* [that's not big time] dealing crack who – fed up of listening to me chew his fuckin' ears about him doing wrong – asked me to turn out my pockets. I had six quid. He then turned out his; he stopped counting at four grand. He looked me in the face and said, "See this is in my pocket, this ain't for bills, this ain't no loan. This is just pocket money. I'm saving up to build my own recording studio so I can make music. When you can show me a way that is going to make me money so I can provide for all of my family and do what I want, when I want, how I want, come and let me know, yeah?"

He said no bank in the world would lend him money. He was right.

'I never thought I'd do something like this, but why the fuck should I work as a motherfuckin' chicken fryer when I could buy my own restaurant in a few months?'

With all these kids angling for a shot at the title, the chance to impress by gunning down a rival marks you out as a leader – it wins you followers. With them, you might start a war on a rival crack gang and take over their house, and then you're made – until some-one comes for you, of course.

One memorable example of this featured a character known appropriately as 'Charlie', who was working his way up the crack-dealing ladder in Tottenham. His friend later recalled, 'Charlie had this Rottweiler, looked hard as fuck but was a soppy bastard really. Anyway, one day Charlie comes home to find his dog out of his mind, on his back on the floor, legs up. It had chewed the crap out of his apartment – the reason was it had eaten an ounce of Charlie's coke that he hadn't hidden well enough. Even tough Charlie loved that animal but he still took him out back, put his gun to its skull and blew its head off. He had nightmares afterwards.

'Anyway, a couple weeks later we had been selling on the street when this big kid with a hoodie rolls up and asks us for some weight, an ounce. We were standing by these phone boxes; the kid said he was waiting for his mate with the money. Sure enough, his friend showed up a few minutes later.

'Charlie said they'd have to wait because he didn't wanna take them inside. But the big kid said he wanted to make sure the ounce was legit. At first Charlie said no, but the thought of all that cash was damn powerful, so he let them in. Besides, we had been sell-ing on the street a long time so it was a break for us.

'We climbed the stairs and as soon as I opened the door Charlie asked me if I had tied the dog up. Before I realized what he was trying to do I had said "What dog?" We walk in and instead of going to the bathroom where his piece is, Charlie walks into the kitchen still talking about that fucking dog. Normally he comes out of the bathroom waving his gun and that's enough to make sure everything goes smoothly. For some reason he didn't this time.

'The two buyers are in the lounge and the big kid says "Where's the coke?" and Charlie says what about the money? The big kid reaches in his coat and pulls out a pistol. He tells Charlie to get the shit and points the gun at him. Charlie tells them to get fucked and so they go through the place looking. They find a bag of coke in the cupboard and then Charlie makes his move, going for the gun arm of the big kid, but the kid just pulls away and shoots Charlie in the side. They grab the stuff and split.

'Charlie's bleeding and holding his side. There was more blood than I ever knew was in somebody – my shoes, shirt, hands were all bloody and Charlie looked like he fell in a big tank full of red paint. I drove us to the hospital. Charlie lost a kidney which left him too weak to deal any more.'

Despite the hazards, dealing crack in Haringey was just too attractive an option to pass up. The police were seen as less of an inconvenience than rival gangs and robbers (at least we didn't usually shoot anyone without good reason and most smart dealers could take enough precautions to avoid prison). I desperately wanted to make it as unattractive an option as possible by making it impossible for anyone to set up shop on my patch.

SEVENTEEN

ABOLISHED

Just before Christmas 1999 we had a run of three crap raids – all we netted were a lonely crack addict, a stolen bus pass and a Turkish guy with a big bag of weed. So it was not the best time to get word on the police grapevine (which works at broadband speed) that I was about to be 'abolished', sacked from my present position and sent back to my old job as a uniformed sergeant. I was gutted: the team was just bonding; things had been going really well. We'd kept the cells full and had been gradually reclaiming the streets. My immediate boss, Detective Inspector Gordon Green, called me into an office and said, 'You're spending too much money. We can't afford this so we're going to have to send you back.'

'I disagree, guv – there's only five of us, we can't have spent that much.'

DI Green pointed out that I was supposed to keep our costs down. It was at this point I played my trump card. I took a breath and played it for all it was worth. 'Do you realize that in the three months since I've been doing this, only one black person has been shot – and we've recovered the gun.'

I knew that this was an unanswerable truth which proved we were having an amazing effect. For the three months of the same period last year we had had fourteen shootings, two of which resulted in murder. Next, I asked to see the big boss, Chief

Superintendent James. I knew that this argument might work on him more than anyone as he was passionate about the hands-on approach to destroying criminal networks. DI Green looked at me thoughtfully for a moment. 'Let me see what I can do,' he said, 'but honestly it doesn't look good, it's been decided.'

This was a load of bollocks – and just in time for Christmas, too. The lads already knew by the time I ambled glumly into the dusty dark stock cupboard we called our office. I saw the long faces and asked what was up. Colin stood up, looked at me a bit awkwardly and said, 'Harry, if those bastards want to give you the fucking sack then the bastards will have to sack the fucking lot of us.' Coming from macho Colin this was praise indeed.

Darren raised his eyes skywards at Colin's efforts at a loyal speech and added, 'Yeah, Harry, if you go we all go, right lads?'

I was deeply touched. 'Lads, what can I say . . . well, let's just see what happens. In the meantime they haven't fired me yet so it's business as usual, right?'

Inside I was absolutely devastated. The words 'You're bound to fuck up and be back in a couple of weeks' haunted me and I was now sure that was exactly what was going to happen. And we were only seventeen houses on our way to the century. All of the good work we'd done would soon be undone. With the pressure off the dealers would soon reclaim the streets as their own. It would take something truly extraordinary to change the minds of the powers that be.

The next day we hit a house in Copperfield Drive, a couple of streets north of Ashmount Road, in an early-morning raid, only to be confronted by a wild-eyed and wild-haired Bulgarian man who spoke no English. The only thing we managed to get from him was a pot of Bulgarian tea while we repaired his front door. He'd just moved in; our target had fled the country. This only deepened my growing depression. I hoped that management wouldn't get to hear about this raid as it would only add weight to the wrong side of the scales.

Our intel told us that a place on Falkland Road was a minor crack house and so we decided to hit it without the use of the TSG. Falkland Road is on the 'Haringey ladder', a series of parallel streets laid out so that each street looks like a rung with a series of alleyways connecting them all – perfect for burglars and crack dealers. It's a stone's throw from Ducketts Common, where crack dealers handed out gear to punters.

I was still in a bad mood about my impending abolishment so, working off my aggression, I crashed through the door at full tilt only to find that we were totally outnumbered. Shit. Move fast, I thought, don't give them time to think. Luckily the rest of the squad cottoned on; we quickly got them all sat down and the back-up arrived before they realized they outnumbered us two to one. All of them appeared to be long-term crack-heads so their minds weren't working too well. I grabbed a mobile phone that kept on ringing and answered it. A voice at the other end said, 'Dave?'

'Yeah.'

'You serving?'

'Yeah.'

'Got a party bag for me, one white, one brown?'

'Yeah. Come now.'

Two more guys turned up so we nicked them as well. The house was full of crack, pills and skunk seeds; the forty-three-year-old owner looked about twenty years older than she was. On the charge sheet she bizarrely gave her occupation as an antiques dealer.

We took our bounty back to the factory. 'I'm not in the mood for any shit from any fucking custody sergeant tonight,' I told Greg. 'If any of them open their mouths and spout any of their sarky shit, you come and find me, right?'

'Sure thing, Harry.'

We walked into the packed reception. If I saw the custody sergeant's face wrinkle with disgust at the sight of our latest haul I would not be impressed. 'Just one word,' I thought, 'just one word.'

Unbeknownst to me, Chief Superintendent Steve James had just marched into the lobby behind me and grabbed Adam. Speaking in a loud voice, making sure he had everyone's attention, he pointed at us and said, 'These lads are the ones stopping the shootings; they're responsible for the massive drop we've had in crime in the borough recently. They are doing a great job.' He marched off again.

Everyone stood there, gobsmacked. In that simple action, James had done us a massive favour. The story that we were stopping the shootings whizzed round the nick in no time at all. Before this, many of our fellow officers didn't know what we were up to or realize the effect we were having. One of the custody sergeants had morphed into a new man. I'd previously suspected he'd thought we were just making his life difficult by bringing him dozens of particularly annoying prisoners. First, he stunned me with a friendly smile, and then he said, 'Right then, let's see how quickly we can get this lot done then, eh?' To my great relief, the hostilities between us were over.

The next day DI Green made a very rare journey to Haringey Drugs Squad's office. 'Sergeant Keeble.'

'Sir?'

'I want you to write me a report on your time here and tell me what effect you think you've had – good and bad. Do you think you could do it by the end of the week?'

'Yes, sir.'

'Very good. Crack on.'

It wasn't hard not to laugh at his pun but I suspected something strange was up. I spent the rest of the week in the run-up to Christmas writing my report about the people we'd arrested, the houses we'd closed, the effect this had on the neighbourhoods and how many more we had on our hit list, as well as comparing it with the situation before and spelling out what would happen if we stopped closing crack houses. I wrote about how communities needed to know that they could talk to us about the problems they faced from crack houses, that if a member of the public gave us an address we would check it out and then shut it down ASAP without having to involve them any further.

Then I got pissed with the rest of HDS, left the alien world of Haringey and went home for Christmas.

EIGHTEEN

MORE RAIDS AND A REPRIEVE

We'd been slowly working our way down the list towards a house in Plevna Crescent when it suddenly shot to the number-one spot. There had been a serious stabbing in the street and a trail of blood literally led to this address. We screeched off in the Primera for a rapid recce while the TSG set up back at the factory.

Plevna Crescent is right at the centre of the Tottenham Triangle, at the crossroads of the north-to-south and west-to-east railway networks, a minute from South Tottenham and Seven Sisters train stations – crack central. There was an under-fives' day-care centre in the crescent so we had to be on our guard. Luckily the target address wasn't next door; it was a small, one-bed ground-floor flat. It had its own front door with a peephole. As we watched, a young Mediterranean woman rang the bell; the door was opened almost instantly and she stepped inside. A few minutes later, two young men wearing expensive leather jackets, jeans and the latest trainers turned up. They looked as guilty as hell to my trained eye.

'OK, I've seen enough, let's get this one over with,' I said. I was still depressed about my impending abolishment and had resolved to get through as many crack houses as possible before it happened. We zipped back to the factory where I briefed the TSG and we drove full tilt back to the address, my red enforcer bouncing around the boot. I made a mental note to fasten it down in future.

We charged straight down the garden path, watched by a surprised pensioner which was fine by me. The more people that saw us at work the better. The door imploded first time; it slapped the hall wall with a tremendous crack and we steamed inside.

There were three men in the house, which was littered with drug paraphernalia, knives, porn videos and booze. One of them had a horrendous scar down his cheek where his face had been sliced open; most likely he'd been glassed in a pub brawl. Once we'd secured the place and the guys were cuffed I let the TSG go (this keeps the costs down).

The electric was hotwired and so after identifying the owner we nicked him for that. A check made over the radio revealed that he'd failed to register his address under the new Sex Offenders Act, so we nicked him for that too. Sounds bad, doesn't it, being on the Sex Offenders Register? The crimes are not always as awful as you'd think. I heard that one guy ended up on the register after he'd got drunk down his local and pinched a girl's bottom. Her boyfriend called the police and had him prosecuted. He was eventually convicted and that meant he had to go on the register.

As it was a council-owned property, I'd called in a council representative who showed up in a van with metal grills for the windows and a steel door. Within minutes the grills were up and the borough had their flat back. Once the three men were in the back of the van, several neighbours came over for a chat. One of them said, 'If we'd known this would happen I would have reported them earlier.'

'Well, spread the word. You show us a house like this and we'll close it down straight away.'

It was a perfect job, exactly as it should be.

The next raid wasn't quite as perfect but it was convenient, as we were able jog across the road from Wood Green police station. It was the home of a small-timer whose name had popped up on various intel reports and drug-related incidents. By living just across the road from us she was asking to be raided but it also made sense to us for another reason. She was so well connected in the drugs scene that once she was bailed she would spread the news to everyone she knew. Once word got out that we were raiding everyone – small, medium and big time – this would send a clear message that it wasn't safe to be involved in drugs at any level in Haringey.

We hit it at dawn with two covering the rear and the rest of us at the front. The door opened cleanly and I was immediately horrified to see the place was immaculate – not a good sign. I wondered whether I'd got the right address as we ran around the house until we got upstairs – it was in a mess, a real crack den.

As I crashed into the kitchen I ran into a terrified cat which performed a very impressive version of the wall of death round the kitchen, screaming as it went while the five of us stared in amazement. After a couple of loops it made a bolt for the open front door and zipped out into the street. We looked at each other, shrugged our shoulders and carried on.

It turned out that the suspect's mother lived downstairs, hence its neatness. The mother said she was glad to see the back of both of them, daughter and cat.

We were in the custody suite and actually having a laugh with the custody sergeants for once (about the cat) when DI Green spotted me and called me into his office. My smile collapsed. This was it, I thought – back I go to the old section. The rest of the squad watched me trudge glumly after Green.

'Have a seat, Harry.'

'Thanks, guv.' It was a nondescript office – broken blinds half open, a desk piled high with neatly organized papers, cabinets, coat-stand, a lukewarm radiator that rattled and needed to be drained. It had started to rain and there was a definite chill in the air.

'You must be awfully tired. All these houses and people you've been arresting. Coffee?'

'Not at all,' I said and added a 'no thanks' to the offer of coffee. What was he trying to say, that I was burned out already and should be grateful for my abolishment?

'What did you think when you heard you were going to be abolished?'

'I was gutted, of course.' What was he getting at? Why didn't he just get it over with?

DI Green slurped his coffee. 'I wondered whether you'd had enough.'

'What do you mean, enough?'

'Whether you were perhaps exhausted? You've really been going at it, you know.'

'No, not at all. We have a few long days each week but the squad's coping brilliantly and we've been making real inroads into the borough's crack trade. Look, guv, don't be offended, but can we get to the point?'

'Yes, of course. You've impressed the right people with what you've accomplished. Those same people liked what you had to say in your report. It fits with certain political thinking at the moment.'

Now my heart was pumping. Green paused, took a sip of coffee and hit me with the bombshell that made this meeting so memorable.

'We'd like you to keep doing exactly what you're doing for a little longer. We're launching a new Met-wide campaign called Rat-on-a-Rat and I want Haringey Drugs Squad to be a part of that.'

I was stunned. 'So carry on . . . as we are?'

'For now, yes.' Green took a sip of coffee. 'We might even be able to throw some more resources your way.'

'For how long?'

'We'll see how the Rat-on-a-Rat campaign goes and have a review of things then, OK?'

I walked out, punched the air and ran down to our stock cupboard. I booted in the door; the entire squad jumped as if they'd all been shocked in the arse. 'Lads, they love us! We've gotta carry on as we are!'

'What?' said Greg, getting up from a sofa he'd made from a pile of dusty boxes.

'Just had a meeting with Green and he said the chief super loves what we're doing, wants to see more of it and wants us to form part of the Rat-on-Rat campaign, busting as many crack houses as the public tell us about. We'll even get some extra resources.'

'No fucking way!' said Colin.

'Oh yes.'

'Do we get a new office?'

'Don't be ridiculous. But pass me some of those boxes, we need to make another desk.'

NINETEEN

PEST CONTROL

RAT-ON-A-RAT: DAY ONE, MONDAY 27 JANUARY 2000

'Students at Middlesex Poly smoking weed, you say?'

No shit, Sherlock.

'Yes, well, thanks for the call, we'll look into it.' I sighed as I hung up and scratched my head. As far as I was concerned the students could smoke dope till the cows came home. I wanted our focus kept firmly on crack cocaine. Most people are rightly afraid of grassing on crack dealers, but the Rat-on-a-Rat scheme worked because it made it clear that people could call us with total anonymity. Unfortunately, along with some good tips we also got a lot of prank calls, timewasters, some threats and the odd loon.

The best story was the man who reported that he had been attacked by a pack of marauding squirrels. He wasn't crazy: he had just realized that the hungry rodents, who are excellent foragers, had found somebody's stash of crack and eaten the rocks, thinking they were nuts. Apparently, squirrels on crack behave just like human users – they become incredibly aggressive towards each other and even attack humans.

Now, with a bit more official financial flexibility, I was able to get a TSG liaison officer to come to our office and help me organize the raids. John was an excellent planner and really got behind us; closing crack houses was just the sort of thing the TSG liked to do. Together, based on the information we'd received via the Rat-on-a-Rat campaign, we planned a series of seven raids aimed at delivering a disabling blow to the crack-house structure in Haringey.

Unfortunately, it was just then that we lost Colin to the CID, as he made detective. He was replaced by Tina, a tall and fiery twenty-five-year-old streetwise English-Jamaican with a razor-sharp mind who couldn't wait to get as many collars as possible in the shortest possible time. She always seemed to be cold, hungry and in need of a cigarette and kept her private life private, as did Adam.

First up was a flat in a housing estate above the Tesco in Seven Sisters Road; its unusual position gave the impression of a small city in the sky. It was another place, once again, within the Tottenham Triangle. All the security was suitably fucked, the door entry-system a mess of wires and the lock was missing, a necessity for any successful crack house. Bouncers were on the stairwells and the block was circled by catchers in the High Road below. John suggested we play the crack dealers at their own game and send a couple of our own guys to compete.

Because we had the backing of the powers that be, this meant we were being watched very closely; now we were under pressure to get good results for the sake of the stats, which I could understand, but it was a bit different from what we were used to (i.e. being ignored unless something went wrong). As a result we decided to hit the flat in the evening when it would be at its busiest. This way there was a chance of picking up some decent collars. John reckoned that the TSG could take care of the door, so we could save some time and money by not using the Ghosties on this one. We also had the bright idea of bringing a bloke from the electricity company to make the meter safe. They were hotwired so often and so badly that it was only a matter of time before someone got fried.

We debussed outside the supermarket at 9 p.m. and the TSG

charged the door with the Enforcer. It didn't even flex. Shit. They hit it again. Nothing. We had checked it out and were sure there was no New York latch. What we hadn't spotted was that the door had been fixed so it opened outwards, with the door frame behind it. We needed the Ghosties to sort this one out. 'Get a crowbar!' I yelled. 'And tell the catchers to be on the lookout!' Meanwhile various windows had been flung open all across the estate; suddenly we had become the night's entertainment. Insults rained down on us from above. In the darkness, I couldn't see anything up there. Not a good situation. I took a peek through the target's letterbox. I could see one man, smoking a cigarette at the top of the stairwell.

'Police! Open the door!'

He gave me the finger.

'We'll be coming in anyway in a minute.'

He shrugged and gave me the finger again.

'Cheeky fucker. Where's that fucking crowbar?'

By this point the whole estate was watching us. This didn't look good. 'The DI ain't gonna like this,' Adam added unhelpfully.

Eventually, the crowbar was handed over; we jammed it in at the edge of the door and hammered it in with the enforcer. Finally, after we frantically yanked it back and forth, the wood scraped, screamed and then cracked, giving just enough for us to kick it in.

We strolled in – there was hardly any need to announce ourselves. The bloke at the top of the stairs was the only one there, although it was like the *Mary Celeste* with crack pipes, half-drunk beers and fags that had burned down in ashtrays without being smoked or thrown away. But no one else was in the property.

I was just thinking that this was hardly a glorious start to our new campaign when Greg gave me a shout. 'Harry! You're gonna want to see this!' I walked into a large bedroom to find Greg standing holding a copy of a CD. 'Check it out, Harry,' and he pointed at the wall. Computers and CD burners lined the side of the room; on the other side were thousands upon thousands of CDs along with a handful of master copies of the latest big film releases of the day and computer software. 'That's at least half a million quid's worth,' I said and smiled. Not bad at all. 'Let's get this lad down the station and close the flat.'

The guy from the electricity board re-looped the meter and we bagged the evidence, which besides the CDs included a stash of crack and some stolen credit cards. We dragged our captive off to the station (he gave us abuse all the away) and were gone within the hour.

The next day's Rat-on-a-Rat raid was in Harold Road, just round the corner from Ashmount. This place was home to a couple of addicts in their thirties (they looked nearly twice their age) whom we had encountered on several occasions, and their home was a quiet haven for drug-taking and sex; there was no security – if someone slammed the front door the knob would fall off and bounce down the stairs. We had no trouble here; they were polite without giving anything away and were nicked for handling stolen goods and possession of crack and heroin. We hung around for a bit to see if anyone else came round, which they did, so we arrested them too.

On the Wednesday we went back to the Ashmount Road house, which had reopened for business. The cheeky bastards were making good use of the steel door we had used to seal off the property. As we studied the address from our observation point Sam, who was with us for a couple of weeks on attachment, spotted a face she recognized. 'He's wanted, Harry.'

'You remember what for?'

'Let me take a closer look at him and maybe it'll click.' I agreed and Sam followed the suspect on the road. Suddenly she dropped back, turned and waved for us to join her.

As nonchalantly as we could we quickly caught up with Sam. 'We think he's a crack dealer wanted for attempted murder; he poured petrol over one of his prostitutes and put a match to her. His brother runs the crack house at Somerset Gardens[8].' This was serious Prince of Darkness stuff.

---

8 We'll get there, don't worry.

As I've already mentioned, Mark Lambie was known as the Prince of Darkness, head of the Tottenham Man Dem (TMD). Before the Broadwater Farm riots, the TMD were just common thugs, but afterwards they got organized. Lambie, who'd laughed his way out of court after being acquitted of Keith Blakelock's murder, had worked his way to the top of the TMD.

The TMD had been at war with the Hackney Man Dem from London Fields and Haggerston. The fighting had started in 1997 over the accidental shooting of a sixteen-year-old studying for his GCSEs; Guydance Dacres caught a bullet in the head as he danced at a New Year's party in Hackney. The same bullet also hit and injured a teenage girl. It had been accidentally fired by a wannabe teenage gangster who had been showing off his 9mm to a girl.

Despite there being 300 witnesses, no one saw anything. At the trial the accused shooter, nineteen-year-old Anthony Bourne, a member of the TMD, walked free after telling the court, 'I never had a gun that night. I've never had a gun in my life.' Well, if he didn't then he soon fucking did. Bourne went to lead his own gang, 'The Firm', and became Lambie's number-one enforcer.

In revenge the Hackney Boys hunted down another sixteen-year-old, Kingsley Iyasara, street-name Popcorn. He was kidnapped and taken to a tower-block rooftop where he was beaten with clubs and baseball bats before being shot in the stomach at point-blank range. He bled to death, alone. Then the TMD starting picking off these murderers one by one; in June 1999 one made the mistake of driving his red Beamer convertible through the streets of Hackney. He was overtaken by two sports motorbikes. One blocked his way while the pillion passenger on the other shot their target dead in the chest.

Lambie eventually stopped these tit-for-tat shootings. For him, life was all about money and power. He didn't see the sense in maintaining a gang war and, as long as the HMD didn't interfere with his business, he kept the peace.

He had no problem hooking up with other gangs and had been working with groups across North and South London from the

PDCs, the SMS, LGM and the Ghetto Boys. He also hired the Harlesden Clicks as his own version of the Baker Street Dozen to run his errands, find people and provide info. He didn't so much care about respect as money. Anyone got in the way of business, they wound up dead.

Lambie was untouchable. He never saw the drugs, never went to crack houses and almost never touched the money, which was expertly laundered by his team. He was at the top of the pyramid. Taking him out wouldn't have changed a thing in Haringey, though. Nobody would have noticed at street level; the addicts were there and the supply was there.

Then, in 2000 he, vanished. We didn't know it but he had moved to South London, from where he ran his North London empire, so even the newly established big-budget Operation Trident, who had him down as their 'prom-nom-one', couldn't get a bug on him or even a photo. He was an enigma, and some even believed he was a 'Juju man', a kind of witchdoctor whom bullets bounced off. He was certainly lucky. Three hitmen thought they'd found Lambie in a Caribbean restaurant called 'The Place to Be'. Acting friendly they said, 'Someone here called Mark?' Lambie was sitting at another table and kept his mouth shut. Two other guys nodded. Mark Spence, an unemployed painter, was shot dead. Mark Verley died in hospital a short while later.

We certainly couldn't pass up the chance to bust what might be one of the TMD's top psychos. We quickly arrested him. He was exceptionally pissed off and quite right too. It was a good collar. Was this house one of Lambie's? I hoped so. I liked the thought that even though the cops had no idea where he was, we were about to piss him off by screwing up his business.

That night we came back with a larger-than-usual flotilla of TSG. Thanks to a trade secret, the Ghosties made short work of the steel door and in charged twenty TSGs accompanied by the thuk-thuk-thuk of the descending chopper. The lads watched and waited, leaning on the side of the Primera while I followed the TSG inside, where once again it was mayhem.

It was a truly surreal feeling as I walked around with my radio, deliberately not getting involved with the fighting but keeping clear, trying not to trip over the broken furniture, milk crates and piles of rubbish so I could assess and direct the operation. It was an even match and the TSG called for support.

I clicked the talk button on my radio and said, 'Deploy the second wave.'

I could hear them coming. It was the sweetest music: the sound of many boots on the garden path, the clattering of shields and batons. I felt like the Duke of Wellington as another twenty troops poured in. This was more like it. As they piled in one of the TSG caught my eye; it was an old friend I hadn't seen for ages. 'All right, Harry! How's things?' he said, as he waved his baton cheerfully and dived through the door into the swirling smoke.

It was at this point that I got a call over the radio from a nervous uniformed inspector who'd come along with the TSG to see what was going on. 'Is everything all right in there?'

'Don't worry, everything's perfect, guv.' Once again the tables were turned as the dealers and crack-heads alike scattered in fear. They didn't have a chance.

A few minutes later we had the house under control and I was speaking to a much more subdued Lesley Ballantine. This time we arrested him for all the stolen property, cannabis, crack and heroin we found. Not all of the charges would stick but it got the message across. 'And we'll keep coming back,' I said loudly so that every one of the thirty or so people could clearly hear. 'No matter how many times we have to, we'll be back.'

Friday's target was a property on St Ann's Road, a famous crack house situated in a large first-floor flat on a major thoroughfare that cut straight through Haringey, just across the road from St Anne's Hospital. Now that Ashmount Road had closed it was the busiest little crack house in Tottenham, especially as the addicts who normally scored from Ashmount now headed straight over to this address – which was exactly what we wanted. This place was open

24 hours, seven days a week, 365 days of the year. We planned to hit at night, when it would be at its absolute busiest.

Like Ashmount Road, it was secured by a steel door. According to our sketchy intel, the occupants protected themselves with bouncers and a machete, as well as smaller knives and possibly guns (although we had no way of knowing about any of these things for certain). But we had heard the same thing time and again and knew full well to expect there to be some kind of weaponry. As one ex-dealer put it: 'Crack has caused nothing but shit for the drugs trade. It's brought all the heat on everybody: the dealers, the sniffers, everybody. Before people started taking this shit, everybody sniffed and was polite and sensible and that was that. But now kids are killing their mothers and everybody to get something for the pipe. People are scared to go out because of the guns and shit. Dealers sit at home with their own pieces waiting to get robbed by kids.'

What we did know was that they had a bouncer at the door who checked the punters as they came in. Another bouncer stood behind him and a third stood with those queuing to score. It was a fast turnover house with only a select few allowed to stay and smoke; most punters came and went in a matter of minutes. This was in part thanks to the way crack was packaged – a seemingly innocuous thing but it was a development that transformed the drugs trade. Suppliers who wanted their product to reach their clients undiluted sold pre-packed rocks in tamper-proof wraps to their middlemen. Arguments over purity were avoided and there was no need for scales and cutting equipment to be kept on site. Sealed packages also saved precious dealing time. As one buyer commented: 'Crack houses are like a regular business now. Dealers don't give out samples. People come in and know what they want. The stuff is pre-packaged, it's good, and they know the price. They pay the money and leave. Next customer.'

I paid a visit to the housing association that owned the property and they agreed to close the building after we'd turned it over. Next, we booked in our man from the electricity board and then looked at our best way in. After a short discussion, the answer was clear: I wanted us to go in fast, which would mean debussing in the road.

On 4 February 2000, the night of the raid, I went to take a look at the place on my own. As I stopped to pick up a newspaper in a local supermarket I was impressed to see that the owners had restocked their shelves in line with local demand. Amazingly, along with stacks of every flavour of Nutriment, reams of cheap foil and boxes of straws (these are handy for making homemade pipes), they were actually selling the little metal pipes that crack smokers use for £2.99 with the legend 'I ♥ London' written on the bowl (these pipes aren't illegal). They also had plenty of butane mini-blowtorch lighters which are preferred by most crack addicts because they think they are less harmful to the lungs than a normal lighter. Bic lighters are even less desirable. All lighters, however, are thought to be less harmful than the sulphur from the match. This is part of a strange obsession amongst crack users about what's 'good' for you.

The activity in the crack house was intense. People of all ages were coming and going, from teenage girls to middle-aged men. A heavy-set black man with a scar above his eye opened and closed the door as people came and went.

It felt as if we had created a sense of desperation, forcing addicts to go on 'missions' to score because we had closed their local crack houses. Now, they had to find new places where they could score a decent hit for a good price. For young girls, it's a complicated process of manipulation, charm and bravura. The crack-head on a mission has to travel through labyrinthine housing estates, often following cold trails, sometimes risking their lives in a desperate hunt for a smoke.

A girl who looked to be about fourteen years old walked towards the house, dragging her right arm along the side of the building as she went. She was tiny, half-starved; the outlines of her bony legs were hard to distinguish in her dark jeans, which were unwashed and worn thin. There was desperation in her eyes. Some words came to mind when I saw her, something a prostitute had once said: 'Even if you live in some posh village and were born with a silver spoon in your mouth, you are going to kill your mother for that hit. If you are a sweetheart on the outside and you take this drug, it will make sure that the dark side comes out, the side of you that you don't want others to see. But it makes you not give a toss one way or the other.'

If there was any dignity before that girl started using crack then I could see no sign of it now.

Another lost girl in a faded blue jacket exited as the other entered. Suddenly she dived down onto the pavement, ghostbusting for all she was worth. She came up, knees dirty from the wet pavement, and wandered away. I couldn't stand it any more. I drove back to the station in the Primera.

At 10 p.m. the convoy pulled up perfectly in sync, not too close, so that there was enough space for each group to cleanly debus. The thirty TSG officers were divided into groups; we had studied the building plans and each group was given a room to attack.

The Ghosties were already working their magic as the TSG pounded towards the door. This was fast. It was like watching the mechanics change the tyres on a Formula One car and refuel in record time. The steel door was open in seconds and the TSG ascended into the smoky vortex. As I followed, and even though I thought I was used to it by now, I almost retched at the wall of stench: the piss, the stale dampness, rotting food and the irrepressible odour of crack cocaine. The smoke billowed out behind us as we plunged in. I was delighted to see that by the time I made it to the top of the stairs, the TSG were in control.

They'd had a bit of unexpected assistance from the chopper. A pair of crack dealers had tried bailing out of the first-floor window when the helicopter came down on them, the million-watt light blazing. It stopped them dead. By the time their eyes had adjusted the TSG were there and they yanked them back inside.

Among the dealers were a thirty-three-year-old technician, a seventeen-year-old student from Birmingham armed with a knife and forty-year-old Patrick Jarrett (son of Cynthia, of Broadwater Farm riot fame), with about ten rocks in his jeans pocket. None of them gave us any grief and I got on quite well with Patrick. A fifty-four-year-old addict called Leon whom I'd encountered before greeted me like an old friend (this wasn't the last time I'd arrest him either). This was quite helpful as once Leon said I was an all-right copper the others relaxed and did their best to be civil, making our job a lot easier.

As soon as I judged everyone was secure I told the TSG they could go. Keeping thirty men on overtime was an expensive luxury I wanted to keep to a minimum. A couple of hours later, just as we were about to leave, a man with a rucksack on his back, clearly the worse for wear, half-staggered, half-strode straight into the flat and into my arms. He was Jamaican, the same height as me, and had a shaven head. He stank and wasn't happy to see us; he racially abused Adam, Taylor and Tina before putting up so much of a struggle that we had to put him on the floor. He had been carrying a Stanley knife. One more for the cells.

The custody sergeant greeted me with a smile. 'Crikey, Harry, how many tonight?'

The next day a uniformed inspector asked me why I had released the TSG after the raid and not waited until we had finished clearing up. He'd had a complaint that we'd put ourselves at risk by sending them away too early – this wasn't something that had bothered them over the last five months we'd been operating, though. 'To save money,' I explained. Although he accepted my curt explanation, this blast of cool air was not appreciated.

Chief Superintendent Steven James, however, was marvellous. He'd asked to see me about the use of the chopper. I assumed this would have something to do with the expense but I was surprised to hear that I had used the chopper so much (the chopper squad had given me my own radio) that some locals had complained about the noise. James told me that we might end up with some more complaints, as he had now ordered the chopper to fly for ten minutes every day twice a day just because it unnerved criminals. Criminals assumed that it was flying over them for a reason – if you're a gangster carrying a gun or a few ounces of crack you think it might be there for you. I was sure that every time it flew over Haringey about a hundred or so criminals dived for cover. It sent out an excellent message to the entire borough which said we were here – loudly.

TWENTY

THE LOST GIRLS

I was in a crack house after a raid, interviewing a prostitute, trying desperately not to look as disgusted as I felt. She was less than a foot away from me. For the umpteenth time, she put her hand beneath the waistband of her tracksuit bottoms and scratched between her legs. Something was making her itch pretty damn bad down there. She didn't even realize what she was doing until she caught me looking at her like I'd just stepped in shit. But she was beyond caring. She looked utterly pathetic, rodent-like, and I began to feel sick; I tried to stop the thought but it was too late – she should be put down. There was no way back from where she was, a life of delusional hope and unrelenting misery and degradation. I didn't want to talk to her any more so I told her I was done.

There was a fully-fledged whorehouse in Bruce Grove, a big place with a massive living room. It had five rooms for people to sit around and get high but most guys just came for the sex, which is how 'Jay' the K-man advertised it. One teenage girl said, 'He charged £20 just to get in. It was full of us girls, fourteen to six-teen. Some stayed for days at a time, getting high and screwing these guys, just so they could keep on getting high. When they ran out they went begging to the first man who would give them another hit and do whatever he asked, blow-jobs, go down on other girls, you name it. There was a girl who had her own room.

She had no teeth and charged a hit for anyone to do what the fuck they liked. Her room stank of piss and rubbish was just piled up in the corners but she was never short.'

Meanwhile, while I'd been interviewing itchy, two female officers had been thoroughly searching the rest of the prostitutes for drugs. Some of them put up a good fight, scratching, biting and spitting; there was a real danger of getting stuck with a needle. They got to one lady, a thin wastrel; there's no polite way of putting it – she stunk like shit. As they undressed her, the smell grew in intensity until I started to feel ill – and I was in the next room. One of the officers, holding her hand over her mouth, ran from the room while the other told the prostitute that if she had any crack 'down there' she could keep it.

While I was hanging out with stinking prostitutes in this filthy crack house, my wife was preparing to give birth to our son. I hated not being home more and was desperate not to miss the big day. The raids had taken their toll on all our personal lives. At this stage we were averaging about three large crack houses and a handful of minor dens each week. The paperwork with each case was unbelievable; it usually took all night to work through. We were on the job pretty much 24–7 and were permanently knackered. We were drinking too much coffee and snapping at our girlfriends, wives and kids.

Going to work was like travelling to a different planet. I lived in a small pretty village in a leafy part of Hertfordshire and each morning I drove to this other world, a world full of dealers, whores and damaged and violent addicts who threw their lives away in vile cesspits; a world in which I had to be this hard-faced bastard prepared to face death, terrified that one of my men would be hurt or killed or that one of our raids would somehow kick off a massive riot. Each day I tried to transform into a loving husband and fun father once I made it home (which was becoming more and more infrequent). It wasn't easy.

I regretted straight away my thoughts about putting down the young prostitute; it was just a symptom of my weariness and despair at the utter hopelessness of her situation. Generally, the rule was once a crack-head always a crack-head. Many addicts understandably have the attitude that since they are lost there is no reason to try to change. But change is possible.

They had all been babies, children once – they had a chance at a decent life and then something took it all away. I tried to imagine what it would be like for my kids to become addicts, and saw how that could happen – I knew better than most how crack could make that nightmare possible.

Prostitutes remain fundamentally misunderstood. They don't belong to a different level of humanity from the rest of us. Society perceives prostitution as a career that attracts girls from the gutter or the wrong side of the tracks, but it's not only the daughters of troubled and deprived families who are destined to become prostitutes. It can be the well-bred and educated daughters of perfectly ordinary stable families. As one woman put it: 'People don't see we're normal people; we are either dirty or we haven't got the brains to do anything else.' One thing's for sure: before crack got them, they shared the same hopes, dreams and fears as the rest of us.

They hurt too, and suffer more than most. I've seen them beaten up, bones broken; I've seen them dead and I've sent them to prison, which for crack addicts is the best thing that could happen to them. In the last ten years, over sixty prostitutes have been violently murdered by ripper-style killers; later that year three crack-addicted prostitutes would be tortured by a man known as the Camden Ripper before he killed them, cut up the bodies and disposed of them in wheelie-bins around Camden in North London.

It is a sad fact that people don't treat the murder of a prostitute the same way they would that of some other unfortunate woman. Even the police approach the scene with a different attitude. It's not that the case receives less attention from us; officers are simply seeing a different kind of human being. They are stereotyped as all being the same, so it follows that they are killed for the same reason, regardless of where or how they are found.

As I stood in the flat surrounded by filthy mattresses, trying not to gag on the smell of crack, stale sex and whatever was wrong with the stinking woman no one wanted to go near, I told myself over and over that 'Prostitutes are individual people'. In our twelve-month campaign we encountered every kind of sex worker, from the maimed fire victim to the stinking disease-riddled crack addict, from the policeman's daughter to one of the highest-class prostitutes in the UK, who helped run a drugs empire worth several million pounds. Their stories were all so different that the only thing they had in common was their profession and their addiction.

Crack feeds the prostitution trade and vice versa. People do anything for their next fix and with crack there's no chance of overdosing: you can just keep on and on smoking and smoking. Time and again, crack prostitutes told me they had no recollection of the moment they became a prostitute (although they never had any trouble recollecting the first time they smoked crack). As long as they were high it didn't matter. Drug dealers encourage prostitutes because it means with women addicted their sales skyrocket. The dealers are very often pimps as well; they're happy because the prostitutes high on crack are able to work for longer than non-crack-smoking prostitutes and will make every effort to do so to keep their fix regular; they also won't want to leave the crack house for fear of missing out on a fix. Prostitutes also encourage the dealers to find them clients who will share a bit of their fix for sexual favours, which entices customers.

Scores, maybe hundreds of prostitutes disappear all the time. Many of them don't officially 'exist' and never turn up again, and if they do they have to be entered into the thick file of unsolved prostitute murders. They are always in danger, always close to violence. Their stories are shocking, horrific, and lest you ever thought prostitution was a minor offence, here's the tale of fourteen-year-old runaway Mandy.

She was 'rescued' by a pimp. He began by becoming her lover and supporting her. Then he started bringing his 'friends' to see her and asked her to help out with the money. 'He's a mate, he fancies you, just this once.' When Mandy tried to say no he went apeshit. 'Do you think I'm made of money? Why can't you do your bit?' Just the once turned into three or four times and before she knew it she was on the game.

Mandy looked particularly young and childlike, so she attracted men who fantasized about abusing children. She was grossly violated and brutalised. At one point she was imprisoned in a flat for an entire weekend. The man refused to pay and Mandy complained to her pimp, but he accused her of stealing the money and beat her with a broom handle. She stabbed him in the stomach with a pair of scissors. Pimps advertise themselves as protectors but never are in reality.

Donna's experience is typical of the addict's blatant disregard of risk. 'He was panicky; I thought it was the drugs. I should have known better, but I wanted to get high and he had drugs, loads of drugs. What I didn't know was he'd just robbed a kilo off some big-time dealer. We smoked for two days non-stop – until my heart ached.

'We went to this apartment with some other guys, and before I knew anything they had all taken off their clothes and made me do them. Then they brought some more girls over there and we all had sex together.

'One of them beat me, telling me I was a slapper and a bitch until this other guy threatened to beat him up and so he backed off. But as soon as things calmed down, this guy – the guy who helped me – started taking off my clothes. When he saw I was covered in welts and bruises he let me be. I fell asleep. Later, when I woke up, he was on top of me.

'A few days later he was shot and dumped in the Union Canal. I'm sorry he died but he was a total bastard.'

Young women like Donna make up a good proportion of the floating population in the crack houses. Wherever she was and whoever she was with, as long as there was plenty of crack she stayed, whatever the consequences.

Drug addiction and prostitution had turned Lindsey into a pretty tough character. She'll never forget the day she spotted the man who raped her in the Swan pub in Tottenham. The heavy reggae dub music faded into the background as the blood rushed to her head, making her ears sing. Being raped is a working girl's worst nightmare. When it happened to Lindsey she felt that she couldn't turn anywhere because she thought the police had an attitude of 'well, you fuck for a living so what's wrong with the odd freebie?' Nonetheless, she did report it and although they showed concern at the time she felt as though they were secretly laughing at her. They wouldn't have treated her that way if she were a young woman with a family. But that didn't mean she didn't want justice. She still had the scar on her hand from where he'd stubbed his cigarette out on her. Now he was sitting at the bar swigging from a pint, laughing, joking with his mates.

Spotting cutlery sitting in an open tray she grabbed a fork. As she walked past him she stabbed the fork into the back of his hand on the bar. It went straight through and fixed the hand to the wooden top. Then she grabbed his pint glass and smashed it into his mouth, where it broke and cut his cheek wide open. 'You could see his gums through the slash in his cheek; his skin was flapping as he screamed,' she recalled.

'If I had my way I would kill someone if I had the chance. I'm ready, believe me. You fuck with me and I'll come for you with a kitchen knife, bleach, a baseball bat, CS gas and my lighter – whatever I've got. Thing is, though, I don't want to go back to prison. The other night this guy pulled my hair and I went and headbutted him right there and would have killed him but for the thought of prison. You have got to put up a fight. I mean I've had a gun at my head and a knife at my throat and been strangled in crack houses. When I saw this guy beating another girl I ran outside and smashed his car windows with a bat. When he ran outside the both of us beat the bastard up.'

The crack-house girls never enjoy their job. They are always frightened, in fear for their lives; the only thing that keeps them going is the crack cocaine for which they'll do anything. Often they are disgusted with themselves. 'Plenty of times I have gone and bought bottles of bleach and scrubbed my skin so bad that I have brought blood to it. If we didn't have crack then the disgust of what I'd done, of letting strangers shag me, would wash over me and the agony of that would be utterly unbearable. I'd be sobbing while being fucked, utter misery – only the crack could blow it all away.'

And that's the problem. Crack keeps them there. They are using sex to get the drug because that's the only way they can get it – as far as the male is concerned his first hit of the night goes straight to his dick. It becomes a power game; the men say, 'If you don't give me sex, I won't give you the drug.'

Women try to get men to smoke a lot of crack quickly, as this tends to make them impotent, but this is dangerous because some men get upset and violent when they don't get an erection. Girls also risk retribution by finding ways of scamming a man's stash of crack: 'A lot of girls will pull the screen so that the residue falls to the bottom of the pipe. The man won't know what's happening. The pipe belongs to the girl, and the guy might smoke what appears to be a hundred quid's worth but most of it falls to the bottom.' The unsuspecting man will still get high over time. 'When it's all over she may do him but she will walk out with the pipe and 90 per cent of the drug.' What remains in the pipe is the residue, which is essentially refined crack. The risk of course is that if they get caught the man will hurt them, often during sex.

Some of the more experienced girls have quite sophisticated survival techniques. 'I never let blokes on top of me. Most girls, they think it is easier to let them be on top but no way, they could do anything. When *you* are on top you know that you have got their arms and legs, you can lean down and headbutt them or bite them. You get some that pile on top of you and try to smother you. I always make sure that my own arm is by my throat so at least I know I can use my other arm to force him off me. And you can always kick them in the bollocks anyway. You have to get them in the position you want.

'If someone comes in giving me grief they are going to get grief back, simple as that. It's either him or me and it ain't going to be me. I always have a plan and think about scenarios. It's me or them. A man came and turned nasty and told me he wasn't going to pay me. I simply told him he had to and if he didn't I'd throw him out of the fucking window. I meant it. I really meant it and would have had no hesitation. He paid me.

'One night this bloke was really high on speed; when they're like this they go on for ever. I said your time's up now. He got abusive so I picked up his clothes and threw them out of the window. Well, what could he do? He begged me to fetch them. I said he had to buy me a smoke first.'

One girl had a Rottweiler that was devoted to her. The dog sat and watched as she got on with it. Sometimes girls work in pairs as a 'double' – this means that at least someone else is present if the client turns nasty. It also works if one of the new teenage addicts is inexperienced, providing a useful education for her.

Then there are of course the dangers from smoking too much crack along with prostitution; aside from the unprotected sex and rape (leading to HIV and other STDs, pregnancy and the high risk that their baby will suffer from some kind of brain damage from all the crack their mother smokes), there are also the beatings (every prostitute we encountered had been beaten more than once), the risk of murder and the psychiatric disorders the lifestyle brings with it (depression and schizophrenia being the two most likely). The joint isolation of addiction and prostitution makes a woman vulnerable to the loss of social services, removal of her children and termination of parental rights, along with expulsion from social support systems, such as family or church. At the moment the stigma of prostitution makes it even harder for those addicted to drugs to give up and return to 'normal life'.

Besides this, smoking crack often leads on to other drugs. A young prostitute discovered that if she was strung out on crack, a shot of heroin mellowed her out. Her arms became riddled with thrombosis. Eventually she was taken to hospital where the doctors told her that to save her life she would have to lose both arms at the shoulder.

Some girls have been arrested over thirty times as part of a revolving-door syndrome of fines and arrests, thin veil for a street licence fee. Although it is illegal for premises to offer sexual services, police intervention is generally minimal and will occur only in response to a police complaint. In 2000, a judge threw out pimping charges against several whorehouses on the grounds that there was an unwritten rule that houses would only be prosecuted if a complaint had been made against them – leading to a reasonable expectation that a well-run operation would not attract police attention. This is a mistake. People don't report crack houses out of fear, allowing hundreds of teenage girls to face all the abuse described above. If anything the laws surrounding prostitution should be tightened and the trade regulated. Those worried about sex tourism should know that it's already here because our laws are so hopeless. Men from all over the world are in London literally getting away with paedophilia, rape and GBH.

That was the thing that bugged me the most, that gave me sleepless nights, that made me so obsessed with closing all the crack houses down – that so many teenagers were in them. Emma, who was fifteen, was totally addicted to crack. She was in a total mess – she reckoned she'd been raped four times, robbed countless more, and that a punter had once tried to strangle her as she slept.

Jill was seventeen and had been making £700 a week for three years. She was charging between £20 and £40 and had had sex for money or crack about three thousand times. She looked like an adult with her hair and make-up and the way her clothes hugged her figure, but when she spoke it was the voice of a child. 'I turn a bloke down if I don't like the look of him or if he don't look right,' she told me, 'if he looks sickly or looks like he's got AIDS.'

She had come from a poor family; her parents argued violently. She was taken into 'care' at the age of ten, where she was bullied by the other kids before being moved on to another home, then another and another where she was abused by her carers before she ran away. She lived on the streets and got into the game and into crack at fourteen. Almost without exception the teenage whores had lived in care homes, which was where the ones we found were sent – this should have rung alarm bells for me.

A few days later, as part of the Rat-on-a-Rat campaign, we almost literally crashed into a house off West Green Road in Tottenham, where our intel told us that a handful of dealers had been operating. I decided that eight of us should be able to take care of the dealers in one house but I couldn't find a way in; the door was secured by a New York latch. Eventually, I came up with the ultimate solution – drive straight through the outside wall in an armoured Land Rover, but we were forced to cancel the raid when our intel changed at the last moment.

Soon after this, we successfully raided a flat in Somerset Gardens. I didn't know it then, but as I marched a cuffed dealer into the back of a Transporter, just a few doors away a little girl was at that moment going through unimaginable suffering.

I didn't know it yet but that little girl was going to change my life.

Her name was Victoria Climbié.

TWENTY-ONE

MORE RATS

For the moment, though, after one hiccup the Rat-on-a-Rat campaign was about to reach its crescendo. The hiccup was a flat in Cordell House, a tower block, impossible to observe without decent camera equipment (which we didn't yet have the finances or the time to acquire). We crept through the estate on the night of 7 February, hoping not to be spotted from the flat's excellent vantage point. It was only when we hit it that we found the intelligence was very wrong indeed. Inside we found a thirty-nine-year-old Nigerian security guard and his white middle-class teenage girlfriend.

He was severely pissed off; his language spat hate – nothing I said calmed him down until I caught Greg's eye. He was smiling. 'What's that?' he said, pointing to the coffee table. There was a small piece of cannabis – enough for a joint or two. I grinned: now we could give him some grief back and forget about fixing the door. We quickly cautioned him for the cannabis and departed, and I apologized to the TSG for wasting their time.

Next on the list was a *very* heavily fortified crack house. Once you saw it, it was obvious, but we wouldn't have known anything about it if someone hadn't called Crimestoppers. It was in the most unlikely place, in a brand-new block of flats near Middlesex University's All Saints site.

To be sure that the information we'd received was correct we drove to the estate in a observation van. The target flat overlooked a large courtyard and to say that it stood out was an understatement. The windows were painted black on the inside so no one could see in or out. We stayed there all day and counted 250 visitors. I got a key to the communal door, and as it was unanimously agreed that I looked most like a crack addict (I had become truly proud of my skinny, filthy crack-chic look) I followed a punter into the building and was disappointed to see that there was no way through the door, which had a steel cover *and* a New York latch. I resisted the temptation to knock on the door for a look around inside and left.

For a while we were stymied for a way in until DI Green suggested I call in Scotland Yard's elite Merlin Unit. Merlin's official codename is CO12 but it is commonly known as the rope team. This specialist unit is used as a last resort to gain entry into awkward places. At first we thought of abseiling down the outside of the building SAS-style, but they actually came up with the more practical idea of using ladders.

Once they'd firmed up their plans I booked them in. I suggested that they work with the Ghosties, who'd been faultless and had built up invaluable experience, but the rope team insisted on working on their own. The Ghosties weren't prepared to be kept on standby so, with regret, I gave them the night off.

Then another blow: I was told that no TSG would be available on the night. I couldn't postpone, as we were on a tight schedule – we either hit it that night or forgot about it and moved on to the next job. There was no fucking way I was missing my one chance to close this very busy crack house. The dealers were on the run, but the demand and the profits were still there so any loss of momentum would set us back months.

I asked the lads if they'd be happy to go in through the front door in riot gear. They were. When I told the rope team the situation, they said they'd be happy to fill in for the TSG. Between us, I thought, we should just about manage. Thinking correctly that this was going to be a spectacular raid, I brought a video camera.

We waited until midnight and snuck quietly as possible onto the estate in an unmarked van. The commander of the rope team told me that the street lights surrounding the flat we were trying to get into could cause a problem because they gave enough illumination for the people inside to see the rope team's shadows once they were close to the blacked-out windows. I took an asp (an extendable truncheon) and solved the problem with a few carefully aimed prods. I made a mental note to own up to this bit of vandalism later.

The rope team, dressed in chainmail suits and helmets and carrying pickaxes and ladders, quickly approached the three double windows that faced the courtyards and veeee-ry gently placed their ladders under each of them. One man clambered up each ladder with another man below and, once in position, turned and gave me the thumbs up. Now the rest of them, dressed in full riot gear, jogged round to the front with the enforcer. The idea was to make the people inside think we were attacking from the front. This would send them into the rooms where the rope team would simultaneously come through the windows and nab them; then one of the rope team would lift the New York latch and let the HDS in.

I grinned at the thought. The terror factor was going to be fantastic. But there was a lot riding on this one. We'd rehearsed the raid several times at the station but something could still go wrong. Any fuck-up, then it would be down to me and the game would be over.

As soon as the lads hit the front door I signalled the rope team. Looking like three coal-mining ninjas they simultaneously swung their pickaxes through the windows and jumped through the broken glass straight into the flat. Immediately I heard the screams of the people inside, who were no doubt terrified to see three storm-troopers dressed head to foot in black armour piling in through the first-floor windows. This was a crucial moment – for a few seconds they would be on their own in the crack house in a room with up to thirty people. The second three-man rope team quickly climbed the ladders and dived in after their colleagues.

At exactly that moment I ran to the front, only to find that my team was already inside. They had stormed in just as two people were leaving catching the doorman off-guard, and to their surprise and my delight they plunged straight inside. The kitchen was full of cutting equipment and scales and when we opened the oven door I almost keeled over when I was hit by a wall of smoke – they had been drying some freshly made crack which had started to toast.

Although most people were calm, a twenty-nine-year-old prostitute had kicked off in the bedroom. She was bone thin and her arms were covered in gaping sores. A hypodermic syringe full of watery-brown fluid was beside the bed; we'd kept her from her fix. Then the man she was with, whom I suspected to be the main dealer, suddenly exploded. Greg got him in a headlock while I dodged karate kicks from the incensed prostitute. Then the man spat at me. 'Get him on the fucking ground, now!' I yelled.

'Can't, Harry,' said Greg as he struggled to hold his captive, 'he'll be cut to shreds!'

He was right; the floor was covered in massive jagged pieces of glass. A couple of nearby officers pitched in and together, after a bit of phlegm-dodging, we subdued him. One of the addicts wouldn't stop coughing – I worried about tuberculosis. TB was on the rise in London (77–79 cases per 100,000 people, which is well on the way to an epidemic) – and 1 in 25 of these was a crack addict. Crack smokers, by the nature of what they did, sharing pipes and breathing in each other's smoke, were highly vulnerable to TB. Despite the smashed windows we were still all standing in a thick smog of crack. I wondered if the deadly germs were floating around in there somewhere. I had to get us outside.

As I left the room, Taylor stopped me in the hallway. 'Here, Harry, take a look at this.' It was an eviction notice for non-payment of mortgage.

'Nice one. Get in touch with the bailiffs and get them to board it up fast.' My contact from the electricity board was there once again, an utterly brilliant guy who came out at all hours to make these addresses safe. 'I live here,' he told me with a grin, 'and really appreciate what you're doing; I'm proud to be a part of it.'

As we chatted to the addicts, one of the prostitutes, who was heavily pregnant, proudly told me that when we arrived she had just finished giving a blow-job in return for a rock and could still taste the semen. Nice.

As we'd filled up Tottenham and Wood Green cells to overflowing, our spitting dealer was dealt with at Islington police station, where despite being charged with possession and supply he was for some inexplicable reason bailed to his mother's address, where he didn't live. I freaked out when I heard this; I suspected he was a major player, so I really hit the fucking roof and tried to argue it out with the custody officer. He hung up on me.

'Christ, this place is busy,' I whispered to Greg as we passed a ground-floor flat in a row of Victorian terraces for the second time. It was the early evening and we were deep in the heart of the Tottenham Triangle.

'Let's do it,' said Greg. But having watched the place a while longer, I wasn't so sure. The people leaving were slouched and woozy, the sign of grass, not crack. But this was one of the Rat-on-a-Rat addresses; I wanted it so we would still be on course for 100 per cent success. That would please the bosses and get us some good press and hopefully more resources.

The flat's kitchen backed onto a garden so I sent Greg and Adam round the back to cover the area for any suspects fleeing to a nearby alley.

I ordered the TSGs in; as usual all hell broke loose as the State's muscle bombed down the street in their vans, piling out and obliterating the door in a storm of glass and wood. Shouting broke out on all sides. The house was packed and people poured out into the garden. Considering they were supposed to be stoned, they were pretty quick on their feet. Greg sprinted after a guy with long dreads; with a grunt, Adam launched himself onto a low wall and leaped onto a young lad as he dived into an alleyway. They both crashed into a wheelie-bin and went down; after a little bit of squirming from the suspect, he surrendered. Greg put his rugby skills to good use and brought down dreadlocks with a tackle that landed them in a nest of aluminium bins – a week's worth of pizza boxes, nappies and rotten food erupted over them.

Their pockets were full of grass and the kitchen was full of bags, scales and cash. As things calmed down, one of the TSGs, a bull-ish lad with a dent in his forehead, complained that too many had escaped from the rear and the operation could have been better planned. I told him that the normal procedure was to have two men at the back but the place had a lot more people than we were expecting. So we were unlucky. The TSG officer shrugged, mumbled something and started to walk back towards the house to join his colleagues when I spotted something – a perfectly still figure on the ground, hidden in the darkness, pressed under a bush running alongside the fence dividing the gardens. What the fuck? Then it clicked: 'Oi!' I yelled at the TSG officer. 'To your left!' He was practically standing on him as everyone looked back at me to see what the hell I was yelling about. The figure tried to make a run for it but the TSG officer was right on top of him and simply grabbed his collar. Afterwards, the TSG, pleased with his arrest and grinning from ear to ear, gave me the thumbs-up.

TWENTY-TWO

PUBLIC RELATIONS

While the gunfights seemed to have stopped, stabbings were happening all too frequently. A few days earlier a fight had erupted outside a crack den between two dealers after a girl smoked from one dealer's pipe and not the other's. One of the men had wound up stabbed in the chest with a screwdriver but as usual nobody wanted to know.

The next big crack house, a drab low-rise council block on Culcross Close, formerly a quiet dead-end street with an old church, had become the site of a never-ending saga of violence. Whilst on a recce disguised as a council worker I spotted a familiar face from the High Road, the flat above the dentist's. He'd obviously been bailed and had relocated.

Culcross Close was now absorbing all the trade from the shrinking crack-house scene, bringing all the mayhem along with it. This meant that whereas we might not have received any calls about a quieter crack house, suddenly Crimestoppers was inundated. For people who smoke crack, time and other people don't exist – they're on a totally different cycle from the nine-to-fivers so sudden bursts of partying, violence and screaming-loud sex tended to erupt at any moment. The church cemetery had become home to a gang calling themselves the 'Graveyard Shift' who hung out there at all hours, scaring the shit out of the locals with their antics.

In one incident a naked man had sprinted out of the crack house and bolted across West Green Road into the Halifax Building Society, where he smashed a fire alarm and bit a bank employee. He was tackled by several brave members of staff who sat on him until the police arrived. The screaming addict chewed his lips and tongue until blood poured from his mouth; he spat over anyone who came within range. Luckily, he didn't have HIV or hepatitis, although the bank employee went through a hellish few days before he got the all-clear.

Incredibly, this naked nut had once been a city high-flier. He eventually came off the crack and I caught up with him while researching this book. 'Ten years ago I was addicted to money,' he said. 'I ate in the best restaurants, went to West End shows – best seats, champagne and coke all the way. I used to wear Brooks Brothers suits, the finest shirts with kick-ass cufflinks. We'd knock back oysters and champagne without thinking about the bill. In a way crack was no different; I exchanged one monster for another.

'That crack house was fucked up. I knew the dealer. He was a mad bastard; his teenage daughter was an addict and this pissed him off big time. He was appalled at his daughter's situation, you know, sleeping around for crack and suchlike. Yet he was the owner of a crack house who seduced teenage girls with drugs, money and charm and fucked them. But he still didn't see himself as the exploiter, even though he struggled with his anxiety and pain as a father.

'For example, one night this little teenage girl showed up. Jenni, her name was. He asked her if she wanted something to taste. "All I wanna do is buy a gram and get outta here," she said.

He says, "No you don't, you want this," and he stands up and his dick is hard. He says, "Suck this," and she says, "Fuck you," and walks out. He throws some wraps at her and says, "Don't come back until you're ready to give me some head!" What a fucker.

'Anyway, this dealer dude had picked up a package that was so big none of us had seen so many rocks at one time in our lives. There had to be ten ounces or more in that bag. But after a day or two of getting high he started to get paranoid, to think we were stealing, either by taking small pieces of rock or by taking cocaine out of the bag.

'When you think about it, there were a dozen or more people smoking every few minutes for days; we were eating it up.

'One night, he went to the toilet and when he came back he looked at the bag and swore some of us took some rocks. He said, "Who took my stuff?" Then he pulled out the gun he keeps around the house and waved it around the room at all of us.

'Totally freaked, he made us turn out our pockets, searched our clothes to see if we were hiding anything. This was serious because the guy was high and we all know this is when you do stupid crazy shit and he was waving a gun everywhere. Finally, he told us all to piss off. That's when I freaked, completely broke down.'

After I'd finished my recce of the door I was on my way back to the street when I noticed that running up the side of the stairs at banister height was an odd cable which led to the crack den. It looked connected. So much was stolen around here, electricity, cable TV, it was impossible to tell what it might be. I made a mental note to warn the TSG and the Ghosties.

When I got back to the Factory I got a call from the chief super. 'I've just had Bernie Grant on the phone,' he told me, 'and he wants to know what we're going to do about this crack house in Culcross Close.' Grant, christened by the *Sun* as 'Barmy Bernie', was the outspoken black MP for Tottenham (he'd been MP for the area since 1987). He was loved by the local community and rightly so as he fought hard for them in parliament.

The chief didn't know that we were planning to raid that very same crack house the following day, so the timing was perfect. 'We're doing it tomorrow, boss,' I said, 'and we're taking the press in with us. You can tell Mr Grant he's more than welcome to come along if you like.'

There was a short pause. 'Errrr . . . I'm not sure it would be a good idea if he came along but I'll ask him. Good work, Keeble.'

We had decided it would be a good idea to bring a journalist, Alison Campsie, who had given us some positive press in the *Hornsey Journal*. I wanted to repay her with an exclusive story. I'd opted for a hard-hitting raid that I thought would generate some good publicity while giving the other crack houses a proper warning that we were coming for them. Unfortunately our press office liked the idea so much they decided to send me a minibus full of reporters and photographers, blowing Alison's exclusive.

A few days before the raid I had an unpleasant shock. On one of my recces I had spotted an old orange VW Camper with blacked-out windows parked up near a primary school at the end of Culcross Close. I had a bad feeling about it so I parked up in the Primera in the next street, watching and waiting. About an hour later I was about to head off when a tubby balding man in his forties showed up. I memorized his face, height and build. He opened the back doors. Inside, the van was empty save for a dirty double mattress on the floor. Not good. I called in the registration. The vehicle was clean but the owner was a suspected paedophile. He wasn't on the run and hadn't actually committed any crime yet, so the only thing we could do was warn the school. This was going to be difficult.

I got hold of the deputy head within a few minutes and briefed her about the situation. She took the news calmly and agreed to call her teachers for an emergency staff meeting. She asked me to attend. Unfortunately, I was in my drug-addict unwashed scumbag attire and wasn't too keen on the idea but agreed to come. At the meeting, everyone remained calm except for one female teacher who completely freaked out.

'We have to tell the parents,' she said. 'If we don't do anything and they find out –'

'Look, I understand where you're coming from,' I said, 'but if you do this you'll cause panic and a witch-hunt. The guy's never been charged. We have to manage the situation. We can watch him between all of us; you get the slightest inkling that anything's wrong, call us and we'll be here in a flash.' We didn't know it yet but the creep was using his van to sleep with young prostitutes; the location probably helped him to get his perverted rocks off.

Meanwhile we still had a crack house to close. On the day of the raid, on the way to Culcross Close, the busload of journalists somehow became detached from the rest of the convoy and arrived after the assault had been successfully completed. It went smoothly with all the usual screaming and chaos and as ever the place was a stinking mess.

By the time they arrived we'd found some ammunition and I posed with a bullet (which I held wearing forensic gloves so as not to ruin any evidence) for the photographers. As people were strip-searched and kicked out, journalists asked them for interviews. One girl agreed and spent the rest of the conversation punctuating her sentences with bizarre karate kicks. Another girl who had stashed her crack in her vagina surrendered it after we told her it might kill her. She was later fined £100.

The guys steadily worked their way through all the occupants, who were either told to clear off or were thrown in the back of the carrier. One of the girls they told to clear off was Jenni. I didn't find out her full story until we researched this book; she was the girl from Woodstock Road we first met on page 53.

At that time she lived in a squat, a two-bed flat in one of Haringey's shit-hole estates. The windows were smashed, the heating didn't work and the wallpaper was steadily peeling off the damp walls as the wetness brought in by the rain spread. Lighting was down to candles and torches, every so often Jenni and the friend she shared with would hear the rats passing through, rummaging through the litter. She was fifteen. After her mum tried to get her off the crack by chaining her to the wall, she had been sent to a care home where she said she was abused. Social services didn't want to know and as far as they were concerned she didn't exist any more. She fled her carers for the comparative safety of the crack house. 'At least you get something for being abused there,' she said.

Since HDS had been closing so many crack houses down, she had run out of places to go and decided that there'd be less chance of imprisonment and fines if she lived in a squat of her own. She was still trying to recapture that feeling from the first blast of crack that sent her to her knees. She had become skilled in the art of deception and manipulation of her punters but was in terrible danger; she'd already slept with a suspected paedophile and worse was to come.

It just goes to show that no matter how much shit you might see, you're only ever picking at the surface. But at the time I was blissfully ignorant of Jenni's plight. I was on cloud nine, having scored six out of six, and my report on the Rat-on-a-Rat campaign went down a storm with the chief super, who passed it on to Haringey Council and the press. Our adventures even got a brief but very positive write-up in *Time Out*. It later came back to me that my report had been adopted into a larger document which found its way into Number 10 Downing Street and formed part of the government policy on crime. As a result, I was suddenly the golden boy and my unit was full of rising stars. Our position was secure. But I hadn't had much chance to rest on my laurels when the super called me to his office.

'That report,' he said, 'on the Rat-on-a-Rat campaign.'

'Yes, guv, what about it?' I replied.

'I'd like you to make a personal presentation to Haringey Council in two hours. Here's the address, don't be late.' And he was gone. Bastard. What a fucking stitch-up. Two hours! I relished the challenge, but could have done with a bit more notice.

I had a think and decided that the best way to do it would be to show them the video footage of some recent raids which included Ashmount Road; that way I could talk them through the process of the raid and I wouldn't need notes for that. Just some stats on the number of arrests we made during the Rat-on-a-Rat campaign.

I put on my normal civvies, made sure I wasn't wearing my nose-ring (it was easily forgotten), grabbed my files and video and hared my way through North London. I arrived at 5.59 p.m., one minute to spare. 'Let's keep this brief,' I thought to myself as I was led in to meet the councillors. Most were in their forties and fifties and their head was a very well-spoken and charming woman whose husband happened to be a respected church figure.

'Sergeant Keeble,' she said, giving me her hand, 'we've heard so much already about the wonderful and difficult work you're engaged in. We're really looking forward to hearing you speak and we promise not to keep you from your duties for long, but it really helps us to talk to those involved, to understand the problems you face.'

'Not at all, I'm happy to be here,' I lied and forced a relaxed smile. Damn, I'd forgotten to ask for a video player. 'Do you happen to have a video player?'

'Certainly, I'll have one brought in. Are we going to see footage of your operations? Wonderful, that'll really give us a clear insight into your dangerous work.'

The room was very large and packed with councillors. I'd never seen so many before. They smiled as I introduced myself and the video was wheeled in. I slid in the cassette, hit PLAY and began my preamble. All eyes were on the screen. 'Aha,' I thought as I rambled on. 'Maybe this isn't going to be that bad; this is having an effect on these people who could be so helpful to our cause.'

Gradually I noticed that some of the faces had turned a deep shade of red. I'd turned down the sound so they could hear me talk and wouldn't hear the police officers swearing, so I wasn't sure what part of the video we'd got to. I turned round to check and saw Darren and Colin studying the enormous stash of porn that we'd found in the living room in Ashmount road. They were on the stairs and the camera had filmed them from above. Colin was laughing and holding up a magazine. The cover picture illustrated the magazine's title perfectly. It was *Double Entry IV*.

In a pathetic attempt to cover this up I leaped in front of the screen. Note to self – *always* review video material before showing it in public!

TWENTY-THREE

INTERLUDE

What I hated most was that more than any other age group, crack seemed to hurt children the most. This was certainly part of my reason for wanting to move into Child Protection after my time was up at the drugs squad. To make certain, I was given the opportunity to spend some time at North London's Child Protection Services office, on a sort of suck-it-and-see experiment. It was known amongst the more macho police circles as the 'cardigan squad' and had a low status; its officers were seen as the 'poor cousins' or 'Cinderellas' of the Met. Like HDS, in the wake of the Stephen Lawrence inquiry they had been drained of resources by the murder squads who were currently investigating ninety-two murders that had taken place in northwest London during the past twelve months.

I opened a file and started to read; soon I actually started to feel sick. The address, in Somerset Gardens, sparked my memory.

I had busted a crack house on the same estate where this little girl lived a few days before the story hit the headlines. I took out the coroner's report, which had been written by Dr Nathaniel Carey, one of the most experienced and esteemed pathologists in the country. I had come across his name in the case of Roger Sylvester (see page 77). He would later go on to give evidence in the Soham murder trial in 2003.

Until 1.30 p.m. on 25 February 2000, he thought he had seen the worst that could ever have come through Westminster Mortuary's doors, but it was then that the tiny, bone-thin body of an eight-year-old African girl was brought into the examination room in a white plastic body bag.

Her wounds told Dr Carey better than anyone else the story of how she had suffered. Her hair was short, in tight curls, and her face puffy, although she was obviously malnourished. Dr Carey worked his way down the body counting the scars, fifteen of which were on the face; some were clustered around her eyes, others around her cheek. These were probably 'blunt force splits'. Dr Carey knew from another hospital report that the girl had been scalded with hot water and there was indeed some evidence of this in the scarring. There was a series of scars on the front of the neck on both sides. They were also scattered across her chest and there was a larger irregular scar close to the right nipple, suggestive of a cigarette burn. The scarring continued down her stomach and when turned onto her front there was an equal amount on her back, some circular and some lengthy, curved marks, particularly around her shoulder blades.

The child's buttocks were riddled with sores and the skin was leathery, a result of lying in her own urine and faeces for extended periods of time. Scars also covered the buttocks, suggesting she had been beaten on her sore skin. From the patterns Dr Carey was able to guess that she had most likely been whipped with a belt and beaten with a shoe.

Her wrists and ankles were cut and worn sore. The feet and hands were swollen. Numerous old scars in this area told Dr Carey that the little girl had been bound several times over the past few months, he supposed by masking tape which had twisted up as she struggled to loosen the bindings. Her legs were also covered in scars, as were her hips, knees and feet. After shaving her head, Dr Carey found a series of blunt force splits several centimetres long on her scalp. He counted 128 injuries in total.

Not one part of her had been spared from pain.

Dr Carey concluded that it was obvious from her weight that she was terribly malnourished, a feature which had contributed to her death from hypothermia. She had been kept in a bath and forced to wear a homemade nappy, and had slept in her own waste. In an unheated room on a cold February night, her body temperature had dropped from thirty-seven to twenty-seven degrees centigrade. Normally the body does everything in its power to maintain normal temperature but the little girl was so poorly fed that her fragile body was simply not strong enough. In the end, her lungs, heart and kidneys all failed.

It was the worst case of deliberate harm to a child Dr Carey had ever seen.

Victoria Adjo Climbié was born near the Ivory Coast's commercial city of Abidjan on 2 November 1991. She was the fifth of seven children. A happy, outgoing child, she showed herself to be intelligent and articulate at school, a child who stood out.

Perhaps this was why she came to the attention of her father's aunt, forty-three-year-old Marie-Therese Kouao, when Kouao turned up at the Climbié house in October 1998. Kouao had lived in France for some years but had returned to the Ivory Coast for the funeral of her brother. She told Victoria's parents that she wanted to take Victoria back to France with her and arrange for her education. Entrusting children to relatives living in Europe who are able to offer better financial and educational opportunities is not uncommon in the Ivory Coast. Her parents agreed once they were sure Victoria was happy to go. They didn't know it but Victoria was a last moment replacement for another little girl called Anna – her parents had second thoughts and refused to let Kouao take her.

After spending five months in France, Kouao (who was on the run after falsely claiming excessive benefits from French social services) and Victoria boarded a flight from Paris to London on 24 April 1999. They travelled on Kouao's French passport, in which Victoria was described as her daughter. The picture in the passport was not of Victoria but of Anna, the child she had replaced. The two children didn't look that similar; Kouao shaved Victoria's head and made her wear a wig so she looked more like the child in the photograph.

From July 1999, the moment she arrived in Tottenham, Victoria was first mistreated by Kouao and then tortured by her boyfriend, twenty-eight-year-old bus driver Carl Manning, who believed she was possessed (as proof of this they claimed she wet the bed). To exorcize the evil spirits she was beaten with belt buckles, bicycle chains, coat hangers and shoes. Razor blades were taken to her fingers and a hammer to her toes. She was burned with cigarettes, bound hand and foot, forced to eat like a dog, had boiling water poured over her and slept on a bin-bag in the bath.

Eventually Kouao took Victoria to the Universal Kingdom of God Church in Finsbury Park where Alvero Lima, a twenty-one-year-old assistant pastor, told Kouao that he would exorcize the devil at a special service. The day before the scheduled service, Kouao brought Victoria, who was then very cold and barely conscious, into the church. A shocked Lima urged Kouao to take the child to hospital immediately. But it was too late.

The subsequent investigation put a large part of the blame for Victoria's death on the 'blinding incompetence' of Haringey social workers who missed an unforgivable twelve chances to save Victoria.

I threw the report down on my desk. I couldn't believe it. While we were demolishing doors and enjoying our success, eight-year-old Victoria Climbié had been going through a living hell just a few yards away.

I was, like most, utterly stunned. I, along with everyone else, wondered how on earth the Met's Child Protection Service could have let this happen.

Now I knew the answer. It turned out that they had fewer people and less money than we did when we started. HDS didn't have any computer technology to speak of but Child Protection was supposed to be a serious department with countless cases requiring major resources. The software was slow and unwieldy; it could take all day just to research four or five cases when they should have been able to do that many an hour.

And there was worse to come. Detectives investigating serious offences against children weren't actually trained detectives. They were simply regular police officers with a job title. Unaccompanied children as young as thirteen, including those we'd rescued from crack houses, were being placed in bed and breakfast accommodation alone and officers were told to close 190 files to persuade an inspector that the department was under control.

Worst of all, I found out that no fewer than fifteen children had died in recent years in the London borough of Haringey *while in our care*. Nine children had died while they were either in council-run children's homes or with council-approved foster parents or adoptive parents. In one of the worst cases a mother rang social services and told them she was going to harm her two children, aged eight and nine (who were already on their 'at risk' register). She was ignored. The next morning she set fire to her house and both of her kids burned to death. A six-year-old girl was murdered, smothered to death after her stepfather stabbed her crack-addicted mother in the heart, killing her. In another case, a two-and-a-half-month-old baby was on the child protection register when she died in agony from blood poisoning caused by severe nappy rash. She had been seen by social workers twenty-eight times in the weeks leading up to her death but was allowed to remain with her crack-addicted mother.

The council had also recruited child molesters, two of whom worked as caretakers in the borough's primary schools (one had seven previous convictions). Eighteen other convicted criminals worked in its social services department, which had failed to check their pasts.

As I looked at the files, I realized I was staring at the faces of kids 'rescued' from the horrors of crack cocaine. What was the point of handing them over to Child Protection Teams only for them to disappear and eventually wind up as crack addicts and prostitutes?

And then, just as I finished reading the coroner's report into the death of Victoria Climbié, the Met's internal investigation branch, CIB, raided the Child Protection Team office and I returned to Wood Green, determined to take my war to child protection. The only problem was that by then my own unit was already under investigation and, as we shall soon see, internal investigations were gunning for *my* scalp.

TWENTY-FOUR

INTEGRITY IS NON-NEGOTIABLE

For the moment, though, Haringey Drugs Squad was flying high; and because of this we were given a detective sergeant from the CID to assist us. Kev, a tough northern lad who grew up on a council estate, proved to be a very welcome addition. A keen and knowledgeable DS, we hit it off straight away. He provided an essential bridge between us and the CID, something that would soon prove to be vital when we hit the drug-dealing mother lode not long after he joined.

Kev was also up to speed on the latest investigative procedures, so while previously we had tended to crash into a house, crack a few skulls and cart everyone off, Kev brought a new level of professionalism which meant we searched premises properly, which sometimes kick-started useful investigations.

Kev fitted right in. At this point our morale was sky-high and we clowned around quite a bit. Not long after he joined us, we raided a crack house and one officer spotted a very bling pair of gold and red trainers and swapped them for his boots. He then interviewed the suspect while wearing them, uncrossing and crossing his legs all the while. The suspect didn't seem to notice; or if he did, he didn't say anything.

At the other end of the scale, we received another, unexpected addition to the team. One Monday morning, our new DI stuck his head round our door. 'Sergeant Keeble, I've got a lady here who needs to collect crime data; take care of her, will you?'

A tiny woman walked in and introduced herself as Sita. She was a university student working on her final-year project, which was on statistics for the social sciences.

'You're more than welcome to join us,' I told her, 'but I'm not sure we'll be much help in terms of data collection.' As it turned out, Sita found it an education all right, but I'm not sure it was the one she was looking for.

I was always keen to show other agencies/people what we were trying to achieve but I was very surprised to be asked to babysit a group of Russian police officers. The DI didn't say who they were exactly and I didn't push it – it wasn't my problem. At the time I had no idea if they had a crack problem in Russia.[9]

Like most visitors, they were amazed by our stockroom office (I had by now become quite fond of the place). But then they pissed me off by yawning, showing extreme disinterest and talking amongst themselves in Russian as they watched videos of us raiding crack houses while I explained to them how we did it. I was extremely relieved when S019 telephoned to ask for my assistance in a firearms raid on Broadwater Farm. 'Amuse yourselves,' I told the Russians. 'I'm off.'

On my way out I was apprehended by the boss, who asked me to take them along. It was like babysitting a bunch of moody immature school-kids. When we got to the Farm I told them to sit tight while I liaised with S019. But for the fact that there was a gun inside it was a straightforward job and all I had to do was stand back and watch as the armed officers approached the flat.

---

9 I later discovered that in late 1999 a Russian gang had hooked up with a Colombian cartel to buy a Soviet-era submarine to transport cocaine direct from Colombia. They planned to distribute the coke to twenty-six Russian crime organizations based in the US and Southern Europe. Russia didn't yet have a serious crack problem, but their law-enforcement agencies were supposed to be helping other countries fight the Russian Mafya causing havoc across the world. From what I could tell, these officers really couldn't give a shit.

Suddenly I noticed that the Russians were no longer in the van. 'What the fuck?' I said out loud. 'Hey, Greg,' I called out, 'you see those five Russians go past?' Open-mouthed, he pointed over my shoulder. I turned around and looked back towards where SO19 were approaching the building. To my utter horror and disbelief, the Russians were following right behind; even worse they were taking the piss, making guns with their hands, ducking behind buildings and giggling like idiots.

For a second I was speechless; my mouth opened and closed but no sounds would come out. 'Wh– wh– what the fuck are they doing?' The officers from SO19 spotted them too, and stopped in their tracks. Their horror and disbelief clearly more than equalled my own. These morons were jeopardizing not only the raid but their own lives as well as the lives of the SO19 officers by clowning about in full view of the whole estate.

The mission was restarted after a swift intervention. 'Please tell me we can lock these idiots up,' one of the officers muttered as he passed by. They couldn't be fucking cops; they were more like a bunch of adolescents on detention. 'Get in the fucking van,' I told them. In silence we drove them back to the station while I briefed my boss over the phone. We never saw them again.

Kev did the recce for the next raid on the Ferry Lane estate where a few low-level crack houses had sprung up. He decided we could do it ourselves. We stormed the address that night; the door gave us no trouble and we quickly fanned out to our assigned rooms. I found a couple of guys in the lounge smoking puff who didn't seem that bothered to see us; no sign of crack and the place looked clean and tidy – not a crack house. I went out, put the door back on its hinges and called Sita over to come and join us.

We arrested one of the guys for cannabis and started to search the house. Oddly enough, I quite enjoyed this, as we normally had to search real shit-holes but this place was spick and span; no danger of a needle-stick, but it didn't look good for Kev's first operation. Because crack houses hardly have anything in them they usually don't take any time to search but this place, being much more like a 'normal' home, took us ages.

As soon as we brought in the dog, however, he immediately snuffled out a couple of small rocks of crack. Things were looking up. Then Kev gave me a shout from upstairs. He'd found a good few ounces of crack stashed in a plant pot in the bedroom. Tina nicked the other guy, an eighteen-year-old wanted by Birmingham youth court, for possession with intent to supply.

Shortly afterwards there was a knock at the door. I shouted the usual 'Come in, bruv, it's open,' and two young lads walked in. One of them spotted Sita but wasn't alarmed – she hardly looked like a police officer, just a very attractive teenager; although I didn't intend it, she made an effective lure and he smiled before pushing the door open. His face dropped as the door swung off its hinges and I appeared in front of him, clamping my hand on his shoulder.

'Welcome to the warrant party, bruv.'

Kev spotted they'd come in a BMW; a quick search turned up a dodgy credit card under the driver's seat and so we nicked them both and seized the car as being bought with the proceeds of drug trafficking. This was a rarity for us, as crack addicts rarely have any assets; they spend what they earn straight away. It was the last time we ever saw the car; the company that came to collect it went bust and the BMW vanished, probably into the hands of the receivers. At 10 p.m. two more guys turned up. A quick check revealed that one of them was wanted for perverting the course of justice and was arrested by Taylor.

All in all a decent first operation for both Kev and Sita. 'What did you think of that, then?' I asked Sita.

'Loved it, amazing, brilliant,' she said. With that, Sita became our seventh, albeit unofficial, member of HDS and joined us on raids until she had to go back to university to complete her dissertation.

After a dud at a property on the High Road, Tottenham (the dealers were running scared and had already split by the time we hit it) we learned that a new crack house was opening up near Ashmount Road. We did the recce disguised as council workers armed with clipboards and I decided that we could do it ourselves.

During the Rat-on-a-Rat campaign I had managed to acquire a large Luton van for transportation and had kept hold of it (no one had asked for it back yet). I decided we'd hit the house from the back of the Luton. We made a most peculiar sight in the back of the cavernous van, six burly police officers in full armour while tiny Sita sat in the middle of us all, her only protection a flimsy stab vest. There was no way I was going to let her in until the place had been made safe, which it soon was, and the council boarded it up minutes after we had cleaned it out. It was a great hit: it had barely even opened for business and yet we'd managed to shut it down.

We were right on top of them, and on the next hit almost literally – Nightingale Road was about ten yards from the Factory, so we just jogged over the road. It was a good hit as we caught Freddy, a prolific thirty-eight-year-old Afro-Caribbean dealer with a good collection of rocks. He made bail but we caught up with him again a few weeks later.

When we ran into Freddy for a second time it was when we raided a house in Bruce Castle Road, just next to Tottenham Cemetery. My wife was due to give birth the next day and I was particularly keen for everything to go smoothly, so I could clear off pronto and spend two weeks on paternity leave.

My family life had been hellish over the past few months. My wife knew what my work involved and while we both wanted to have kids more than anything, her being pregnant during this time was a big strain for her, especially as I was spending more nights in crack houses than I was at home. I wasn't going to miss the birth and those two weeks – no matter what.

Hoping to catch the dealers in action we hit the address just after midnight. It was me, Kev, the famous five, a sergeant from Wood Green who wanted to see what a crack house was like, two constables from the CCTV department (there to bolster numbers) and a dog handler. One of us smashed in the front window with a brick as a distraction; while the people inside were all panicking looking at the broken glass we stormed straight through the front door and were on top of them before they could say, 'What the fuck?'

We had two couples, a twelve-year-old girl and a nice collection of rocks. One of the men was Freddy. We said our 'hellos', cuffed him and the others (except for the girl, who was terrified) and started to search the place properly. Taylor found a large wad of cash in a jacket in the hall; he brought it into the lounge where he counted it in front of everyone so we could all agree on the amount. Meanwhile, the dog handler ran round the house and turned up a couple of ounces of crack. A good score for us.

I looked at Kev and said, 'Great, so I can fuck off now, can I?'

'Go on, mate, and good luck.'

Greg ran me back to Wood Green station, where I dived in my car and hared off home.

Kev was just tying things up at the bust when Taylor called him back into the lounge.

'Kev, we got some missing money.'

'What do you mean?'

'Well, I counted sixty, and now it's forty. We're twenty quid short.'

'Check it again.'

It was £40. 'Couldn't have been a miscount?'

'We all saw it, Kev, definitely sixty.'

'Sure?'

'Yeah, sure.'

'Anyone in here alone with the cash for any length of time?'

'Just the dog handler.'

I had hammered it into the lads that 'integrity is non-negotiable' and now they were pushing it to the limit. 'Could have been a miscount,' said Tina.

'You all saw me count it and agreed,' said Taylor. 'Now we've counted it again and it's short.' He shrugged his shoulders. 'It's short.'

'You guys gotta all agree,' Kev told them. 'Either you're telling me some money's gone missing or you're not. Which is it?'

After some more discussion, the vote went in favour of missing money.

Once the prisoners had been dropped off, Kev rang the duty officer, who called in the Department of Professional Standards (DPS).

I'd just made it home when I realized I'd left my wallet at work. Screaming and kicking the car didn't help. I had to get it back. Then I got the tip-off that the DPS would be at the station first thing in the morning. I was a bit worried because I'd gone home without completing my duty state, which meant that the DPS could have me up on a discipline charge. Besides that, if they caught me at the station then they would insist on interviewing me whatever the circumstances. But I really, really needed my wallet and so I zipped back down to the station at 8 a.m., snuck in, grabbed it and was creeping out into the car park when the duty officer appeared in the doorway behind me and called me over. I waved at him cheerily as if responding to a goodbye, jumped in my car and burned rubber all the way to the High Road.

As I suspected, the DPS demanded to speak to all those involved, even though all the people they wanted to talk to had worked through the night. The squad had to remain on duty until they arrived. Two of the guys told me they were rude and abrupt from the moment they arrived. I was appalled. The squad should have been commended for coming forward and setting an example for the Met's slogan, 'Integrity is Non-Negotiable'. They were searched, their cars were turned over and they handed over every twenty-pound note they had on them for forensic analysis. This came to £80 and was locked up at the DPS's property store at Colindale police station.

Once word got around that we were subject to an investigation we were suddenly no longer the golden team. When I got back from paternity leave two weeks later[10] I was told I wouldn't see out the rest of my time as head of Haringey Drugs Squad by Darren, who had spotted our jobs being advertised on the Intranet! 'Good fucking God,' I thought, 'that'll teach us to show integrity in future all right.'

---

10 It was a boy, six pounds, seven ounces.

TWENTY-FIVE

SPRINT FOR THE LINE

It has often been reported that the effect of a crime clampdown in one borough would immediately lead to an increase in related crime in neighbouring areas. Not so with the shootings in Haringey. By July, although guns continued to play a major role in drug-dealing, there had still been no further recorded gun-related injuries or fatalities within the black community in our borough. In the adjacent boroughs of Hackney and Harlesden the shootings continued to increase, but at the same rate as other areas across London.

Harlesden is home to at least fifty-seven ethnic groups as well as Britain's biggest Hindu temple, the Swami Narayan Mission, with real gold leaf on its roof. The Diwali festival there in November attracts 50,000 peaceful worshippers. On the other hand, the huge Stonebridge Park estate on the Harlesden/Wembley frontier is an urban wasteland, a monument to misguided public policy. Its massive tower blocks have few communal facilities and most of the pubs were at the time boarded up.

In July 2000 in Harlesden, eight people had been murdered and twelve wounded in shootings in little more than a year as the Lock City Crew and the Much Love Crew engaged in a pointless war – the papers tried to write it up as a battle for control of the drugs market but in reality it was just a stupid collection of tit-for-tat shootings based on 'respect'. The most extreme example of this was the expelled schoolboy arrested for pistol-whipping his former deputy head teacher in front of other pupils in the dining room of a secondary school.

In August, legendary Jamaican sound engineer Henry Lawes, fifty-one, had popped out for a packet of cigarettes when a blue Daewoo pulled up alongside him. Two gunmen jumped out and opened fire. Lawes fell to the ground wounded after the initial volley. He was finished off at the scene in cold blood.

In another Harlesden incident a car was raked with fire from a Mac 10 sub-machine gun outside a primary school. Two men were hit – one staggered into a shop, the other crashing the car through a police station's gates to seek sanctuary.

It wasn't just Harlesden, of course; the frontline now appeared to be all over town. An hour after the primary-school shooting, two men were shot and wounded on a South London estate. The day before, a man sitting in his car in North London was also shot.

Then there was twenty-one-year-old crack dealer Affar Tikur, who had ignored his mother's pleas that he abandon the drugs trade. He was found in a reservoir with six bullets in the back of his head. Beside him in the water were three red roses, a possible calling card of the all-female Red Rose Gang. In June, twenty-four-year-old Albert Lutterodt was found dead on an Acton street; he too had been shot in the head.

In July, shots were fired into the queues outside the Chicago nightclub in Peckham, South London. Eight people were hit. Despite there being close to 2000 revellers in the club, nobody saw anything. 350 people said they were using the toilets at the time of the shooting. Hundreds gave the police false addresses.

A few weeks later a nineteen-year-old was dragged from his car after a chase through West London, pistol-whipped about the head and shot in the leg. The following day a twenty-year-old man was charged with three counts of attempted murder and other gun offences after a night-time shooting rampage through London's West End in which two bystanders were hit.

One of our crime analysts at Wood Green did a study on two of the addresses we had closed. There was a phenomenal decrease in burglary, robbery and general theft around the area once we had closed the crack houses. Best of all, although there had been a few gun incidents no one had been shot for months. The difference we were making was massive and it surprised and swayed a lot of hardened CID officers who thought we were wasting our time, convinced that shutting down crack houses wouldn't make any difference because the amount of drugs we recovered was relatively small. That was precisely my point. The seizures were secondary; what counted was closing the crack houses. That reduced crime and, in particular, the shootings more than recovering drugs – no matter how much drugs we recovered the streets were flooded; there was always more.

Just as importantly, the closure of a crack house meant the area was almost instantly transformed. Needles left in alleyways and booby-trapped stashes hidden in areas where children might play vanished; the stink of urine, human faeces and vomit disappeared; litter decreased; residents were no longer threatened by addicts and dealers and were no longer propositioned by crack whores; the round-the-clock noise, fighting and general terrifying atmosphere was gone; the houses were repaired and the streets stayed clean and people felt safer. To the local residents it was like a miracle and for once they loved the police. Because we had taken out so many crack houses, we were able to stay on top of the situation; as soon as a new den opened, we knew and were ready to close it. The organized drugs scene in Haringey was getting progressively weaker, but the crack scourge continued to reign in the borough and there were still guns aplenty.

Maria was a crack whore who hadn't yet lost her looks. She was young but had been an addict long enough to seize a dangerous opportunity. She'd been to score from a big dealer in Tottenham, a guy called Tony, who made the mistake of leaving Maria alone with his stash. She was out of the door in seconds, crack squeezed tightly in her fist.

About eight months later, some guy took her to a house in Noel Park to score. Because she was good-looking, she got through the six-foot-high security gate at the bottom of the garden path, past the two guys on the door, past the racks of TVs and stereos people had traded for rocks, and she came face to face with the one and the same Tony. Instantly recognizing Maria, he grabbed her, took her into a back room, fired up his video camera and gave her a huge hit of crack.

For almost four days Tony beat and sexually assaulted Maria, at one point stabbing her in the thigh with a wire coat-hanger. At the end of the fourth day a rival gang fired at the house in a drive-by. Tony's minders went apeshit, threatening to kill everyone and anyone. While Tony was distracted Maria seized her chance and vanished.

After this kerfuffle, intelligence came through that an address was being used by a heavily armed crack dealer. Because there were guns involved a firearms operation was jacked up. This was a disaster from an evidential point of view as we'd have to do a 'dig-out', which meant surrounding the house at gunpoint and calling everybody outside, giving the dealers plenty of time to smoke the evidence.

On the appointed day we surrounded the address just after lunch and called the occupiers out over the loudspeaker. Nothing. After a while the Ghosties rushed up to the door, bashed it in and fell back sharpish. Next we gave the warning that we were about to send the dogs in. As I was ready to give the nod to the handlers, a figure came down the stairs. What had he been doing till now? Had he been hiding evidence? Had he been contemplating a shoot-out?

No, he'd been in the bath and had been trying to dry off before he got outside. We tried not to laugh as he walked out of the door in a towel and slippers in the line of fire of half a dozen weapons and was cuffed, but he was smiling. I knew then that we weren't going to get anything.

We ran the dog around and turned it over. There was loads of stuff in the house and it took us ages. It was totally clean. Could he somehow have got word? Eventually we had to let him go. He looked at me and leant over as he sauntered past. 'You have a nice day now, won't you?' Cocky fucker.

Shortly afterwards, I was sitting at my cardboard desk when I received a letter from the court. We would usually be notified of the final result of our cases and this one was one of our parade-room regulars, a habitual criminal we'd arrested who'd later jumped bail. He had been charged with possessing drugs, reckless driving and failing to stop after an accident. He was sentenced to twelve months probation, received a six-month driving disqualification and had to pay £50 costs. Under the heading 'FAO Drug Squad', someone had scrawled 'Why do we bother?' Despondency with the system was commonplace in 2000, but I was less concerned about arrests and trials. What seemed to be working was our making it impossible for dealers to set up houses. Even the guy we'd turfed out of his bath would have been unnerved by his visit. Sure, he was clean then (pardon the pun) but what about the next time, and the time after that?

A property on Seven Sisters Road had come to our attention as an enormous, full-blown, *very* busy crack house on the edge of the Tottenham Triangle. Unusually, it was run by white guys. In my experience, 95 per cent of crack houses are run by black guys.

Because of its size, we decided on a simultaneous hit from the back and the front – both entrances were being used for dealing with many customers preferring to approach from the secluded alleyway, which was strewn with drugs paraphernalia and stank of human waste. Punters stopped at a secure six-foot gate from where they would be admitted before making their purchase in the kitchen.

This raid was going to be a nightmare to co-ordinate; trying to get two groups of twenty men bursting with testosterone to simul-taneously attack and demolish different doors was going to be tricky. Fortunately, the TSG and the Ghosties loved the plan and were right behind me.

On the night I took the rear entrance while Kev took the front. We jogged down the alleyway, the only sounds our boots clonking on the hard ground. As we neared the door, a couple of punters took off. A lucky escape; we couldn't nab them as our timing would then be off. I checked that Kev was in position using my phone. It was time to go.

The Ghosties swung the enforcer. It hit the gate with a crash that woke up the neighbourhood. I heard Kev's team hit the front door – a dog started barking. The gate hadn't moved. The Ghosties hit it again. Nothing. By now shouts of 'Police!' and screams of terror could be heard coming from inside as Kev and the lads started cracking skulls.

'Come on!' I shouted. 'They're on their own in there!' Fuck. The door wasn't budging. This was unbelievably stressful – Kev was inside, maybe outnumbered, and we were stuck behind the garden gate. The Ghosties were going mad trying to force it, sweat pouring off them. The shouting intensified as the battle poured out into the garden. I was on the verge of ordering the Ghosties to kneel down next to the fence so the TSG could climb over them when the gate was suddenly thrown open.

A rake-thin crack addict stood gasping at us. For a second he stared; twenty-odd men in riot gear waiting in the alley stared back. 'Shit!' he cried in disbelief.

'Not your lucky day, is it?' I asked as the nearest TSG grabbed him.

Kev appeared. He had a massive grin on his face. 'Hello lads, having a spot of trouble, are we?' Luckily Kev's group had no trouble at all containing the people inside. They'd even caught a dealer trying to flush his stash down the toilet, tackling him just before he was able to yank the chain.

We studied the garden gate from every angle and couldn't see why it hadn't caved in. It must just have been the toughest gate in Haringey. The unlucky Ghostie found himself the subject of some pretty cruel piss-taking which everyone except him found hilarious. It was 3 a.m. by the time everything had calmed down and we'd booked our prisoners in, and we went home shattered as usual – me even more so, as my new son was doing a good job keeping us up at night.

The next day, I stifled a yawn as I gazed up at a house in Hampden Lane, a busy residential street on the edge of the Tottenham Triangle. We'd been given intelligence on the house as suspect. Normally I would have gone and confirmed that it was gospel in person but I kept getting called away by work every time I popped down for a look. According our intelligence, it was a small operation. Apparently the info was good and I decided that was enough for me. I planned to raid it with just the HDS guys, no TSG or Ghosties.

I was completely knackered. I knew I wasn't going to see out the year as leader of HDS now, thanks to the DPS investigation, which plodded along interminably, all for the sake of twenty fucking quid. Something like that should have taken twenty minutes to sort out, something along the lines of: 'It's probably just a miscount; thanks for reporting it, just keep a careful eye on things in the future.' Because this death sentence was hanging over me, I had ratcheted the pace right up to eleven, *Spinal Tap*-style. Despite the looming investigation, the unit was working together as if we shared the same brain; we hardly needed to speak as each job came up, as we all knew what to do and what was expected of us. Nevertheless, we were all exhausted and this was inevitably going to lead to mistakes.

We charged the door, which imploded instantly, and almost just as instantly my blood started to run cold. It was too twee and tidy for my liking. We plunged into our assigned rooms. It seemed no one was in until Darren, who'd charged, called down, 'Up here, Harry!' I ran upstairs to find Darren with a worried look on his face and two very petrified twelve-year-old boys skipping school.

'School's cracking down on truancy,' I told them. They looked like they were about to burst into tears. I could have cried too and my stomach churned with fear. This was a right royal fuck-up; we definitely had the wrong address. To make sure, I ran the dog round but nothing, not a crumb.

One of the kids didn't live there so we took him home and explained the situation to his parents. They took the news very well and were quite glad we'd caught their son out.

Next, I needed to placate what would most likely be a furious homeowner. I went into charm overdrive, got the front door fixed pronto, did a follow-up visit, bought the kid's mum a present, helped her choose a pricey new front door and crossed my fingers she wouldn't make a complaint. Luckily she didn't, otherwise I was sure I would have been instantly booted out of HDS with a big black mark on my file.

It turned out it wasn't our mistake – intelligence had got the door number wrong. The crack address was three doors away. We added it to our 'to raid' list and moved on.

Incidentally, that same year a Manchester drugs squad was given a tip on a supposed crack house. They raided it and nicked a load of dealers before they realized they were in the wrong street – they had raided the wrong house and were successful anyway. They then went to the correct address and shut that one down too. It's a sad reflection of the war on drugs when you can just walk up to a random residence and score crack. I mean, our neighbourhood was as rough as it gets, but that's just ridiculous.

The following day, I was running up several flights of stairs, my foot aching from kicking in doors, my ears ringing from the noise of the chopper hovering just outside, its million-watt searchlight strobing through the windows. We were after a busy crack dealer in bedsit-land – a bit of a nightmare in that they were located somewhere in this massive Victorian property full of tiny flats. Because it wasn't possible to tell which one/s were dealing we'd been smashing every locked door we came across.

Although the innocent residents would no doubt be pretty ter-rified and then pissed off at having their door bashed down, I was sure they would be relieved to lose their crack–dealing neighbours along with the incessant stream of aggressive addicts who tramped up and down the stairs night and day.

I'd booked in the chopper to slow anyone trying to escape or throw their stash through the window; its dazzling beam was doing an excellent job of temporarily blinding anyone who looked out of their front window, buying us a precious few seconds. We worked like a team of raving lunatics: bang, in goes door, we dive in; bang goes next door, we dive in, over and over, each time not knowing what scene awaited us.

Bang, the door went in. I stopped. A teenage girl, pregnant, was sitting on the corner of her bed in a tatty room, shit-brown carpet, ancient wallpaper, bay windows which rattled like a pneumatic drill thanks to the chopper's rotors. I was on the verge of holding back and apologizing when I spotted the pipe. Fuck. I never got over the fact that young girls were so gripped by the crack that they kept smoking right through their whole pregnancy. Her baby was going to be born an addict and develop God-knows-what illnesses. We found a load of money and crack in her bedside drawer; she told us she was dealing on behalf of someone else. 'Tell it to the judge,' I said. She did; he bailed her and she vanished.

Meanwhile, Darren had burst into another bedsit and caught four young men trying to throw their stash out of the window. Not quick enough, guys. The helicopter had done an excellent job of slowing them down, keeping them back from the window for a crucial few seconds. Once again the fear that crack dealers sent out into the communities had been put right back from whence it came.

TWENTY-SIX

PAYDIRT

Kev had set up a raid in College Park Road, in the shadow of Middlesex University, my old stomping ground. I had parked my mother's Morris Ital in this street for the entire three years I was at uni and I felt almost guilty raiding this address as it was so close to 'home'. All we found was some cannabis and a false driving licence, so at least the taxpayer wouldn't foot the bill for the smashed door.

I had previously taken a couple of phone calls about dealing taking place on the university campus but, having lived there for three years, I knew it wasn't the sort of thing that warranted our attention. I really wanted to stay focused on the crack trade which had been tearing communities, apart as opposed to a bunch of university students smoking a few spliffs.

I wasn't too thrilled when one day Kev rolled into the stockroom office and told me he had a cannabis factory in his sights. I tried to put him off but he was resolute; his conviction was such that I reluctantly agreed and he headed off with Tina to do a recce in Park Avenue North, a street just outside the Tottenham Triangle which ran parallel to a railway line.

I was desperately trying to catch up with paperwork. My desk looked like it had been hit by a paper avalanche and I was bored out of my mind. When Kev and Tina returned to the office a short time later, they were both grinning from ear to ear, looking pretty pleased with themselves. I threw down my pen and, with some relief, pushed my paper mountain to one side. 'What's up?' I asked.

'You can smell it as soon as you hit the street,' Kev said.

'The address literally stinks — and it's really busy,' Tina added. 'We can't ignore it.'

I quickly 'filed' the paperwork and scrambled the entire squad so we could all have a look. At that time a very capable new probationer called Abby had joined us, and she came along.

The address looked totally wrong: Park Avenue North was a leafy street filled with spacious three- and four-bedroom houses. The road finished in a dead end opposite the railway line. But as soon as I turned into the street I recognized the sweet herbal smell of high-quality marijuana straight away. 'Christ,' I said more to myself than anyone, 'that's fucking potent.'

We set up an observation post in the back of a van; Abby and Tina took first watch. They reported that there was a lot of activity, people coming and going; a lot of 'stuff' was being carried out of the house and loaded into cars.

'No time to lose, then,' I said when they reported back. 'Let's do it.'

As Tina rushed off for a warrant, I suspected that this might be a bit 'different' from our normal raids but I had no idea just how extraordinary this was going to be.

The following morning, Abby watched as several black bin-bags were loaded into a white Transit van by two men. She called it in and I scrambled the squad. 'We've got to do this now!' I yelled and we leaped into the car and hared our way through the streets of North London in the Primera. A team of Ghosties was right behind us. I hoped it was enough.

We parked up opposite the observation van. The door to the property opened and a white woman in her early twenties stepped out into the street, locking the door behind her. She was hot: blonde, with a perfect figure that got the pulses of all of the male members of HDS racing. She walked right past us and into Priory Road, a wide, busy thoroughfare, and started to run for a bus.

'Let's pick her up,' I said. 'We know she's got a key, makes our job easier.' We took off after the bus in the Primera and swerved in front of it, forcing the driver to a halt. Kev ran on board, flashed his warrant card at the outraged bus driver, found the girl upstairs and took her back to the house. This is the best and most civilized way to raid any house – get the keys. That way, once we're inside, anyone else who shows up won't know we've paid a visit until my hand's firmly clamped to their shoulder.

I waited in the van, keeping lookout. Almost as soon as Kev had stepped inside he rang me. 'It's a biggy,' he said. 'Better come and have a look.'

My heart racing, I ran up the street. Kev was waiting for me in the doorway; his grin said it all. I stepped over the threshold and gazed in wonder.

It was as if we'd just stepped into the Amazon.

It was a jungle.

Everywhere I looked, floor to ceiling, the whole place was covered in green.

The first two reception rooms on the ground floor were full of plants. Above them a gentle whirring sound revealed that lights on timed electric rollers made sure every single plant was fed exactly the right amount of light. An automatic hydroponics system took care of water and food. A huge water barrel sat at the top of the stairs alongside a massive main junction box, the source of the factory's impressive electrics.

Upstairs was the drying room, with dozens of enormous plants draped over ordinary clothes dryers. Every other available space was crammed with growing plants.

This was huge. It was beautiful.

The meter had, of course, been hotwired. It whirred like mad, its numbers spinning in a blur, a result of the massive amount of power this place was consuming.

The girl refused to say much except to tell us that her name was Gemma Anderson. She denied all knowledge of the cannabis factory, a brave effort considering we'd all watched her leaving the property. I wasn't sure if it was the marijuana but I was starting to feel quite light-headed. While we were trying to get some answers out of Gemma, her mobile rang. I snatched the phone and ran through the house looking for Abby; I found her upstairs. 'Answer,' I said quickly. 'Pretend to be her and be ill; get whoever it is to come over.'

This was a gamble: Abby was a probationer who had never been thrust into such an awkward position before and she had to be very careful not to entrap the caller, whom she quickly and correctly guessed to be the main man. Abby did brilliantly. He was initially suspicious but once Abby said she wasn't well he became concerned and offered to come round. 'I'll be there soon as I can,' he said and hung up. This was perfect evidence-wise as he'd have to use his front-door key to get in so straight away we'd have him linked to the address.

We quickly put everything back as it was, parked the Primera and the van further down the street, closed the door and waited. Gemma, meanwhile, still refused to say anything.

After about an hour, Tina called me over to the window. 'Here, Harry,' she said, 'saw this one leaving the house yesterday.' A tall black man was walking up the street, checking over his shoulder. We all moved back from the windows and waited as he keyed open the door, HDS waiting for him in the hallway. As soon as the door had opened far enough, we pounced. The complete look of shock on the guy's face was incredible, like someone had just kicked him between the legs with a stiletto. He tried to back out but it was too late; the element of surprise meant we had a firm grip and we dragged him in, kicking and swearing, and cuffed him.

He gave out a good deal of abuse before he calmed down. After we'd grilled him for a short while, it was obvious he wasn't going to say anything. Kev had retrieved a set of car keys from our suspect's pockets and tried them on the cars parked nearby. They fitted a sleek, brand-new, silver Jaguar XKA 2000 – sixty grand's worth of car. There was much argument over who would get to drive it back to the Factory.

Next we had to start dealing with the crime scene. I called in my contact from the electricity board and ordered a skip so that we could clear out all the plants and equipment. It would take three skip-loads, each packed to their absolute limit. Police officers were photographed by the press staggering down the stairs with bin liner after bin liner packed full of grass. It took us three days to search and clear the house. Poor old Taylor had to document everything. It filled three lorries.

Just before we began the clear-out, a Home Office official turned up and asked if he could have a look around. The next thing we knew he was joined by ten boffins in white coats and they started poking around our crime scene. This was in the days before hydroponics had really caught on in terms of growing weed; this was one of the very first such marijuana 'factories' that we had found and this, combined with the sheer size of the find, meant that interest levels were high.

In Bruno's car (the codename we gave our male suspect) we found a number of receipts for hydroponics goods and when we questioned him again he told us he was a 'hydroponics salesman', which caused much mirth amongst those present; even Bruno cracked a small smile.

That night we started to uncover the identity of our two suspects. Kev led the interviews – first Gemma then Bruno then Gemma then Bruno – trying to find a way in, something, anything that would take us further. While Kev made it clear that the evidence was plentiful, our prisoners kept schtum.

'I hope this isn't going to be all we've got to show for this raid,' I said to Kev during a break. 'Two people not saying anything.'

'We'll get something, mate,' Kev said. 'We've got their diaries, after all.'

We kept them in the cells overnight, ready to start the interview process all over the next morning.

Meanwhile, later that night, in the Jaguar we found a reference to an address in Islington. When we checked it we found it belonged to Bruno's girlfriend; he didn't live there but we were interested to see that she was likely to be the sister of a very glamorous celebrity. We'd later suspect her of money-laundering but she fled the property shortly after our initial visit and we were unable to trace her, despite her celebrity connections.

The next morning, we sat down with Gemma's diary and started calling the numbers contained within it. Our opening line was 'I'm trying to find Gemma; I'm in a bit of trouble, the Old Bill are looking for me,' and so on and hope that eventually someone would give us an address or contact number.

On about the fifth call a woman answered. 'Hi,' I said, 'I'm a mate of Gemma's; I'm really worried about her.'

'Why, what's up?'

'She's been nicked. The Old Bill are looking for me; we've been growing cannabis plants together but I don't know her home address and I've got to get there before the Old Bill and make sure it's clean.'

'Oh my God, that's terrible; hang on a sec, I've got it here somewhere.'

This was when we discovered that Gemma was a prostitute. But she was the complete polar opposite from our crack whores, a very rare creature indeed. As I studied the names and numbers it soon became clear that she had a lot of high-class clients. We made some very delicate calls to her clients, who paid upwards of £300 a night for her company, in an effort to identify her. Kev had great fun talking to a deeply embarrassed United States sheriff who had enjoyed her company on more than one occasion.

Gemma was not only very beautiful; she was extremely professional, intelligent and street-smart. As we picked apart her flat we found false ID squirrelled away in various hidey-holes. My jaw dropped when I opened the wardrobe. Inside was a hundred grand in cash – in dollars, pounds and other currencies. Then we found an A4 sheet covered in lists of numbers.

Bank accounts – lots of them.

We also recovered safety deposit keys. Kev found us a financial investigator who set about tracing the numbers. We put it together, piece by piece, until we were sure which banks held Gemma's accounts. Tina and I then went to Harrow Crown Court to get Production Orders under the Proceeds of Crime Act (1995) which forced the safety deposit companies to confirm whether Gemma had an account with them. To our surprise and delight the judge also handed us warrants as well, so we would be allowed to access them ourselves.

In the end we had three addresses for some very discreet, very expensive 'storage centres' in Belgravia, Kensington and Mayfair. Each one confirmed that Gemma had a safety deposit box with them; we immediately hit them with our warrants, explaining that we were authorized to search the boxes and confiscate their contents.

A short time later I was standing in the vaults of a private bank with a bunch of keys and a sports holdall. My heart pounded as I pulled open the very large, mortuary-sized drawer. It slid back silently. I looked across at Greg. 'I think we're going to need a bigger bag.'

It was so tightly packed with cash that as the drawer opened the money rose up over the sides. We started to count it but it was just too much; after a couple of hours the bank manager came down and told us we had to leave otherwise the massive three-foot-thick steel door, which was on an unstoppable timing mechanism, would lock us in the vault overnight. We gave up and staggered out with a bin liner filled to the brim and hastily bundled it into the car, grinning like madmen while debating how much we thought we had.

We soon realized that we had a problem. We needed to find a good place to stash it.

The normal procedure when you recover a large amount of money is to store it in the chief superintendent's safe but there was no way all this cash was going to fit. It was already really late and in the end, for want of anything better I drove us to Paddington Green police station, which has the most secure police cells in the country.

I explained the situation and they asked us to wait in the canteen. As we drank our tea, other officers stared at our bag overflowing with cash and our two unfamiliar faces and obviously thought, 'What the fuck are those two up to?' Eventually, a senior officer couldn't contain himself any longer. 'Er, excuse me, can you tell me what you're doing here?'

Finally, at about 10 p.m., we were presented with a cell and we locked it in overnight. When I spoke to Chief Superintendent Steve James the next morning he gave me a telling-off, but I didn't know what else to do.

'Where should I put it, then?'

'I don't care!' he bawled. 'Just don't leave that amount of cash in any more cells, or in my station!' Very fucking helpful.

Next, I had the bright idea of opening a bank account. I called Natwest in Wood Green and spoke to the assistant manager, and she agreed we could deposit the cash with them. Great, problem solved, finally. I went up to the Factory with the cash to meet the guys and see if there were any developments.

Meanwhile, the assistant manager had called the bank manager. He was a suspicious sod who smelled a rat. He'd never heard of anything like this before. 'They're not police; they're criminals, just trying to get access to the vault so they can rob us,' he told his assistant.

As it happened, he was right to be cautious; not long ago a robber had arranged a meeting with a bank manager in Wood Green to request a substantial loan. Once in his office the robber produced a gun and suggested they come to a completely different kind of arrangement.

The manager called the Flying Squad, who readily agreed that the police would never behave like this and it was definitely going to be a robbery. They jacked up an armed operation and surrounded the bank and placed armed officers inside.

By now I felt like I was permanently attached to this bloody binbag, or 'bling' bag as Adam called it, and I was only too glad to be getting it down to the bank. I was just heading down the corridor at the Factory with it when a voice came from behind me. 'Oooooh shit!'

I turned, and an officer ran up to me. 'What are you up to with that?'

I explained.

'Don't go anywhere. The Flying Squad are waiting to ambush you!'

Finally, once the armed officers had been called off, I was able to go to the bank and safely deposit the cash. It took three tellers two days to count the money – and that was using counting machines. It came to £365,000. Only one note was forged. And there were more keys to more banks.

The house had been bought for a hundred grand in cash by Gemma. During our search we uncovered some videotapes of Bruno and his girlfriend on holiday in Marrakesh. Much of the film featured Bruno visiting cannabis fields, beaming at the camera, giving the thumbs-up. That was going to go down really well with the jury.

We were gradually generating new leads and coming up with new names which needed investigating, but for some reason I got nothing but grief from the senior management team. For example, I had three car-loads of exhibits I needed to stash somewhere. One supervisor told me to move it to Highgate. When I took it to Highgate I was then given a bollocking by a different manager because it wasn't a secure enough area and I had to take it back again. No one was able to offer me a reasonable solution to any of these problems, partly because it was such an unusual case.

Eventually, we got a detective inspector to review the case and he reported that we'd done a top-notch job; Kev, with his CID knowledge, had been our saving grace, along with the guys' usual selfless dedication to duty. There was one small thing that he found I'd done wrong: I'd signed a form that should have been signed by a DI. I thought this a minor issue as I'd been given permission to sign the form by a senior officer, but the DI said it would cause me a 'problem'. The next day I was given a roasting for exactly this.

During the bollocking, a senior officer said, 'What's the point of carrying on with this investigation? What are we going to get out of it?'

I couldn't believe it. I still had safety deposit keys and links to accounts in Luxembourg. I couldn't contain myself. 'About two million quid!' I told him. This figure, I felt, was a conservative estimate of what we would eventually find. That amount of money would become public property and would be poured back into the police service or a local government department – it would have made a massive difference wherever it went. I thought the senior management would have all been fighting over the cash, trying to divert it into their favoured areas. We could have used it to create one hell of a fantastic drugs squad.

Then we discovered that this wasn't the only marijuana factory Gemma and Bruno were involved with. We raced round to find that everything had been cleared out and the guy who was running the house had quickly rented out the property to a group of Poles. The Poles let us in for a look-round and shortly afterwards their landlord walked in. We searched him and found some cannabis, so we nicked him and turned over the house. It was clean, but the garden told a different story; a massive pile of roots had been concealed in a compost heap. We reckoned these were cannabis, so I sent them off to the boffins at Kew Gardens for analysis. They agreed and gave us a certificate to show the judge.

Unfortunately, the investigation started to stall at this point; pressure came down from above to leave it alone. I was frustrated and furious; senior officers felt that the chances of getting any more good evidence were dwindling – for some reason this job had become a nuisance to them.

Nevertheless, I kept at it for as long as they let me and we eventually recovered a million pounds in cash along with a tonne of marijuana. It was still the biggest cash score of the year in the country bar none.

The trial took place at Wood Green court in 2001. Gemma told the judge that she had earned all that cash from prostitution, not from marijuana. Prostitution wasn't illegal, so technically she'd be allowed to keep the money she claimed she'd earned legitimately.

'That may be the case,' the judge said, 'but I'm sure your earnings didn't total 1 million pounds. How much do you charge per hour and how long have you been a prostitute?'

After some wrangling, it was agreed that once Gemma had served her sentence she would be able to walk away with sixty grand. Not bad!

A couple of years later, I got a phone call out of the blue. A woman asked me, 'Are you Harry Keeble?'

'Yes.'

'You prosecuted my daughter, Gemma.'

I waited, not sure what to say.

'We haven't spoken since the day she walked out of our home, when she was only sixteen.'

'I'm sorry,' I said, still unsure of what to say.

'Would you tell her I'm here? That I'll be waiting for her if she wants to talk. Just talk, that's all.'

I agreed. On the day Gemma was released, Tina was waiting for her to return her belongings. Tina told her that her mother was waiting in a nearby pub, alone. 'She just wants to talk. She's desperate to see you.'

Gemma looked at Tina – beautiful, her eyes cold.

She didn't say anything, just walked away.

Bruno was sentenced to three and a half years. The remaining £940,000 was ploughed back into central government. After the case had finished I put in a request for commendations for the officers on my team. I thought this would more or less happen automatically; after all how often do you hear of a drugs squad making a profit of a million quid?

This proved to be much harder than I ever imagined. But before we come to that, we still had a job to finish.

TWENTY-SEVEN

ALL ABOARD FOR THE CRACK EXPRESS

Despite the the occasional icy blast from my superiors, I was full of confidence and it was at this time that I came up with a very novel way to raid a crack house.

The address was in Woodstock Road and it had top notch security; a New York latch secured the door. The guy running the house was a known 'face' who had used the latch before. This would make going in through the front very difficult, and because there were no alleyways which would give us access to the rear, we were struggling to come up with a solution when inspiration hit me like an enforcer.

Train.

The rear of the house was right up against a railway line. If we could persuade a railway company to lend us a train which would stop just outside it would be a perfect way in – cut a hole in the mesh fence and straight through the back door. I made a few calls and eventually a well-known train company said they were prepared to let us have one for the night for three grand. Needless to say, that was beyond our budget so I called a few journalists and asked them if they wanted to come on a very special raid by train. The general answer was, 'Hell yeah!'

I called the train company back and told them that the media were coming so they would get about a hundred grand's worth of publicity. They agreed to let us have the train for free.

It was all aboard the Crack House Express for a dress rehearsal so we could practise debussing from a train. Unfortunately, it was then that track safety experts spotted a Jarvis depot from where we could simply walk along the tracks if supervised. Bugger. I was crestfallen – but that was that.

In the end, after some discussion with the rope team, I opted for another 'spectacular'. Officers wearing chainmail suits took running dives through the front windows. It was brilliant; the dealers had just finished setting up the house and were utterly terrified to see these psychopathic, heavily armoured raiders crash straight past their newly installed defences. The rope team were shocked to run into a fifteen-year-old girl inside. She was so scared she'd wet herself; it took some time to calm her down again.

We'd hit the address so early they hadn't even started operations, which was terrific, although the downside was that we only recovered a small amount of cannabis. But Woodstock Road had been saved from the scourge of crack and I was happy.

Although our focus was almost entirely the crack houses, we were sometimes dragged into other operations. An unusual situation arose when we received reports that drugs were being dealt from a house inside the Tottenham Triangle. It was no crack house, however, but was occupied by members of Reclaim the Streets, political activists who campaign for the 'community ownership of public spaces'; they describe themselves as 'a resistance movement opposed to the dominance of corporate globalisation and to the car as the dominant mode of transport'. We contacted a specialist unit to see if they wanted to come along. They did.

As far as I was aware they were a peaceful group who were known for their 'spontaneous' parties where a thousand or more people took over a busy high street for a few hours and had a good time before dispersing peacefully.

However, they had recently come to attention during the 1

May riots that took place in central London in 2000, where after four days of peaceful protest about 1000 unruly protestors took part in a planned disturbance that would eventually land ninety-five people in jail and leave nine police officers badly injured. Perhaps most infamously, the protestors outraged millions when they defaced Winston Churchill's statue in Whitehall by making a Mohican for his head out of some turf and pouring paint over it.

Although there was no suggestion that Reclaim the Streets were behind the rioting, a certain department was keen to learn more about all of the large groups involved in the four days of protest. Raiding this house would give them a chance to have a nose around to see what they could find.

I studied the address and it looked like a harmless squat: brightly coloured drapes hanging over the windows, political posters and various young people, obviously (from their dreadlocks and clothing) living the alternative lifestyle.

I opted for a low-key raid, just the Ghosties and the squad. We hit it at 9 p.m. on the dot; I leaped into the front room only to wind up toe-to-paw with the most massive Alsatian I'd ever seen. Fortunately, he was more terrified of me than I was of him and he hid in the corner after a few half-hearted woofs.

The house was a mess of old mattresses, unwashed plates, political posters and slogans scrawled on the wall; takeaway dishes littered the floor and the kitchen was an unwashed nightmare. The combination of joss-sticks, decomposing food and rising damp made an interesting change from the rancid smell of crack.

We nicked the occupier for cannabis and then found another character outside who had ten tabs of ecstasy in his pocket. Upstairs, we found a forty-five-year-old woman with another ten Es on her. We suspected (rightly as it turned out) that she'd just sold the guy we'd picked up outside ten Es. Although the specialist unit got to have a good look around, I'm pretty sure there was nothing of interest for them.

★

A far more dramatic break in our routine came when we were ordered to police the 2000 Mardi Gras Festival, the biggest gay party in the UK, which that year was taking place in Finsbury Park.

It was a lovely sunny day and all we wanted to do was watch the show as tens of thousands of people poured into the enormous park to watch Kylie, All Saints, Billie, assorted drag queens and the Mardi Gras Marching Band. Chief Superintendent Steve James had other ideas, however. As well as us, he had dragged his management team down to the park to get them to take part in arresting people for drugs in a sort of away-day management–junior officer bonding session.

Steve James was a great policeman, a real trailblazer, and he wanted the senior management team to have a more hands-on approach and muck in with more junior officers. While I admired him for this attitude, some of the management didn't and they spent the day trying to keep out of the way.

James told us to go and sit on a small mound and watch the queue. Everyone was being searched and he told us that when we saw people hiding drugs in their socks we were to make a note of them and nick them once they were inside. We sat down and watched as dozens upon dozens of people hid their tiny piece of cannabis for their own personal use in their socks.

We looked at each other. 'This is bollocks,' said Greg. We knew this was ridiculous on so many levels. For a start we were going to make the police look bad by nicking loads of mainly law-abiding people for a tiny piece of cannabis which was for personal use. On top of that, the costs and time associated with processing those people arrested, followed by a court appearance where they would receive a tiny fine, were just not worth it. If we were operating a New York-style 'zero tolerance' policy then I would have had no problem with this, but we weren't and so I did.

Chief Superintendent Steve James was on a mission, however, and in no time at all he'd arrested three people for possession. I went and found another member of the management team, told him we hadn't seen anyone hiding cannabis in their socks and asked if we might have a look around inside instead to see if we could find anyone of real interest. He agreed, and in we went.

The main arena was just one big colourful, noisy and extremely enthusiastic party zone. People of all creeds and colours (often painted in luminous shades of fluorescent paint) were dancing together while All Saints mumbled their way through their bland hits. We were in civvies but were suspiciously plain-looking compared with the majority of the crowd. We couldn't spot anything drugs-related and one member of the team (who shall remain nameless) managed to blag an invitation to the VIP tent and got thoroughly smashed on free booze. Lucky bastard.

'Let's try the rave tent,' I said and we marched over; the bass rattled my bones as soon as I stepped inside. It was packed with hundreds of people dancing, steam hanging in the air.

'Want any pills, mate?'

Bingo.

This was more like it. I ignored him and walked around a little more, and was offered a good selection of ecstasy several more times. I led the squad back outside.

'You guys follow me. Watch me at all times, and as soon as you see me grab someone you grab them too.'

I knew this was going to be 'griefy': we were in plain clothes and the loud music meant we couldn't shout 'police', so all people were going to see was a bunch of 'thugs' picking on a hapless raver. But at least it was going to be more interesting than nicking people with a little piece of cannabis in their sock.

We plunged back and once again I was approached by someone with E. I ignored him and the next one as they didn't sound too confident; they were probably occasional dealers who sold now and then at these types of events. I wanted to find someone more hard-core and struck gold when a character bounded up to me and insistently offered me drugs.

'What've you got?' I yelled over the music. He thrust his hand into his pocket and came out with a fistful of Mitsubishis[11]; this particular 'brand' of ecstasy had been linked to the deaths of two young Danish clubbers, one American and a thirty-year-old German in 2000. It was a 'rogue' version, weaker than normal, and as a result these people had taken several tabs too many in an effort to get high, causing their hearts to give out.

As soon as he opened his hand and I saw the pills I grabbed him. Thinking he was being robbed he kicked off straight away; he really went berserk when the rest of the squad jumped in. Ravers stood stunned as we half-carried, half-marched him off and stuck him in the police van. He had a good assortment of drugs on him – lots of E, some heroin and cannabis: a good collar.

'Any more for any more?' I asked the lads, nodding back at the tent. They were all up for it and we marched back in, same routine as before. This time two guys came up to me, one white, one black, both very confident. 'Want any pills, mate?'

'What've you got?'

His hand came up with the dodgy Mitsubishis and I nabbed him. Even before the guys arrived his mate had landed a couple of meaty smacks on me, thinking I must be a lunatic to want to try and rob them on my own. I clung on to his friend for dear life. Then, as HDS piled in, these two showed us they really knew how to fucking fight. They were the slipperiest pair I've ever tried to hold on to. Whenever a limb came free they successfully used it to punch, elbow or knee us in some vulnerable point. To the crowd they looked horribly outnumbered, as if we were attacking them and they were simply defending themselves.

Frustrated to the extreme, Darren lifted the guy who was whacking me off his feet and threw him out of the tent. Somehow, he gripped onto me at that moment so we both went spinning into the crowd outside. The rest of HDS soon followed with the other

---

11 This particular 'brand' of ecstasy pill has Mitsubishi's company logo imprinted on it – otherwise it has nothing to do with the car company of the same name.

guy. I was too busy fighting to yell police, let alone grab my warrant card. Tina was reaching for her asp, her extendable truncheon, as we battled, our opponents screaming for help as stunned festivalgoers looked on.

I didn't realize it at the time but the music had stopped and London Mayor Ken Livingstone had appeared on the stage, hugged Kylie Minogue and called for a peaceful celebration, which that year was dedicated to human rights.

We weren't setting a very good example.

Suddenly an arm gripped my throat and dragged me backwards, loosening my grip on my opponent so he could get in a good whack on my solar plexus. 'What the fuck?' I wheezed. I had been grabbed by a have-a-go hero who thought we were beating up two innocent partygoers for no good reason. I fought to catch my breath.

'Police! We're police, let me go!' and, thank God, he did.

Eventually we sat on them both, got them in arm-locks and marched them through the festival; they screamed abuse and begged for help the whole way while we shouted back, letting everyone know that we were police. Meanwhile Mayor Ken continued to deliver his message of peace and harmony. All in all, we made quite a spectacle.

We finally got them in the back of the van. I was bent over, huffing and puffing and nursing a variety of bruises when Steve James came up to me. 'How many did you get then, Harry?'

'Three, guv.'

'Three?' he exclaimed incredulously, 'Is that all? With the whole drugs squad? I got three myself!'

I didn't say it but now I wish I had. 'Yeah, but while yours are all at home watching telly, mine will be in the cells.'

When we got the lab results on the duelling duo's ecstasy I could believe it. 'Fuck me!' I exclaimed, slapping my forehead.

'What's up, Harry?' Greg asked.

'Those cheeky bastards weren't selling Mitsubishis; they were knocking paracetamol out for fifteen quid a time!'

This made sense. I had recently read an article in which a famous pop star bragged that he had taken a half-dozen Es one night. Well, if they had been Es he would have been dead; as it happened he probably woke up the next day feeling fresh as a daisy with no headache.

So we did them for deception instead.

TWENTY-EIGHT

THE DEATH OF ASHMOUNT

I was with the squad outside a lovely little Victorian terraced house in Glynne Road. Pity, I thought to myself – that looks like an original door. Oh well, *c'est la vie*. We were getting quite close to the magic 100 by this stage and I was starting to think that maybe, just maybe, we'd nail them all.

This house was a low-level distribution point rather than a full-on crack nightmare and we charged it no problem; the door was ruined but I soon had a smile on my face. Upstairs we caught two suspects in the front bedroom, their cash, crack and electronic scales scattered across the bed. They'd hotwired the meter and admitted they were squatting. However, although it looked obvious to us (and anyone else in their right mind), we still had to convince the Crown Prosecution Service and then a jury that they were dealing. Whatever happened in the end, it was a good bit of disruption work.

When we got back to the Factory I was told that Ashmount Road was up and running again. 'They're gluttons for punishment,' I replied. This time we would make sure it was shut down for good.

We planned to raid it on Friday night, and after spending some time watching the house to calculate numbers we booked four van-loads of TSG. After another massive briefing session at the

Factory we kitted up in the back yard and trundled off to Ashmount Road, only to find it totally deserted. The usual stink and paraphernalia littered the surrounding area but there was no sign of life. 'What the fuck?' I said. 'How can it be empty on a Friday night?'

'Maybe they were tipped off?' Greg replied.

'Someone might be watching the station,' Adam added. 'I wouldn't put it past them.'

This was always a concern; someone probably spotted our massive convoy snaking through Tottenham and put two and two together. I was worried that Adam might be right; perhaps some of Lambie's troops were being paid to watch the station and text ahead any sign of activity. Drug dealers at the higher end of the game are smart and are always evolving the trade, seeking out ways to deal with new police tactics.

For example, because we'd shut down so many houses we'd made it hard for some dealers to operate and so they'd started renting cars belonging to crack addicts in return for a fix. These are known as 'rock rentals' and are generally hired out for three or four hours at a time (although some are loaned overnight or for a weekend); crack is sold through the rear window, with one man driving and another in the back handling the drugs and cash. This proved to be an ineffective way of dealing, however, and never really took off, although cars were regularly hired out to criminals on the run and dealers who needed to pick up large consignments.

We later returned in force to Ashmount Road on another Friday night, with thirty TSG, the chopper, the dogs and so on. The raid, although extraordinary to most, was routine for me now; I knew what we'd find inside. It was as busy as it had ever been. I marched confidently into the clouds of acrid crack smoke and expertly co-ordinated the TSG so that after two minutes of utter mayhem, during which time some people leaped out of the first-floor windows, we had everyone on the floor in cuffs; and although many were shouting and screaming they weren't struggling. Many of those who had put up an intense fight struggled to catch their breath.

This was always a bit of a worry; there was the very real danger that one of these characters would die from lack of oxygen. This was something the Met had learned from the Roger Sylvester case (see page 77); that when people are involved in a punch-up or struggle violently for some time, some of the metabolic process becomes anaerobic. In other words, while the person resists being restrained they don't take in enough oxygen and this creates an 'oxygen debt' which the body tries to pay back as soon as the exercise has ended and normal breathing is resumed (this is why we continue to breathe heavily for some time after we've stopped exercising).

When people struggle violently high levels of lactic acid are built up, and if the TSG, as they were sometimes doing, ended up sitting on the person or holding them down in a way which constrained their breathing, they were not able to take in enough oxygen and the point was quickly reached where the person lost consciousness and could not be revived. This condition is sometimes known as 'positional asphyxia'. This is what investigators thought had happened to Roger – he was not a drug user but a normal, fit young man. Long-term crack addicts have weak hearts, and when high their heart rates work overtime, so there was a very real danger that one of them would collapse and die at some point. It was vital to get control of everyone quickly, making sure they were sitting up and breathing all right.

Once I was satisfied everyone was all right and had said 'hello' to a few familiar faces and received half a dozen fairly cheerful replies of 'It's fucking Jim Carrey again!' I marched back to the entrance and checked the electricity meter; as usual it had been looped. This was the last time. I'd brought the guy from the electricity company and a couple of blokes with pneumatic drills. They dug up the road and cut the supply permanently. Try and get round that, you bastards, I thought smugly.

We arrested various people for theft, handling stolen goods and possession, as well as a prostitute in breach of bail and in one case an immigrant who'd overstayed his welcome (not too dissimilar to the characters I described on pages 98–100). Then I hunted for the most familiar face of all, the owner, Leslie Ballantine. He was arrested (he'd jumped bail from the last time we'd nicked him) and then I threatened him with a CRASBO. 'What the fuck's that?' he sneered.

'It's a Criminal Anti-Social Behaviour Order,' I replied. This earlier version of the infamous ASBO had been introduced in 1998. CRASBOs are used when criminal activity is anti-socially related; it was perfect for the irresponsible owner of a house who repeatedly rented it out to crack dealers. It would give us the authority to prevent Ballantine from entering his own house; if he did, we could put him away for five years for breaking the CRASBO. Ballantine was forced to hand over his keys and the council put steel sheets on his house.

Before the raid I'd asked for a charging centre, a special custody suite where all the prisoners from one large job can be taken together and processed quickly, saving us from having to stay up all night searching for cells in police stations across London in which to stash and process various prisoners. Usually, this would leave us completely knackered by the time we got round to doing the paperwork, filling out a massive amount of forms explaining what had happened, how and why the person had been arrested and so on. Looking at these sheets the next day, they'd often be covered in wobbly lines where we'd fallen asleep and the pen had run across the page, or they were heavily stained after one of us had fallen asleep and drooled all over them.

My request was refused and I was told to use Haringey's custody suites. On the night these were full up, however, and so we were forced to wait in the crack house in the hope that we could find a custody sergeant at another station prepared to accept us. After two hours of ringing every borough in London, just when we were about to consider ringing outside the Met to Hertfordshire, Wandsworth was able to help. So we embarked on a massive cross-town drive to deepest South London.

When we arrived we were met, thank God, by a cheerful custody sergeant who couldn't believe that we'd travelled across London to deliver four minor crims. 'I was hoping for some excitement,' he told us as we marched in our addicts, already quivering for a fix, 'some hitmen or coke barons, not a bunch of minors!' He turned out to be one of the best custody sergeants I ever had the pleasure to meet and we managed to get everyone processed just before the rush hour. We drove home, dead beat.

I was exuberant, however. We had done it. The One-Way crack house in Ashmount Road was finally dead. The fear that had soaked the area for so many years would now finally evaporate for good. Unable to live in his own house, Ballantine was forced to sell it. He immediately blew the proceeds and died from a massive drugs overdose soon afterwards.

Although this was a huge triumph for HDS, permanently shutting down one of the largest, most persistent and damaging crack houses in the capital, the event was soured the next day when at the tasking meeting I was criticized for not having arranged a charging centre!

I couldn't fucking believe it. Barely able to contain myself, I told them through gritted teeth that I'd requested one but had been turned down. While they accepted my explanation the icy atmosphere did not thaw at all.

But I was still happy. We only had one crack house left to go.

TWENTY-NINE

THE CENTURY

The house in Stonebridge Road was at the exact apex of the Tottenham Triangle, the heart of crack-land. It was 30 June 2000, nine months after the official formation of HDS, and here we were, already close to reaching the century.

I wanted to use the TSG but they were committed to another job. I either had to scrap it or wing it. The rest of the guys agreed: there was no way we were aborting this raid, and so we decided to fly blind one last time.

Big mistake.

The target was in a low-rise council estate which backed onto Tottenham High Road; we did the recce early when it should have been good and quiet. Our target was hard to find and we heard and smelt it before we saw it; the two-storey property was in a nook in the curvy estate which was shaped like a lower-case 'e'. It was busy; the door snapped quickly back and forth to allow people to come and go; a faint cloud of crack smoke puffed out each time it opened. I took this as a sign of how effective we'd been, that there was such a scarcity of places to buy, smoke and party that any new house that opened up was instantly swamped 24–7.

As I breathed in the acrid smell of crack, I swallowed hard; bile bubbled in my empty stomach. 'Looks like a nasty one, Harry,' said Greg. 'Should we leave it until the TSG are free?'

I should have done. I should have known better, but I was on edge; I was knackered beyond belief. I wanted it over before the DPS concluded their investigation and the squad was abolished.

'Nah, we can handle it with the Ghosties,' I said with more confidence than I felt – and more to myself than to Greg.

I decided to hit it in the evening, when it would be at its busiest, and, knowing we were taking a risk, I went back to the estate for another recce. As I slouched towards the address, it looked quiet. Odd, I thought. The lights were on but there was no activity. I pushed my luck and walked right up to the door. A quick look over my shoulder and I pressed my ear to the mottled glass door-pane.

Murmuring, perhaps three people. Easy. Boring.

We must have caught the tail-end of an all-night party on our early-morning walk-past. I passed on the good news at the briefing which was being led by a new face, Hannah, who'd joined us on attachment. The briefing was straightforward enough; Hannah knew that we'd all seen the target and we knew the routine. We were soon climbing into the Primera and on our way, tailed by the Ghosties and the dog squad.

Hannah was lovely, but far too quiet. I wasn't sure whether she had the necessary aggressiveness to storm a crack house without the TSG.

'Hannah,' I said, 'we're about to raid a house containing a load of crack-heads and dealers; I'm a bit worried you're going to be too quiet. When we go in, you've got to scream at them as loud as you can, let them know there's no messing with you.'

''Kay, Harry,' she replied quietly.

I took a deep breath and yelled at the top of my voice, 'POLICE, NOBODY FUCKING MOVE!' Hannah jumped out of her skin and literally hit the roof while Adam, who was driving, swerved slightly.

'Bloody hell, Harry,' he said. 'You trying to give us a heart attack?'

'Just a demonstration. Your turn,' I said, looking at Hannah.

'POLICE, NOBODY FUCKING MOVE!' She sounded like a slightly peeved squirrel.

Tina decided to show her how it's done. I thought the car windows were going to shatter into smithereens. My ears ringing, I said to Hannah, 'Try again.'

We spent the rest of the journey screaming our heads off in the car while pedestrians kept stopping, thinking we were yelling at them. People turned their heads in astonishment as we sailed by doubled up in hysterics. Hannah wasn't exactly going to put the fear of God into the criminals but at least they'd be able to hear her now.

The High Road was as busy as ever and we caused a bit of congestion as we pulled up by the railway bridge at South Tottenham station, just shy of the rear of the target address. As we climbed out and slammed the doors, still grinning from our shouting game, a train screamed over the bridge.

Without saying anything I led us to the address. As we approached I spotted a group of young men lurking close by. They looked up and froze as they saw the four fully armoured Ghosties striding towards them carrying the enforcer, then the seven of us – me, Greg, Adam, Kev, Darren, Hannah, Tina – marching across an open section of the estate, *Reservoir Dogs*-style, Bear the sniffer dog not far behind.

I felt all-powerful, adrenaline filling my veins, my chest swelling with pride and the confidence I had in my team; I had that 'I could take on the world' feeling I got when I felt the police were about to do what it was they were supposed to do and crush a much-hated public enemy and bully.

The men, pale, baggy-eyed and skinny, split as we drew close, saying nothing; they didn't want trouble and they knew we'd brought it in bundles.

A smidgen of worry caused my heart to flutter at this point; maybe they'd spotted us debussing and warned the occupiers, and the target flat was empty – perhaps our last crack house was about to go with a fizz rather than a bang and they'd hang around ready to take the piss once we emerged empty-handed.

I threw a look over my shoulder; they were walking away, unhurried, looking back at us as they went. Something felt wrong but I had no idea what it was – just a copper's gut feeling.

I shrugged it off; too late for doubts now. The Ghosties crouched by the door as we lined up behind them on the walkway. I nodded and they swung back the battered red enforcer. With a crash the door flew open and smashed into the wall, torn from its top hinge. We were in.

As we stormed inside I caught sight of a New York latch; we were lucky it had been left off the hook. In the next instant, however, my attention was grabbed by the terrifying scene that awaited us.

It was fucking packed.

No going back now. I didn't hear Hannah scream so I yelled, 'POLICE, NOBODY FUCKING MOVE!' along with the rest of the gang. Fuck going into assigned rooms, we'd have to fight our way through this mob. It was two-to-one and they were ready for a fight, *Gangs of New York*-style, the Crack-Headz settling a score with the Boyz in Blue. It was as if they'd been waiting for us.

We all knew this was bad; there was no going back and we had to put them down hard and fast, no time to waste. Greg was bouncing one unfortunate lad off the walls, while Tina had laid into anyone and everyone within her reach. I could see the panic on Hannah's face; it looked like she wanted to say, 'What have I got myself into?' I marched round pushing people back, yelling at them to sit. Adam was already wrestling someone on the ground in the lounge when someone charged towards him, about to kick him while he was down. Running forwards, I turned myself into a human battering ram and slammed my target so hard in the kidneys that he dropped to the floor, gasping in pain. I span round and took in the scene.

It was absolute chaos. The air was thick with crack, making the room hazy; the windows were covered; lights swung and flicked on and off as people crashed into them. I saw maybe two dozen faces screaming; I launched myself at them, pushing people back and down. 'Sit the fuck down! Shut the fuck up!' I didn't want anyone to grab hold of me; I had to call for back-up. I grabbed my radio and yelled for assistance. This was totally out of control. We were losing here. All four of the Ghosties were wrestling with a bunch of characters on the verge of pushing them back out of the front door.

I ran back down the hallway past a couple of crippled crackheads. Through the open door I had a view right across the estate. Windows were being thrown open; people were rubbernecking to see what all the noise was about. The kids whom we'd passed earlier were running back towards us. What the fuck? Were they coming to back up their mates?

Then I saw two uniformed PCs sprinting behind them. Yes! I'd never been so pleased to see a pair of coppers. I hoped they could fight.

They did the Met proud; full of fresh adrenaline, they gleefully steamed straight in and turned the tide – just the sight of uniformed reinforcements was enough to calm some of our opponents down and we steadily began to take control. I recognized a lot of familiar faces, a few of whom had literally pissed themselves, and arrested one guy for intent to supply crack (he eventually got twenty-eight days for possession). The property, which apparently belonged to a guy in prison for sex offences, was an absolute tip. What shoddy furniture there was had been smashed and overturned, glass and foil were scattered across the floor, and the bathroom was covered in puke and shit; it did not make for pleasant searching.

We split everyone into male and female before strip-searching them all in a cleared room. As we had found before, one of the younger women turned out to be too gross to touch, a distinct smell suggesting a very nasty case of bacterial vaginosis and, hearing my officers' gagging, I spared them from the most intimate part of the search and we turned her loose.

Eventually we got through them all, carted everyone off and

waved in the guys from the council who sealed the property by fixing a steel door over the entrance and drilling grills over the windows.

The guys and I compared and contrasted our injuries as we walked back to our vehicles. When we got to the car I turned to Hannah. 'Top job. In any event I was never going to hear you shouting in there,' I said.

'The sight of all that lot kind of took the wind out of my sails,' she answered, which, although not funny, started us all giggling, burning off the last of the surplus adrenaline; exhaustion would soon follow.

A few minutes later, I was walking back across the estate to check the property was clear. The excitement over, everyone had gone to bed and, apart from a flickering street lamp, it was now in complete darkness. I then spotted a shadow against the wall. It was the stinking prostitute; it looked as if she were ghostbusting the pavement for crack.

It didn't know it then, but it was Jenni Doyle. And it wasn't the pavement she was ghostbusting – she was picking her way through her own puke. She had swallowed her stash during the raid and thrown it up once we let her go, and was now searching for those precious rocks.

THIRTY

THE PRINCE OF DARKNESS

19 APRIL 2001

Mark Lambie walked up the staircase of the house in Turner Avenue, a quiet cul-de-sac on the edge of the Tottenham Triangle. Screams came from the upstairs bedroom.

Inside, a grim scene met the scar-faced thirty-two-year-old Prince of Darkness. Two Jamaican men in their twenties, Gregory Smith and Towayne Morris, were each strapped to a wooden chair with masking tape. They were covered in blood and burns. Two of Lambie's associates were standing beside them. One held a claw hammer, the other an empty kettle – its boiling contents having just been poured over the two men.

Lambie was trying to 'persuade' Smith and Morris to hand over twenty grand in drugs and cash. Smith finally broke when a heated iron was placed on his chest. He told them to go to Wakefield Road, not five minutes' drive away, just off Ashmount Road. There was a house that had been used as a hairdresser's. There was money there, he lied – lots of it.

A posse tooled up and went with a half-naked and shoeless Smith to the hairdresser's. They turned the place over, beating the people inside and taking cash and jewellery, but there was nothing like the amount Smith had promised. Just as Smith was about to become the focus of their rage, the door opened and in walked a customer. The gang fell upon him, pistol-whipping the unfortunate man unconscious before searching his pockets. Smith seized his only chance and ran for it out the back.

Tottenham police station was as busy as ever when Smith, covered in blood, burst through the doors begging for help, yelling at open-mouthed officers that he'd been tortured. A short time later, Detective Inspector Peter Lansdown from Operation Trident started grilling Smith for information. Suddenly, after months of having nothing to pin on Lambie, Lansdown had a witness prepared to give evidence against the elusive gang leader.

Within hours he had another. Lambie's gang were in the middle of moving Towayne Morris to a safer address when they spotted a police car, panicked and ran. Morris ran towards the police and threw his body across the still-moving car's bonnet, leaving bloody red streaks as he slid off.

This was the beginning of the end for the Prince of Darkness.

After we'd been disbanded and assigned our various new posts, the care of Haringey Drugs Squad was passed on to another detective sergeant who made sure he kept the heat turned right up, and with some style. He agreed to take over one of our 'spectaculars', in which the rope team abseiled down the side of a block of flats and crashed through the windows of a seventeenth-floor flat.

HDS had hurt Lambie's North London empire. By eliminating the crack houses we had significantly reduced his cash-flow, and he had emerged from his South London hidey-hole, crawling back to Tottenham to extort and rob as much cash and drugs as he could from whoever he could.

Without the crack houses, he and his associates had fewer places to hide out and, desperate for cash, he had taken risks, providing officers from Operation Trident with a golden opportunity. They nailed Lambie in May 2002, when he was sentenced to twelve years for the kidnap, torture and attempted extortion of Smith and Morris.

By then, of course, both I and the whole squad had moved on to pastures new. We had learned of our imminent abolishment when a mass email advertising our jobs was sent out a few days after our last desperate battle to close the crack house in Stonebridge Road. Not the most sensitive of organizations, the Met.

Although we left the squad, there were a great many loose ends to tie up; various court cases were slowly rumbling their way through the interminable UK justice system. One loose end bothered me far more than any other – the DPS investigation of the missing twenty quid.

We were all interviewed six months after Kev had first reported it (lightning fast those boys at the DPS). Kev and I made 'no comment' interviews and read out prepared statements stating that our officers had come forward voluntarily, and that the DPS had not followed the correct procedure and had treated us poorly.

They criticized me for not staying on the scene (even though there were two other sergeants present and my wife was about to give birth) and we were all devastated (and incredulous) to learn that the DPS had passed on their evidence to the Crown Prosecution Service to see if we should face trial. We spent another six months with this cloud hanging over us while the CPS made up their minds. The decision, when it finally came, was that the missing money was 'probably down to a miscount'. Despite this, and despite my vociferous protestations that we had done nothing wrong, we still received 'words of advice', an official bollocking which left an unpleasant stain on all our records and no chance to argue.

But it didn't end there. Oh no.

After our words of advice, I asked the DPS for the four twenty-pound notes we had turned in as evidence, so I could return them to the lads. About twenty further requests later I had drawn a blank and was at a loss. Many people would have left it there. It wasn't as if I didn't have enough to worry about with my new job; I was about to head off to Africa to nail a child abuser who'd raped his twin daughters 150 times.

It wasn't as if it was a lot of money either, but to me it was the principle – what was right should be seen to be done. Besides that, I could smell a rat. By Christmas 2002, I'd still not received an answer, so I wrote to the then deputy commissioner Sir Ian Blair at the start of 2003, explaining everything exactly as we had experienced it.

A week later I received a reply in which the deputy commissioner's staff officer explained that the money we had handed in to the DPS had 'gone missing'. He arranged for me to have a meeting with the head of the DPS so they could explain what had happened.

At that meeting, there was a pile of paper two feet high on the table (it was actually 4163 pages). That was the result of the investigation into the missing twenty pounds (an investigation which I suspect cost the taxpayer several thousand pounds). I demanded to know why our eighty pounds had gone missing, only to be told that it had been stolen from the DPS property store! They sent the boys a cheque and said that the DPS theft 'had happened too long ago to investigate and we've tightened our procedures since then anyway'.

'So you're telling me my officers have done nothing wrong; have shown integrity; have trusted the DPS to do an honest and thorough job. Yet it takes you two years to decide that it was probably a miscount, during which time someone has stolen the money from you, and my officers still merit words of advice?'

And I thought integrity was non-negotiable.

The other thing that caused me no end of frustration was trying to get my officers two commendations for their work – firstly for recovering a million in cash and a tonne of high-strength, home-grown marijuana and secondly (and by far the more important) a recognition of the fact that throughout the time we had been operating there had only been one injury (the guy shot outside the house in Ashmount Road) and no deaths of any black people due to shootings in Haringey (well, none we knew about anyway). The

London boroughs of Southwark and Lambeth saw fifty and fifty-six people shot respectively in 1999 and 2000.

Besides our success in stopping the shootings, Haringey had seen the number of arrests for supplying crack rise by 50 per cent, a statistic yet to be matched. The number of people arrested in possession of an offensive weapon had increased 69 per cent.

I thought the powers that be would want to plaster our story across the *Evening Standard* and in the police magazine *The Job*, so some commendations would provide a perfectly welcome excuse. Commendations are not really that big a deal; it usually takes one email and a 'well done' certificate is printed off which then takes about five minutes to present.

Sixty-three emails later I still didn't have an answer. I know it was this many because I've kept them (not being quite able to believe it at the time). Eventually, I wrote to Sir Ian Blair again and I was chuffed when his staff officer told me that the team should be commended for the million-pound seizure and for making Haringey safer (I think we struck a chord with Ian Blair as when he became commissioner he came up with a new mission statement for the police – Working Together for a Safer London).

In the end, however, no one was ever given a commendation for reducing gun crime. Steve James, the one person who had commended us for precisely this while we were in the middle of our operations, had since moved on.

James was prepared to take risks and get close to teams on his patch; all too often, some managers these days are not the hands-on type because they're on the promotional trail. There's nothing wrong with working your way up the career ladder, of course, but many senior managers don't want to get too close to anyone or any team, just in case it all goes pear-shaped and they're tainted as a result. Perhaps our brush with the DPS had resulted in this stand-offish behaviour.

Finally, after six years of arguing, I went to collect the commendation certificates for the cannabis operation at a ceremony held at Tottenham Hotspur Football Club. I was shocked to learn that Kev and the financial guy, who'd spent more hours on the cannabis case than anyone else, were not included. The lighting was too low, which made the room feel drab, and quite a few people who'd been invited didn't show up. Although the DCI gave a good speech, I left the club clutching the commendations feeling as if it hadn't been worth going. It was a depressing anticlimax.

On the upside, everyone from Haringey Drugs Squad had made detective (including me) and Kev and I did everything we could to make sure the guys were transferred to their favoured departments (which they were).

And, of course, we had achieved what we had set out to do. Our borough was relatively clean of crack houses, but while we were toasting our success and the local kids reclaimed the playgrounds, other boroughs were suffering for not having tackled the crack house and several turf wars had kicked off. Hundreds of teenage gangs roamed estates across London and talked about people getting jacked (robbed), being blazed (shot) and how they were after 'the Cris life' (Cristal champagne, the ultimate in underworld chic). These kids boasted they'd kill to get it – and on 27 November 2000, one of them did. The Met got the murderers eventually, but it wasn't easy.

When the detective constable stood over the suspected murderer who sat opposite him in the small interview room, he had no idea what was about to happen to him. He knew the case was particularly vicious; the innocent victim had been stabbed with a broken bottle and had slowly bled to death on a filthy stairwell on a decaying London estate, a hideous way to die. A 120-strong team with unlimited funds had been set up, solely devoted to catching the killer. The suspect was eventually caught within the boundaries of the notorious North Peckham estate, a few hundred yards from the scene of the murder.

Scrawny, with a pockmarked face full of hatred, he sat next to his solicitor and stared coldly at the detective. The DC paced up and down the interview room a couple of times and then sat down, leaned over the table and asked the suspect a question. The suspect looked at his lawyer, who nodded as if it were all right for him to answer. Then, in one lightning movement, the suspect's arms shot out and grabbed the surprised detective's lapels, and he headbutted him right between the eyes. As the detective staggered backwards, blood gushing from his nose, the suspect stood up, folded his arms across his chest and said, 'Well? What are you going to do about that?' The suspect was fourteen years old. The murder victim was ten-year-old Damilola Taylor.

By this time, I had had some success working for Child Protection, preventing cases not dissimilar to that of Victoria Climbié that involved 'witchcraft'. As well as Victoria, I often thought about Damilola Taylor and hoped that by eliminating the crack houses from Haringey, we had saved many other children from a similar fate. And if HDS could drive them out of Haringey, then other units could do it across the country, leaving nowhere for the crack dealers to go – at worst they would be forced into dealing in the street, which was exactly what happened in Haringey where they were swept up in other operations.

The new HDS focused on this and did a fine job of clearing them out while keeping on top of the crack houses. Street-dealing was a lot less attractive to the foot soldiers because the chances of being robbed, stabbed, shot, killed or arrested were much higher.

I still think it's a mistake for the Met to enforce such rapid leadership changeovers every six months. The one error most new leaders make is to try to stamp their mark by changing a perfectly effective system before moving on.

Within a few years, it was clear that crack was back in Haringey and was there for the long haul. The shootings gradually returned, an average of twenty-two people being shot and seriously wounded each year between 2002 and 2005; countless shootings were once again being reported and, more than ever, children across London were being caught in the crossfire.

Joel Smith was a twenty-three-year-old crack addict and member of the Mus Luv Crew, who drew their guns at the slightest provocation; a fearsome sight, muscular and heavily tattooed, he specialized in raiding crack dealers. Shortly after midnight on 13 September 2003 he approached an address in Harlesden, North London, with an accomplice. Inside was a former crack dealer. Smith was convinced he was still dealing and planned to rob him. He banged on the door. Eventually, forty-one-year-old Bertram Byfield walked down the corridor to answer. He was annoyed; his seven-year-old daughter Toni-Ann was due to start at a new school the next day and needed her sleep.

Byfield told Smith he wasn't dealing; Smith refused to believe him and raised his gun. As Byfield stumbled back into a bicycle propped up in the hallway, the killer fired. The first bullet hit Byfield in the side of his body; the second passed through his penis and into his leg; the third hit him in his side again. Suddenly, Toni Ann appeared in the hallway; she looked at Smith, screamed, turned and ran. Smith didn't hesitate. He took careful aim and shot her in the back; the seven-year-old cried out as the bullet travelled down through her body and exited her abdomen. The gunman ran. Both father and daughter were still alive when neighbours found them a minute later – but they died together on the floor before the ambulance arrived.

Smith was turned in by associates who were appalled when he told them what he had done. He was sentenced to life with a recommendation that he serve at least forty years, meaning he won't be out until 2045, when he'll be seventy-two years old.

In an attempt to deal with the seemingly unstoppable rise in crack-related shootings, the Met formed the highly secretive Special Projects Unit, a secret squad made up of thirty detectives. Their remit is to track and trap contract killers and major drug and arms dealers. Known as the Met's 'most sensitive unit', they have faced, fought and convicted several Jamaican contract killers brought in from abroad to kill leading gang figures for between £10,000 and £20,000 a pop. The SPU has sometimes found themselves in the strange position of ensuring the safety of a top gangster, only to then have to hunt the same person they were trying to protect when the gangster tries to exact revenge. It's a murky and dangerous job, but they have had some success; they claim to have prevented thirty-five hits from being carried out in the capital in one eighteen-month period.

In 2005, things took a turn for the better in Haringey when the new head of the recently created Proactive Drugs Unit, Detective Sergeant Ian Baker, took a leaf out of my book and proved to be a man on a mission. Two years later, on Valentine's Day 2007, he shut his hundredth Haringey crack house, adapting our approach with the CRASBO to the new, improved ASBO to help keep the houses out of the hands of the dealers. DS Baker's team also managed to nab a kilo of uncut cocaine from a crack house in St Ann's Road, just at the bottom of the Tottenham Triangle (where we had closed a massive crack house in February 2000, see page 155).

DS Baker told reporters, 'Clearly it is good for Haringey that we have had an impact on 100 separate communities.' Too damn right; my advice to him would be to keep going, don't have anything to do with the DPS, and don't hold your breath for any commendations. I'd feel much more comfortable living in Haringey with someone like DS Baker at the helm of the fight against drugs than in other boroughs where the drugs squads focus on other areas, or simply don't have the resources to tackle the crack houses head-on.

Today, the crack-house phenomenon is still not under control. I have seen the grim little floral tributes to murdered children and teenagers fastened to lamp posts on estates all over our capital. Meanwhile, officers from Operation Trident are overwhelmed by crack-associated gun crime while other drugs departments don't have the time, resources or know-how to shut down crack houses. In 2004, Sir John Stevens, the then Commissioner of the Met, attended a much-publicized raid on a crack house in Notting Hill. The building was back in operation as a crack den twelve hours later.

It seems as though every single one of the UK's most tragic, appalling and senseless murders since 2000 have been crack-related. Danielle Beccan (fourteen) died in her mother's arms after being shot in a drive-by by two young men embroiled in a gang war over crack-house territory. Ainlee Walker (two) was tortured to death by her crack-addicted father; her body had sixty-four separate injuries. Mary-Ann Leneghan (sixteen) was repeatedly raped before being tortured to death by a gang of crack users. WPC Sharon Beshenivsky (thirty-eight), shot dead on her daughter's fourth birthday by gun-men robbing a bookie's with guns, one of which was a Mac-10 (one of the robbers had convictions for dealing crack; all of them were already on bail for firearms offences). Jesse James (fifteen), shot dead on a Moss Side estate, an innocent victim of mistaken identity. Letisha Shakespeare (seventeen) and Charlene Ellis (eighteen), killed in a botched drive-by shooting, the result of an escalating gang war. These are just a few of the victims killed by crack.

Then there are the people dying for their addiction – often as a result of the danger they put themselves in to get their fix. In Ipswich in 2006, five prostitutes aged between nineteen and twenty-nine, who had sold themselves to pay for their addiction, were killed. Steve Wright was convicted of their murders in February 2008.

Crack-related deaths have increased nine-fold since 2000 as the crack houses spread out from London and infested other large cities. They then moved to suburban towns, particularly in the north of England (where the number of drug-related deaths dou-bled in 2006) and, most recently, to Scotland, where despite some officers raising concerns about crack back in 2000, the authorities were completely taken by surprise and are only now trying to deal with the problem before it spirals beyond their control. Perhaps it already has.

For instance, in Aberdeen, the number of crack users has rock-eted by more than 600 per cent over the past five years as London dealers targeted the oil-rich city. Crack sold in the Aberdeen area fetches up to five times the London prices. The trade in Aberdeen alone is worth around ten million pounds a week.

But not to worry, because local health officials have offered crack users acupuncture, reflexology and aromatherapy, along with advice and medical treatment to help them beat the drug. Yeah, right, that'll sort out the crack addicts all right – people battling the most addictive substance known to man, so addictive that they'll choose crack over relief from starvation any day of the week. There are 4000 registered heroin addicts in Aberdeen. Ninety-five per cent of them now also use crack. Despite local police recording a 700 per cent increase in seizures of crack cocaine, last year drug deaths in the region more than doubled to 48. So although the police are recovering loads more drugs, they're seeing a rise in drug-related deaths – you don't have to be Sherlock Holmes to realize that the area is flooded with crack.

Overall, shootings in the UK have tripled since 2000, with 11,000 offences occurring in England and Wales each year (*that's thirty every single day*). In London in 2006 *two people were shot every day* – that's *double the number for 2005*. Dr Karim Brohi, one of the UK's leading surgeons in treating knife and gunshot injuries, recently began campaigning for doctors to be given better training and resources to deal with the increased shootings. At the moment, he argued, patients are dying unnecessarily because hospitals are not geared up to deal with bullet wounds. This violence is steadily spreading to places like Aberdeen – or anywhere else where the crack trade has recently taken hold.

Trigger-happy gunmen are no longer afraid to shoot those brave people who are prepared to testify against them – and their relatives. The gunmen know that the police can't afford to put entire extended families into Witness Protection.

Many stories that would have been front-page news two years ago are fading into the background. Black-on-black shootings rarely make news headlines. Who has heard of the case of Jason Greene, who started his day on 18 July 2006 by taking his two young boys to school? By 8.30 a.m. his sons' uniforms were splattered with their father's blood. His murderer was eighteen years old.

Ultimately, this is what has motivated me to write this book. We *can* defeat the crack dealers. While we might not be able to stop the influx of crack into the UK, we can make it impossible to sell; we can close the crack houses and imprison the dealers by catching them at it, thereby stopping the shootings and making neighbourhoods safer, as our tiny under-funded squad did in Haringey, one of the roughest parts of the UK. There were just six of us in HDS, while other similar borough intelligence cells had more than twenty staff just processing information. Some kind of balance needs to be found so that we can stay on top of the dealers.

Remove the crack house and crime falls; not just drug and gun crime but prostitution, robbery, assault, burglary – crimes which affect thousands of people. Just think of all the teenagers, policemen and law-abiding citizens we are going to lose to crack-related gun crime in the future. Your children, your friends, husbands, wives, colleagues – killed for nothing.

Meanwhile, Pete Doherty, the UK's most famous crack addict, 'music genius' and role model to thousands of teenagers, is making crack cool. Doherty is following in the footsteps of some pioneering members of the So Solid Crew; Shane Neil recently became the third member of the band charged with dealing crack cocaine and possessing a gun. Thanks to this kind of publicity, dealers are starting to offer crack in nightclubs in an effort to turn it into a mainstream drug like ecstasy, 26 million pills of which are popped by 750,000 users each year. If we let the dealers succeed then we will pay for it with our children's blood.

EPILOGUE

Until I went to Africa to hunt for child abusers, I had never heard of Guinea-Bissau but I'm pretty confident that it's soon going to become one of the most infamous countries in Africa (and that takes some doing).

Guinea-Bissau is a pocket-sized (pop. 1.6 million), impoverished West African country sandwiched between Senegal and New Guinea, facing the Atlantic. Since winning its independence from Portugal in 1973 (thanks to weapons supplied by communist Russia, China and Cuba), Guinea-Bissau has been wracked by a series of civil wars, revolutions and massacres. In 2005, the country held its most democratic attempt at an election to date.

Things were looking up, but times were of a harshness most Europeans can't even begin to imagine. For the average person, life ends at forty. Crops fail, people starve. There's almost no medical care. Phone lines are all but non-existent and there's very little electricity – even the president relies on a petrol-driven generator which screams in protest outside his office every time it's fired up.

Guinea-Bissau's remarkable 350-km-long coastline is strewn with more than seventy uninhabited islands, creeks and swamps amongst which local fishermen have to hunt ever longer for depleted fishing stocks which are currently being swallowed up by European boats further out at sea (various European nations won enormous concessions in 2001). Fish had once been the main income generator for most of the people in Guinea-Bissau; after this, it was cashew nuts.

Things took an unexpected turn, however, when in 2005 local fishermen in Quinhamel, twenty miles west of the capital Bissau, came across dozens of heavy bricks of tightly packed white powder floating in the sea. They often recovered flotsam and jetsam as they fished and occasionally they found something worth taking back to their village.

They returned home with the packets of white powder and, with no idea as to what the substance might be, they divided it up between them and experimented. Some used it as fertilizer while others got a shock when they added it to their daily meal of fish and rice in an attempt to add flavour.

Some days later, a handful of shipwrecked Colombians turned up in Quinhamel to buy back what was left of their cargo. They also showed the villagers how to use it properly. They taught them how to cook crack, which the Guineans christened *qisa*. Sold by some of the villagers for three quid a hit, it became an affordable treat for many of their fellow countrymen. As usual, the crack provided its famous 'one hit and you're hooked' effect.

Guinea-Bissau had started its descent into a new kind of hell.

The Colombians returned with two and a half tonnes of cocaine. Guinea-Bissau was just what they had been looking for – a lawless 'safe zone' from where they could smuggle thousands of tonnes of coke into Europe. The island-strewn coastline provided them with perfect cover; loads dropped from the air would be collected by fishermen with good local knowledge who could easily retrieve them while evading any police patrols.

Mind you, they didn't have much to worry about as there was no law-enforcement agency to speak of. The country's only prison had been destroyed during the civil war seven years previously and had never been rebuilt. The tiny police department did not have enough desks to furnish their office (sounds familiar), their four unreliable jeeps needed constant repair, and staff went unpaid for months at a time.

In no time at all, the cartels had bribed all the right people and hooked up with the military. In one massive shipment, they doubled

Guinea-Bissau's gross national product. Local officials were paid in cocaine, which they sold to their countrymen for a massive profit. They were delighted to discover that turning it into crack doubled the yield.

The new coke barons met little resistance. In one instance, a two-and-a-half-tonne shipment was flown into an old military airfield (the Portuguese left behind several runways but no planes or radar). Police raced to the scene and came upon two local soldiers who had 635 kilos of coke packed into their army vehicle. The remaining 1.8 tonnes got through because the police did not have enough petrol to pursue the other traffickers.

On another occasion 674 kilos of cocaine, worth about 18 million pounds, was seized after a gun battle fought on the streets of the capital, Bissau. It was hidden in the treasury vaults for safekeeping, from where it mysteriously vanished. Prime Minister Aristides Gomes said that he had ordered it to be burned, but as the fire was being stoked seven or eight police officers wandered off with blocks of coke under their coats. I can see how this would be an easy temptation; especially as they hadn't been paid for three months – their families were starving; fish prices were increasing. One brick of cocaine could keep them fed for a lifetime.

Today, Guinea-Bissau is on the way to becoming Africa's first narco-state. Smugglers have taken advantage of the established old marijuana-smuggling network from Morocco to the UK. Thousands of small-time mules flying from Madrid hide the drugs in souvenirs or in their stomachs. In Guinea-Bissau, gangs of pony-tailed Colombians drive their luxury cars through the dirt roads of the capital, and spend night after night partying at cocaine-funded clubs and restaurants. Their mock-Roman villas line newly built streets on the outskirts of the city; satellite dishes adorn the rooftops, which are tiled in the Spanish style. Twenty slightly smaller homes (where swimming pools come as standard) are being built for those local officials who took bribes.

At the other end of the scale, Guinea-Bissau has recently opened its only drug-treatment clinic, which is struggling to deal with hundreds of *qisa* addicts. 'Until twelve months ago I hadn't heard of *qisa* or crack,' said the clinic's director, Pastor Domingos Te, 'but now it's out of control.' He talked about some case studies which sounded identical to the hundreds I had encountered in London: kids stealing from families, women offering their bodies, people murdered for their stash and so on.

The true scale of Africa's first crack epidemic remains unknown but without any real law enforcement and with the Colombian cartels in control, it's decimating the tiny country. If a smuggler is ever captured (a rarity), tried (once in a blue moon) and convicted (better chance of being hit by a snowball in the Sahara), they are immediately freed with the help of powerful friends and the lack of a secure place to keep them.

Interpol estimates that over a third of the cocaine which reaches Europe is trafficked through Guinea-Bissau. In 2007, it was estimated that 300,000 kilos of cocaine was boated or flown to Guinea-Bissau from Colombia. Government officials and high-ranking military officers are turning into the Pablo Escobars of West Africa. In fact the Colombians are repeating exactly what Pablo Escobar did to the US in the eighties, except they are doing it to Europe in the noughties.

What, I hear you ask, have we, the UK, been doing about this? I'm glad you asked because nobody seems to want to talk about Guinea-Bissau or the effectiveness of the UK's shiny new Serious Organized Crime Agency (SOCA). With 4000 staff, it took over drug investigations from Customs, along with the roles of the National Crime Squad, National Crime Intelligence Services and part of MI5's remit in April 2006. Unfortunately, the result has been that smuggling drugs into Britain is now easier than it has been at any time over the last three decades.

As I mentioned earlier (I think these figures are worth repeating), according to the government's own date, less than three tonnes of cocaine was seized in 2006–07 compared with over nine tonnes in 2004–05 and one tonne of heroin seized in 2006–07 compared with nearly two and a half tonnes in 2004–05. Now more readily available in the UK than ever, the street prices of coke and crack have dropped, making them all the more accessible to the young and the poor.

Thanks to the sheer volume of consumption and the entrepreneurial skills of the dealers, who have taken crack to the suburbs and the nightclubs (marketing it as a 'fun' drug), the drugs trade in the UK is now worth some £8 billon a year; it has become an important part of our national economy (generating as it does cash, employment and recreation for tens of thousands of people), so much so that if we could remove the illegal drugs trade at a stroke, it would probably undermine the UK's economic and political stability.

The government's own figures, released very quietly in 2007, reveal there are an estimated 332,000 problem drug users in the UK – almost one in ten of fifteen- to sixty-four-year-olds (in my opinion this is a gross underestimation). The number of sixteen-to twenty-four-year-olds in England and Wales who admitted taking cocaine in the previous year almost doubled from 1998, up from 3.2 per cent to 6.1 per cent in 2006–07. In 2007, shortly after the chief constable of Cleveland admitted that crack cocaine use was now at its highest ever level, the government's own research revealed that drug dealers and smugglers believed (correctly) that the risk of arrest was low.

Meanwhile, Guinea-Bissau, a country which was desperately struggling to get back on its feet, has been knocked down again. And we've literally missed the boats, hundreds of them. Unless we take the war to the crack houses and dealers in the UK, the only place where law enforcement has the potential to be truly effective, we're screwed.

Now, although I'm in a different police department, I still sometimes find myself wandering through London's inner-city estates in civvies, past the sad floral tributes to young victims of crack. It usually takes no more than ten minutes before I'm offered a rock. I think about where that rock has come from, the terrible suffering it has caused on its journey to get to the dealer's palm. I think about Jenni, who eventually made it, but only just (she'll be on medication for the rest of her life for hepatitis but has got back in touch with her mother and is living something resembling a normal life). I think about how crack is destroying kids, families – our country.

Just before I was about to take my war to child abuse, I was called into the superintendent's office. There, waiting for me, were two senior officers leading Operation Crackdown, a short-term Met initiative designed to tackle the drugs trade. The superintendent asked me to talk them through what had happened in Haringey over the past twelve months. When I'd finished, one of the officers stood up and held out his hand. 'You've just been snapped up, mate,' he said with a grin.

They wanted me to join their task force. Deeply flattered, I thought about it for some time, but what had happened to Victoria, and the knowledge that hundreds more kids were suffering unnecessarily, haunted me deeply, and so I declined.

I still think that if we keep bashing doors, keep breaking up networks, keep nicking everyone, then it might not be too late – we can still win the war on drugs and get our neighbourhoods back. But for me it has to be a war of total attrition. No short-term initiatives. I really think it's that simple. As I left the meeting and strode down the High Road, I balled my fists. There was no time to lose. Child protection here I come.

REFERENCES

OFFICIAL REPORTS

Request made by the authors to the Metropolitan Police under the Freedom of Information Act for Data Relating to the Victims of Shootings for Selected London Boroughs 1996–2006, published by the PIB Crime and Core Unit and Performance Directorate Helpdesk, April 2007

Assisting Guinea-Bissau: UN statement made at the International Conference on Drug Trafficking in Guinea-Bissau Lisbon, 19 December 2007

Cocaine and Coups Hunt Gagged Nation, Reporters Without Borders, November 2007

Cocaine Trafficking in West Africa: the threat to stability and development, UN Office on Drugs and Crime, December 2007

Community-led innovation in addressing the problems caused by crack cocaine in London, The Greater London Authority, April 2004

Could a Tuberculosis Epidemic Occur in London as It Did in New York? Andrew C. Hayward and Richard J. Coker, University of Nottingham, Nottingham, United Kingdom, *Emerging Infectious Diseases*, Vol. 6, No. 1, Jan–Feb 2000; and St Mary's Hospital, London, United Kingdom

Crack Cocaine in London, qualitative research focussing on Brent, Camden, Lambeth and Westminster, Craig Ross Dawson, Draft Report for the Home Office, September 2003

Drug Trafficking: West Africa, Africa Research Bulletin: Political, Social and Cultural Series, Vol. 44, Issue 7, pp. 17175A–17177A, August 2007

Drug Trends 2000–2001, United Nations Office on Drugs and Crime Caribbean

House of Commons Hansard Debates for 5 March 1993 (Corruption Scandal at Stoke Newington Police Station)

Haringey Crime and Drugs Audit 2001–2004, Haringey's Safer Communities Partnership, 2004

Heroin and Crack Cocaine Markets in Deprived Areas: Seven Local Case Studies, Supplement to Home Office Research Study 240, 'A Rock and a Hard Place: Drug Markets in Deprived Neighbourhoods', Case Report, 19 January 2002

Metropolitan Police Crime Figures for Financial Years 1999–2005

Reluctant Gangsters: Youth Gangs in a London Borough by John Pitts, Vauxhall Professor of Socio-legal Studies, University of Bedfordshire, 2007

Report on Haringey's Crime and Disorder Audit 1998–2001 and Strategic Recommendations, *The Haringey Safer Communities Partnership, 2001*

Report on Haringey's Crime and Disorder Audit 2001-2004 and Strategic Recommendations, *The Haringey Safer Communities Partnership, 2004*

Tackling Crack – A National Plan, Home Office, 2002, London

The Crack Report, Turning Point, 2005

The Victoria Climbié Inquiry: Report of an Inquiry by Lord Laming, Presented to Parliament by the Secretary of State for Health and the Secretary of State for the Home Department by Command of Her Majesty, January 2003

Working with Black Crack Users in a Crisis Setting, Webster, R., City Roads, 1999, London

MEDIA REPORTS

The authors consulted a number of sources including national and international newspapers and magazines as well as specialist publications. Below are listed those which proved to be most useful and which correspond with some of the most significant aspects of Harry's story.

'America's most wanted: armed, dangerous and living in London' by Tony Thompson, *Observer*, 4 June 2000

'Doctors address our violent times', www.bbc.co.uk, 28 March 2007, http://news.bbc.co.uk/1/hi/health/6500955.stm

'Fifteen children died in Haringey's care', *Evening Standard*, 5 February 2000

'Four jailed for yardie gang murder', www.bbc.co.uk, 22 February 2000 http://news.bbc.co.uk/1/hi/uk/652357.stm

'Fugitive gang enforcer arrested in push-in robberies in Bronx', Diane Caldwell, *New York Times*, 2 March 2001

'Government in crisis (I): victory to the traffickers: heroin and cocaine prices on the street are at record lows as seizures plummet', Paul Lashmar, *Independent on Sunday*, 25 November 2007

'Murdered girl was "at risk"', Justin Davenport, *Evening Standard*, 10 March 2005

'Paedophile worked on Climbié council', Paul Sims, *Evening Standard*, 15 September 2004

'Police concern as drug deaths double', *Aberdeen Evening Express*, 31 August 2007

'Police fear influx of yardie drug dealers', Dan McDougall, *Scotsman*, 2 June 2003

'Pushers' paradise, the drugs trade in the continent's first narco-state is booming', *Economist*, 7 June 2007

'Scandal of paedophile's school jobs', Tim Miles, *Evening Standard*, 21 November 2001

'The primary school where crack dealers and yardies came calling – for the headteacher', Nick Davies, *Guardian*, 17 July 2000

'Terrorist attacks drove Jamaican drug mules to UK', Tony Thompson, *Observer*, 6 January 2002

'Turf wars. The death of Dean Roberts in a London street on Monday continued a spate of killings linked to Yardie-style gangsters', Nick Hopkins, *Guardian*, 8 July 1999

'Women's jails suffer rise in drug "mules"', Ian Burrell, Home Affairs Correspondent, *Independent*, September 11, 2001

'Yardie terror grips London. A wave of gang violence is sweeping from the ghettos of Jamaica into Britain – with tragic results', Ed Vulliamy and Tony Thompson, *Observer*, 18 July 1999

FURTHER READING

Hardly any books in the UK cover the crack trade. Two excellent books, each very different (one told from the criminal's perspective, the other from the police's), that cover some aspects of the crack phenomenon and were consulted by the authors are:

Powder Wars: The Supergrass Who Brought Down Britain's Biggest Drug Dealers by Graham Johnson, Mainstream Publishing, new edition (6 October 2005)

Guns and Gangs: The Inside Story of the War on Our Streets by Graeme McLagan, Allison & Busby (30 May 2006)

Also by Graeme McLagan, *Bent Coppers: the inside story of Scotland Yard's battle against police corruption*, Orion, new edition (1 April 2004), proved to be a useful *aide memoire* for Harry, with particular reference to his time at Stoke Newington.

One of the most fascinating books on the crack trade in the United States is *Dark Alliance: CIA, the Contras and the Crack Cocaine Explosion* by Gary Webb, Seven Stories Press US (10 July 1999). Five years after its publication, the author was found shot dead in a hotel room. Although the official verdict was suicide, some conspiracists have since argued that Webb was murdered for exposing too many painful truths.

Behind the Eight Ball: sex for crack cocaine exchange and poor black women by Tanya Telfair Sharpe, Haworth Press Inc, US (2005) is an American study which documents the plight of female addicts who sell themselves for crack.

INDEX

'Jay' (crack dealer), 161

Jayne (crack user), 87–8

Jenni (crack user), 178

'Jerk Chicken' fast-food restaurant, 21

Jez (crack dealer), 129–30, 134

Jill (prostitute), 169–70

John (crack dealer), 132

John (TSG liaison officer), 149–50

Johnson, Ashanti, 102

Johnson, Avril, 102–3

Johnson, Graham, 40

Johnson, Kirk, 102–3

Johnson, Zhane, 102

Julia (drug mule), 9–13

Junk gang, 7

Keeble, Diana, 195

Keeble, Detective Sergeant Harry:
  about, ii
  Africa mission of, 244, 253
  council presentation by, 182–3
  disrupted family life of, 162, 195
  Drugs Squad post accepted by, 30–1
  Drugs Squad post left by, 198, 242, 243
  Hendon graduation of, 19
  Muswell Hill arrival of, 25
  police force joined by, 18
  promoted to sergeant, 25
  returns to Hornsey, 190
  Romford probation stint of, 19
  son's birth and, 162, 195, 198n, 243
  Stoke Newington arrival of, 17
  see also Haringey Drugs Squad

Kev (fellow drugs officer), 191, 193, 194, 195–7, 204, 209–10, 211, 212–13, 214, 217, 237, 243, 245–6

Kick Off Head Crew (gang), 72

'Kid' (crack dealer), 131

King, Clayton, 72

Kingston, Jamaica, 8–9

Kouao Marie-Therese, 187–8

Lambeth, London, 77, 78, 245
  Community Relations Council, 73

Lambie, Mark ('Prince of Darkness'), 1, 13–14, 76, 152–4, 241, 242
  moves to south London, 154
  sentencing of, 242

Lansdowne, Detective Inspector Peter, 242

Lawes, Henry, 200

Lawrence, Stephen, 43, 126, 185

Leneghan, Mary-Ann, 250

Leon (crack user), 159

Lewanowski, Detective Constable Roy, 20, 21–2, 42

Lewis, David, 70–1

LGM (gang), 154

Lima, Alvero, 188

Lindsey (prostitute), 165–8

Littlejohn, Fabian O'Neil, 99, 100

Liverpool, 39–41
  international trading-hub status of, 40
  Toxteth in, 39–40, 73, 76

Livingstone, Ken, 227

Lock City Crew (LCC) (gang), 14, 69, 70, 71, 99, 199

London:
  Broadwater Farm Estate in, 72–3, 74–7, 92
  central, riots in, 223
  Clissold Park in, 17
  Finsbury Park in, 224
  Hackney in, 77, 78, 199
  Haringey in, see main entry
  Harlesden in, 19, 130, 199–200, 248
  Harold Hill, in, 19
  Lambeth in, 73, 77, 78, 245
  Mardi Gras held in, 224–7